SPELLING
CONNECTIONS
W O R D S   I N T O   L A N G U A G E

The Heber Valley, Utah, near Wasatch National Forest, east of Salt Lake City. Horseback riding is a popular recreational activity in Utah, a state of great open spaces and grand natural beauty. Riders enjoy Utah's rugged snow-capped mountains, multicolored canyons, and sparkling rivers and lakes.

Walter B. Barbe, Ph.D.
Editor in Chief, *Highlights for Children*
Adjunct Professor, The Ohio State University

Azalia S. Francis, Ed.D.
Professor of Education, University of North Alabama

J. Richard Gentry, Ph.D.
Associate Professor, Elementary Education and Reading
Western Carolina University

Christine San José, Ph.D.
Language Arts Editor, Zaner-Bloser, Inc.

Senior Editorial Advisor

William H. Nault, Ed.D.
Author, *Caswell-Nault Analysis of Courses of Study*

Grade-Level Author

Barbara L. Rogers

Book 6

1

Project Director: Judith A. V. Harlan

Word Editor: Janet L. Keen
Grade-Level Editor: Mary E. MacEwen

Design and Art: Thomas M. Wasylyk, Director; Jeffrey E. George, Timothy J. Gillner, Amy Langendoerfer, Lisa Austin. Cover design by Ligature, Inc.

Cover photography: Christopher Kean; Photography: © Beth Bergman 1988, 12, 15; Robert F. Jennings, 34, 35, 49, 55, 59, 86, 87; Ron Colbroth, 36; Ira Block / The Image Bank, 41; Jeff Hunter / The Image Bank, 43L; Peter Beney / The Image Bank, 43R; Courtesy of the Chesapeake Bay Bridge and Tunnel District, 44; Photo courtesy of The Port Authority of New York and New Jersey, 45; Randy Taylor / Black Star, 63; Nick Nicholson / The Image Bank, 67; Fred Ward / Black Star, 89; Photograph by Barry Feig, 94; Photo by Focus on Sports, 108; Photography by Bruce Bennett, 110; © Ingbert Grüttner, 111; © Dave Black, 1986, 116; Dave Black / Focus West, 117; Photograph by Paul Cohen, 120; Sygma, 124; Art Resource, New York, 140; Library of Congress, 141T; NASA, 141B; Allan Tannenbaum / Sygma, 142; Herman J. Kokojan / Black Star, 143.

Illustrators: Alex Bloch, Bill Colrus, Robin & Pat DeWitt, Kitty Diamantis, Simon Galkin, Meryl Henderson, John Killgrew, Ron Lehew, Morissa Lipstein, Sal Murdocca, Tom Powers, Scott Sullivan, Fred Winkowski.

The publisher gratefully acknowledges permission to reprint the following copyrighted material:
From *Computers in Our World, Today & Tomorrow* © 1983 by Sandy & Martin Hintz. Reprinted by permission of Franklin Watts; From *Diary of a Young Girl* by Anne Frank. Reprinted by permission of the publisher, Doubleday & Company, Inc.; From *The Mexican Story* by May McNeer. Copyright © 1953. Reprinted by permission of the publisher, Farrar, Straus & Giroux; From "The Quarrel" from *Eleanor Farjeon's Poems for Children*. Copyright © 1951 by Eleanor Farjeon; copyright renewed 1984 by Eleanor Farjeon. Reprinted by permission of Harper & Row, Publishers, Inc.; From *The Story of the Trapp Family Singers* by Maria Augusta Trapp. Copyright © 1949. Reprinted by permission of Harper & Row, Publishers, Inc.; From *Where the Lilies Bloom* by Vera and Bill Cleaver. Jacket illustration by Jim Spanfeller. Copyright © 1969. Reprinted by permission of Harper & Row, Publishers, Inc.; From "Young Man in a Hurry" by Joseph N. Farley. This article was published in *Accent on Youth*, November 1971, by the United Methodist Publishing House.

Phonetic symbols, phonetic respellings, and the pronunciation key used in the Spelling Connections: Words into Language series are reprinted with permission from *The American Heritage Dictionary*, Second College Edition, copyright © 1985 by Houghton Mifflin Company. Definitions, word histories, and etymologies are reprinted or adapted with permission from *The American Heritage Dictionary*, Second College Edition, copyright © 1985 by Houghton Mifflin Company. Houghton Mifflin Company publishes the *Houghton Mifflin Picture Dictionary*, *Houghton Mifflin Primary Dictionary*, *Houghton Mifflin Intermediate Dictionary*, and *Houghton Mifflin Student Dictionary*.

Copyright © 1988 Zaner-Bloser, Inc.

Zaner-Bloser, Inc., 1459 King Avenue
P.O. Box 16764, Columbus, Ohio 43216-6764

Printed in the United States of America.
ISBN: 0-88309-451-7
Reorder number: 360046

Contents

3

Contents

The Writing Process—Proofreading

Every step in the writing process is important. You explore what you know and think and feel. You organize your thoughts, you express what matters, and often you plan to share your writing with others. In order to understand you, your readers must first make sense of your writing; so you need to check for mistakes in spelling, punctuation, grammar, word usage, content, sentence and paragraph construction, and handwriting. This step is called **proofreading.**

To proofread, follow these steps.

1. Read each sentence for errors in spelling or word usage.
   a. Is each word spelled accurately?
   b. Does each word add to the meaning of the sentence?

2. Check the paragraph for errors in grammar.
   a. Is the proper tense used?
   b. Are parts of speech used correctly?
   c. Does each sentence create a complete thought?

3. Check the paragraph for errors in punctuation.
   a. Does each sentence end with the proper punctuation?
   b. Does each sentence start with a capital letter?
   c. Are proper nouns capitalized?

4. Check the paragraph for proper form.
   a. Does the topic sentence clearly state the main idea?
   b. Are all sentences written in a logical order?
   c. Does each sentence add to an understanding of the topic?
   d. Is the handwriting neat and legible?

Use these symbols to correct errors.

⊙ Insert period.

ℐ Take out.

≡ Capitalize.

🆂🅿 Change spelling.

¶ New paragraph.

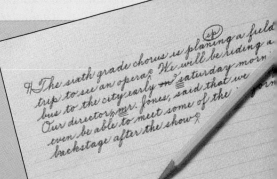

PATHS TO SPELLING SUCCESS

1 Steps for Learning to Spell a Word

1. Look at the word and say the letters.

2. Think about how each sound is spelled.

3. Close your eyes and picture how the word looks.

4. Spell the word to yourself.

5. Write the word.

6. Check your spelling against the spelling in the book.

2 Steps for Spelling Words on an Oral Test

1. Listen as the word is pronounced, used in a sentence, and pronounced again.

2. If you know how to spell the word, write it.

3. If you are not sure how to spell the word, say the word to yourself.

4. Picture what the word looks like when you see it written.

5. Write the word.

6. Look at the word you have written and make any necessary changes.

SPELLING SUCCESS

3 Steps for Spelling a Word When You Are Writing on Your Own

1. Think of the exact word you want to use.

2. If you know how to spell the word, write it.

3. If you are not sure how to spell the word, say the word to yourself.

4. Picture what the word looks like when you see it written.

5. Write the word.

6. Ask yourself whether the word looks right.

7. If you are not sure, check the word in a dictionary.

4 Steps for Spelling Words on Printed Tests

1. Read the directions carefully. (For example, are you being asked to find the correct or the incorrect spelling?)

2. Decide how to mark your answer.

3. Proceed through the test, marking only those answers you are sure of.

4. Return to each word you were not sure of and think about how each sound is spelled.

5. Picture what the word looks like when you see it written.

6. Decide on the answer and mark it.

7. Look over the test and make any changes needed.

SPELLING SUCCESS

1. rapid
2. pattern
3. accent
4. album
5. cancel
6. chapter
7. natural
8. admit
9. advance
10. exactly
11. labor
12. favorite
13. vacation
14. behave
15. daydream
16. trait
17. obtain
18. detain
19. complain
20. survey

Target Skill

The short **a** sound you hear in **rapid**.
The long **a** sound you hear in **vacation**.

A. Write the spelling words that have the short **a** sound. Circle the letter that makes that sound.

B. Write the spelling word that has the long **a** sound spelled with the **a-consonant-e** pattern. Circle the vowel that you hear in that pattern.

C. Write the spelling words that have the long **a** sound spelled by the letter **a** in an open syllable. Circle the letter or letters that make that sound.

D. Write the spelling words that have the long **a** sound spelled by the letters **ai.** Circle the letters that make that sound.

E. Write the spelling words that have the long **a** sound spelled with a **vowel + y.** Circle the letters that make that sound.

WORD STUDY

A. Dictionary Look at the following words. Select the **spelling word** that would follow in alphabetical order. Write the spelling word.

1. **address**　　3. **cycle**　　5. **appoint**
2. **engine**　　4. **camper**　　6. **labor**

B. Vocabulary Write the spelling word that matches each clue to solve the riddle in the box.

1. Rhymes with **last chance.**
2. It was a ___?___ of love.
3. Opposite of **to lose.**
4. An overall look.
5. I'd rather compliment than ___?___ .

Riddle: In this book no words abound, only blank pages where stamps may be found. ___?___

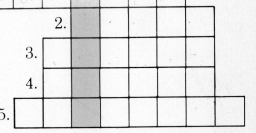

C. Proofreading Vacations are a good time to keep a journal. Find the misspelled words in the journal entry. Write the words correctly.

Chopter 1　　Aug. 15

It took us exacly two hours and twenty minutes to get to Grandpa's house. Grandpa was at his favorit activity, working in the garden. He likes to grow his vegetables in neat rows that make a patern like a patchwork quilt.

Grandpa made a wonderful dinner for us. To acsent the meal, he made one of his famous raspberry pies. After dinner Grandpa showed us photos from his albam. The photos made me dayedream about swimming and fishing in the pond.

The fireflies were out, and I decided to catch a few. Catching these tiny little bugs is not as easy as it may seem. You must labur at it. As you advanse toward one you must always stay behind it. Once in a jar, fireflies behaive like a blinking night-light. This is a natarul trate for fireflies, but I think it is very odd.

Even though I had to cancil my Little League practice, I'm glad we spent our vacation with Grandpa.

rapid *quick*

pattern

accent

album

cancel

chapter

natural

- admit

- advance

exactly

labor

favorite

vacation

behave

daydream

- trait

- obtain *get*

- detain

- complain

- survey

A. Write the spelling words to complete the journal entry.

Chapter 2   Aug. 20

On this day of our __1__ my sister Rosa and I found many interesting rocks. Many of the rocks have a beautiful __2__ of colors. We also learned that if you take two wet rocks and scrape them against each other with a __3__ back and forth motion, paint is produced. We mixed the colors to __4__ a range of colors from pale gray to rich red.

Rosa started to __5__ because I was getting the paint too close to her eyes as we painted each other's faces. So we washed it off, but not before taking pictures for our __6__ .

B. Write a spelling word to complete each sentence.

1. Sixth graders always __?__ politely.
2. Walter made a __?__ of our favorite TV programs.
3. Sheila was lost in a pleasant __?__ of the past summer.
4. I have to __?__ that it's great being back in school.
5. Carlos speaks with a beautiful Spanish __?__ .
6. The __?__ setting of tall pines and flowing streams was very peaceful.
7. The park is __?__ three blocks from home.
8. The first __?__ of this book is exciting.
9. Please __?__ my magazine subscription.
10. The siren gave an __?__ warning of the tornado.

C. Write a spelling word for each clue.

1. Part of one's character.
2. To hold back.
3. Likely to win.
4. Difficult work.

WORDSCAPES: The Writing Connection

Anne Frank hid with her family in an attic to escape Nazi persecution during World War II. They were discovered and sent to a concentration camp where Anne died in 1945, but her words live on in this excerpt from her diary.

> 4 August, 1943 . . . There is so much to tell; everything is so different from ordinary times and from ordinary people's lives. But still, to give you a closer look into our lives, now and again I intend to give you a description of an ordinary day.

A. Begin a journal using what happened today, or during your first week in school, as your first entry. Use the spelling words if possible.

Content Words

abbreviation
apostrophe
capitalization
punctuation
quotation

chisel
engraving
marble
sculptor
woodcut

B. Use the Language Arts Words to complete the sentences.

1. Use __?__ at the beginning of every sentence.
2. Periods, commas, and question marks are all examples of __?__ .
3. TX is an __?__ for Texas.
4. In a contraction, put an __?__ where the letters have been omitted.
5. "The ballot is stronger than the bullet" is a famous __?__ from Lincoln.

C. Use the Fine Arts Words to complete the sentences.

On a trip to New York City, we saw many artists working. A __1__ was making a statue. She carefully chipped off the outer stone of a huge, cold piece of __2__ . Because the stone is so hard, she had to use a hammer and __3__ . Another artist was __4__ an elaborate pattern on wood. Both the marble statue and the finished __5__ would be fine works of art.

11

1. excellent
2. text
3. method
4. regular
5. attend
6. develop
7. dealt
8. meadow
9. cleanse
10. leather
11. sleet
12. feeble
13. indeed
14. employee
15. crease
16. release
17. theme
18. scheme
19. melody
20. gravity

Target Skill

The short **e** sound you hear in **text**.
The long **e** sound you hear in **sleet**.

George Gershwin is recognized as one of America's most popular composers. He was born in Brooklyn, N.Y., in 1898. At the age of sixteen, he began his career playing the piano.

His masterpiece, **Porgy and Bess,** is an opera based on popular songs and jazz rhythms. He combines both **melody** and **text** to **develop** a powerful description of the life of black people in Charleston, S.C., in the 1920s.

A. Write the spelling words that have the short **e** sound. Circle the letter or letters that make that sound.

B. Write the spelling words that have the long **e** sound spelled by a vowel digraph. Circle the letters that make that sound.

C. Write the spelling words that have the long **e** sound spelled by **y.**

D. Write the spelling words that have the long **e** sound spelled by the **e-consonant-e** spelling pattern. Circle the letters that make that sound.

WORD STUDY

A. Dictionary Look at the dictionary respellings. Write the spelling word for each one.

1. /**grăv′** ĭ tē/
2. /tĕkst/
3. /**mĕd′** ō/
4. /**mĕl′** ə dē/
5. /dĕlt/
6. /ĭn **dēd′**/
7. /**fē′** bəl/
8. /thĕm/

B. Proofreading Theater Six needs stagehands. Find the misspelled words in the announcement. Write the words correctly.

**Do you have a skeme
to keep our costumes clean?**

Each employe of the theater does an important job. You are needed as a costume hand for our production of **Davy Crockett.** No experience necessary, just the willingness to atend each performance. Learn how to clense leathr and crese petticoats.

Sign up in Room 6A.

C. Vocabulary Write the spelling word for each clue.

1. **freezing rain**
2. **to let loose**
3. **to grow**
4. **usual**
5. **system**
6. **very good**

D. Vocabulary Put your own **text** to music. Use the spelling words or their synonyms to write a song with at least six lines. Choose a popular tune for the **melody.**

13

WORD SENSE

excellent
text
method
regular
attend
develop
dealt
meadow
cleanse
leather
sleet
feeble
indeed
employee
crease
release
theme
scheme
melody
gravity

A. Write the spelling word that rhymes with the word in boldface print.

1. The rain turned to __?__ and ruined the painted **fleet.**
2. It is not likely we will **offend** if we make an effort to __?__ .
3. The cards will certainly **melt** if they are not quickly __?__ .
4. Within every fold there is a __?__ as in every part there is a **piece.**
5. The situation was filled with __?__ ; before them yawned a **cavity.**
6. When I plan, I invent a __?__ and when I sleep, I invent a **dream.**

B. Write the spelling word that belongs in each set.

1. silk, cotton, denim, __?__
2. frail, weak, shaky, __?__
3. wipe, scrub, wash, __?__
4. normal, average, usual, __?__
5. wonderful, first-rate, splendid, __?__
6. pasture, field, grassland, __?__
7. let go, set free, let fly, __?__
8. worker, attendant, laborer, __?__

C. Use the spelling words to complete the paragraph.

Gilbert and Sullivan were two well-known Englishmen who wrote operettas together during the second half of the nineteenth century. Mr. Gilbert wrote the words for the music, and Mr. Sullivan wrote the __1__ . Their __2__ of working as partners succeeded so well that people everywhere heard their music. A third man worked with them. His job was to __3__ their operettas into stage productions. Mr. Gilbert sometimes developed the __4__ for a musical by making fun of something or someone. The words, or __5__ , flowed easily once the subject was developed. Their songs are, __6__ , still enjoyed today.

WORDSCAPES: The Writing Connection

A. An opera or musical is divided into **acts.** Each act describes a specific part of the play. Acts are divided into **scenes.** The scenes are the different locations or settings where action and dialogue between characters take place. Use the spelling words when you can to outline a three-act play.

Content Words

autobiography
serial
trilogy
journal
novel

violinist
cellist
composer
flutist
pianist

B. Write the Language Arts Words that match the clues.

1. When a person writes his or her own life story, it is called an ___?___ .

2. This word is a homophone for **cereal;** though ___?___ is pronounced like the breakfast food, it means a story or television drama published or produced in installments.

3. From the Greek word **treis,** meaning "three," and **logos,** meaning "word," a ___?___ describes three literary works or dramas that are related by theme.

4. Your own personal record of daily experiences and reflections is a ___?___ .

5. A book-length fictional story is called a ___?___ .

C. Use the Fine Arts Words to complete the sentences.

1. George Gershwin was a ___?___ of popular and classical music.

2. Mr. Gershwin began his career as a ___?___ , playing for musicals and shows.

3. A ___?___ must control her breathing in order to play well.

4. Before the performance, both the ___?___ and ___?___ repaired the broken strings on their instruments.

1. *limit*
2. *permit*
3. *attic*
4. *district*
5. *system*
6. *inherit*
7. *exhibit*
8. *examine*
9. *consider*
10. *item*
11. *ideal*
12. *strike*
13. *empire*
14. *confide*
15. *require*
16. *disguise*
17. *assign*
18. *apply*
19. *satisfy*
20. *classify*

Target Skill

The short **i** sound you hear in **limit**.
The long **i** sound you hear in **strike**.

In an incredible land called the Empire of **I**, the citizens speak only with their eyes, and they use only **i** sounds.

A. Write the spelling words that have the short **i** sound spelled by the letter **i**.

B. Write the spelling word that has the short **i** sound spelled by the letter **y**.

C. Write the spelling words that have the long **i** sound spelled with the **vowel-consonant-e** pattern.

D. Write the spelling words that have the long **i** sound spelled by the letter **i** in an open syllable.

E. Write the spelling word that has the long **i** sound spelled in the same pattern as **design**.

F. Write the spelling words that have the long **i** sound spelled by the letter **y**.

WORD STUDY

A. Structure The Empress of **I** decided to turn back time. Change the underlined verbs from the present to the past tense by dropping the silent **e** and adding **ed.** Write the spelling words in the past tense.

   In order to escape the aliens, the Empress of **I** <u>disguise</u> herself as a streetlight in downtown Denver in the year 1950. She <u>examine</u> the situation and <u>confide</u> to her subjects that the empire would be safe there. To transport the empire back in time, she <u>require</u> their cooperation.

B. Dictionary The friends of the Empire of **I** are the **y's**. They may sound like either the long or the short **i**. Write the spelling word for each dictionary respelling.

   1. /əp lĭ′ /   3. /sĭs′ təm/

   2. /săt′ ĭs fī/   4. /klăs′ ə fī/

C. Structure One day the Empress of **I** misplaced all her vowels. Decide which vowels are needed, and write the completed spelling words.

   1. __ ss __ gn   5. __ nh __ r __ t
   2. __ t __ m   6. __ tt __ c
   3. c __ ns __ d __ r   7. __ xh __ b __ t
   4. l __ m __ t

D. Proofreading Some spelling words are misspelled. Write the words correctly.

   The Empress commanded, "Strik the time-warp button!" and suddenly the entire empyre zoomed backward. They traveled back in time to an idel place. The Empress immediately applied for a permet to occupy this distrect.

WORD SENSE

limit
permit
attic
district
system
inherit
exhibit
examine
consider
item
ideal
strike
empire
confide
require
disguise
assign
apply
satisfy
classify

A. Write the spelling words that complete the science fiction facts.

1. You may want to ___?___ reading science fiction.

2. Librarians ___?___ stories that deal with time travel as science fiction.

3. Authors ___?___ scientific data to their stories to make them realistic.

4. A space helmet is an ___?___ of clothing.

B. Write the spelling words you can make from the scrambled syllables.

1. **her in it**   4. **is fy sat**

2. **al i de**   5. **am ine ex**

3. **it ex hib**   6. **pire em**

C. Write the spelling word that fits each definition.

1. To appoint.   5. To need.

2. To share a secret.   6. Space under roof.

3. A specific area.   7. To conceal.

4. A method.   8. To hit sharply.

D. Write one spelling word twice in each sentence, using it once as a noun and once as a verb.

1. Please ___?___ us to obtain a ___?___ to fish in this lake.

2. If I ___?___ the pressure on the gas pedal, I will not exceed the speed ___?___ .

18

WORDSCAPES: The Writing Connection

In his science fiction stories, Jules Verne presented many ideas that would only become reality years later.

In 1870 the only submarines in existence were small and primitive. In his imagination Verne created his own, a huge and luxurious submarine named the **Nautilus.** The story he wrote about it, **Twenty Thousand Leagues Under the Sea,** is one of his greatest tales.

Verne's **Nautilus** was powered by electricity and lighted by incandescent bulbs—bulbs that actually were not invented until ten years later.

A. Write a science fiction story in which you describe a futuristic invention. Use as many spelling words as you can.

Content Words

legend
myth
short story
fable
ballad

cartilage
exhale
inhale
respiratory
trachea

B. Use the Language Arts Words to complete the sentences.

1. The ___?___ **of Sleepy Hollow** is by Washington Irving.
2. The ___?___ told how Zeus's anger caused lightning.
3. A narrative poem set to music is a ___?___ .
4. When animals act like humans in a story, it is called a ___?___ .
5. A story not book length is called a ___?___ .

C. Use the Science Words to complete the sentences.

1. The ___?___ system controls breathing.
2. Your joints have ___?___ to protect the bones from wear and tear.
3. When you ___?___ , your lungs expand.
4. The windpipe is another name for the ___?___ .
5. When you breathe out, you ___?___ carbon dioxide.

1. bronze
2. contact
3. constant
4. profit
5. project
6. beyond
7. respond
8. positive
9. opposite
10. opportunity
11. pose
12. oppose
13. notice
14. donate
15. emotion
16. charcoal
17. approach
18. associate
19. stereo
20. video

Target Skill

The short **o** sound you hear in **bronze**.
The long **o** sound you hear in **pose**.

WORD HISTORY

The word **video** comes from the Latin word that means "I see." The word **stereo** is the shortened form of **stereophonic**. **Stereophonic** comes from two Greek words: **stereos**, meaning "solid," and **phōnē**, meaning "sound." Can you see where the word **telephone** comes from? What does it mean?

A. Write the spelling words that have the short **o** sound.

B. Write the spelling words that have the long **o** sound spelled by the letter **o** in an **open syllable**.

C. Write the spelling words that have the long **o** sound spelled by the letters **oa**. Circle the letters that make that sound.

D. Write the spelling words that have the long **o** sound spelled with the **o-consonant-e** pattern.

E. Write the base words from which these words are formed.

1. projection   2. association   3. donation

WORD STUDY

A. Proofreading In this paragraph on using the computer, some of the words are misspelled. Write each spelling word correctly.

   If you aproach the computer with a postive attitude, your progect will run smoothly. You will notise that your computer skills improve with consent practice. If you have the oppertunity, contac a computer instructor who can respand to your questions. You will poffit from expert advice.

B. Dictionary Four of the spelling words stem from a similar origin. They are the words in these dictionary respellings. Write the spelling words.

   1. /ə pōz′/
   2. /pŏz′ ĭ tĭv/
   3. /ŏp′ ə zĭt/
   4. /pōz/

C. Dictionary Read the letters across, down, up, and backward to find the spelling words in the jumbled video screen. Write each word and its part of speech. Use the part of speech that the dictionary lists first. Write **n** for noun, **v** for verb, and **adj** for adjective. (Hint: There are six spelling words.)

```
a o c s e f
s n h y m i
s d a o o j
o e r e t s
c b c d i p
i r o i o p
a o a v n a
t n l c o l
e t a n o d
```

D. Vocabulary Look at the spelling patterns in each group of words. Choose the spelling word that does not fit. Write the word.

   1. **stereo, video, beyond**
   2. **donate, bronze, associate**
   3. **charcoal, video, approach**

21

WORD SENSE

bronze
contact
constant
profit
project
beyond
respond
positive
opposite
opportunity
pose
oppose
notice
donate
emotion
charcoal
approach
associate
stereo
video

A. Write the spelling words to complete this description of a video store of the future. You will need to capitalize one word and add **s** to another word.

VIDEO CONNECTION

My friend Dana and I went to a store called the ___1___ Connection, which constantly ___2___ movies on its walls and has records to listen to on a ___3___ . When we entered, a computerized voice asked, "May I help you? Please ___4___ the speaker on the wall and ___5___ your question."

We were not sure how to ___6___ . Dana went up to the speaker and said, "I ___7___ that you have the album Channel 2000. I would like the ___8___ to listen to it."

The computerized voice replied, "The listening booth is ___9___ the counter and ___10___ the main entrance."

B. Write the spelling word that completes the analogy.

1. **Give** is to **receive** as **loss** is to ___?___ .
2. **Start** is to **begin** as **continual** is to ___?___ .
3. **Hurt** is to **feeling** as **joy** is to ___?___ .
4. **Sharp** is to **dull** as **same** is to ___?___ .
5. **Help** is to **assist** as **touch** is to ___?___ .

C. An animal shelter held a race as a money-raising project. Write the spelling words that can replace the underlined words in the story.

Spectators at the race asked the chairman of the shelter to <u>direct</u> his voice when he announced the winner. The winner received a <u>metal</u> trophy. She was <u>certain</u> she wanted to <u>give</u> the prize money to the shelter. The chairman did not <u>resist</u> her request. He asked all the racers to <u>pay attention to</u> the man with the video camera and wave. He invited them to watch the <u>tape</u> of the race.

WORDSCAPES: The Writing Connection

A record album cover is designed to attract your attention. An artist chooses an eye-catching illustration, while a writer describes the musicians and their music in a way that will capture your interest.

A. Choose one of these record album titles or make up your own. Design a front cover. For the back cover, write a description of the music and the musical group that might have recorded that album.

Wind Songs
The Leopard in the Snow
Solid Bronze Hits
Vision Street

Opposite Sides
Lost Opportunity

Content Words

brochure
pamphlet
publication
periodical
catalog

conservation
erosion
topsoil
depletion
fertilizer

B. Unscramble the Language Arts Words in the paragraph below. Write the words.

1. A hampplet and a churbroe are two types of printed material which are distributed to provide basic information on a subject.

2. A batlipucion, such as a lotacag distributed at regular intervals, is called a lioderpica.

C. Use the Science Words to fill in the paragraph.

Imagine what would happen if you woke up and all of the ___1___ had washed away during the night. Heavy rain can cause ___2___ on unprotected land. With vegetation gone, ___3___ of the soil's basic components will result. The use of ___4___ can help restore the loss. We must create ___5___ laws that will protect this valuable resource.

1. budge
2. smudge
3. suffer
4. stubborn
5. custody
6. customer
7. insult
8. result
9. punish
10. union
11. uniform
12. bugle
13. acute
14. accuse
15. confuse
16. dispute
17. computer
18. community
19. contribute
20. barbecue

Target Skill

The short **u** sound you hear in **budge**.
The long **u** sound you hear in **union**.

The Constitution of the United States of America formed the basis for the **union** of the thirteen original colonies. It provided a **uniform** set of laws for Americans in every **community**.

A. Write the spelling words that have the short **u** sound.

B. Write the spelling words that have the long **u** sound spelled by the letter **u** in an **open syllable**.

C. Write the spelling words that have the long **u** sound spelled by the letter **u** in a **closed syllable**.

D. Write the spelling word that has the long **u** sound spelled **ue**.

WORD STUDY

A. Vocabulary Write the missing spelling words. You will need to add **s** to one word and **ed** to three words.

   The Americans' __1__ refusal to pay English taxes led to revolution. For the sake of freedom, the patriots were willing to __2__ the consequences of war. The English benefited from having __3__ of the colonies. They were __4__ by the patriots' demand for independence. The major __5__ was over who should govern the colonies.
   Merchants __6__ blankets and money to the Continental army, but could not afford __7__ for the soldiers. Each morning a blast from the __8__ awakened the soldiers. The winter at Valley Forge __9__ in __10__ hardship for many of these men.

B. Dictionary In a dictionary, there are two words in dark print at the top of each page. They are called **guide words.** They are the first and last entry words on that page. Write the spelling word you would find between these guide words.

   1. **confer | congregate**   2. **buckle | bug**   3. **account | act**

      4. **punch | puzzle**   5. **smooth | sneak**

C. Structure The possessive form of a noun shows ownership. Usually the possessive of a singular noun is formed by adding **'s.** Complete each sentence by adding a spelling word in the possessive form.

   Leaders of the labor union decided to reenact patriotic scenes for the __1__ Fourth of July celebration. The __2__ printer was broken, so announcements were printed by hand. Employees suggested using the __3__ baseball field for a cookout. The __4__ location allowed room for booths selling patriotic items. One __5__ purchases included a hat and a bumper sticker.

WORD SENSE

budge
smudge
suffer
stubborn
custody
customer
insult
result
punish
union
uniform
bugle
acute
accuse
confuse
dispute
computer
community
contribute
barbecue

A. Write the spelling word that belongs in each category below.

1. picnic, cookout, ___?___
2. argue, disagree, ___?___
3. discipline, reprimand, ___?___
4. mark, smear, ___?___
5. inflexible, difficult, ___?___
6. safekeeping, care, ___?___
7. consequence, outcome, ___?___
8. trumpet, horn, ___?___

B. Write the missing spelling words. Add **ed** to one word and **s** to one word.

These events occurred around the time of the American Revolution: Joseph Priestley's __1__ powers of observation led to the discovery of oxygen; Betsy Ross __2__ to the design of the American flag; and Jane Austen became the first great woman novelist, writing books that __3__ still buy today.

C. Write the spelling words that come from the Latin base word **unus.**

1. From Latin **unus,** meaning "one."
2. From Latin **unus,** and **forma,** meaning "shape."
3. From Latin **communis,** meaning "common." Remember, there is **unity** in com**unity**!

D. Synonyms are words with similar meanings. Write the spelling words that are synonyms for these words.

1. **move** 2. **scold** 3. **ache** 4. **blame** 5. **offend** 6. **perplex**

WORDSCAPES: The Writing Connection

THE PREAMBLE TO THE CONSTITUTION OF THE UNITED STATES

We the people of the United States, in order to form a more perfect union, establish justice, insure domestic tranquility, provide for the common defense, promote the general welfare, and secure the blessings of liberty to ourselves and our posterity, do ordain and establish this Constitution for the United States of America.

A. The Constitution established a set of laws for all to live by; rules to help people get along in a group. Imagine that you have been chosen to write the rules for your classroom. Write ten complete sentences describing rules you would make. Use as many spelling words as you can.

Content Words

encyclopedia
thesaurus
atlas
guidebook
almanac

floppy disk
diskette
hardware
printer
terminal

B. Write the Language Arts Words that go with each definition.

1. A book of maps.
2. A set of reference books.
3. A handbook of information, especially for tourists.
4. A book of synonyms or antonyms.
5. An annual of general information, often related to weather.

C. Write the Social Studies Words to complete the paragraph.

Computer programs may be recorded on a __1__ or a __2__. The __3__ is a piece of __4__ that allows the operator to communicate with the computer. Information is printed onto paper by the __5__.

UNIT 1

favorite
vacation
natural
exactly

UNIT 2

develop
method
scheme
melody

UNIT 3

exhibit
examine
disguise
assign

UNIT 4

opportunity
positive
approach
video

UNIT 5

stubborn
customer
barbecue
contribute

WORD CLUES AND STUDY

A. Write in alphabetical order the spelling words that have the long **a** or short **a** sounds.

B. Write in alphabetical order the spelling words that have the short **e** sound in the first syllable and that begin with the letter **m.**

C. Write the missing syllables. Then write the spelling words.

1. op ___ ___ ___ tu ni ty
2. ex ___ ___ ___ it
3. ___ ___ ___ guise
4. stub ___ ___ ___ ___
5. ___ ___ ___ tom er

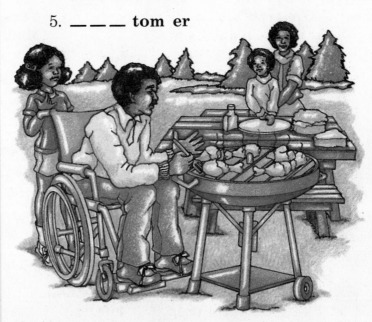

D. Write the spelling words that have the long **u** sound in the last syllable.

FURTHER PRACTICE AND ENRICHMENT

A. Decide which letters are missing. Write the completed spelling words.

1. d __ v __ l __ p
2. s __ h __ m __
3. __ ss __ gn
4. p __ s __ t __ v __
5. __ p __ r __ __ ch
6. v __ d __ __
7. c __ st __ m __ r

B. Creative Writing Writers are inventors in many ways. A writer puts words together to create something new. Through books, writers communicate ideas, create entertainment, express opinions, and provide information.

Put yourself in the place of an author. Decide what type of book you want to write. It could be an instruction manual for a product you invent, a collection of journal entries concerning your thoughts and dreams, or a biography of a famous musician or actor. You decide!

Give your imaginary book a title, and design a cover for it. Use a photograph or illustration that fits the subject. Write a summary of the book that will attract readers. Use some spelling words.

C. Proofreading Write the spelling words that are misspelled. You will have to add **s** to one word and put two words in the past tense.

Costomer stood in line for hours to buy theater tickets for **Vakation Barbique.** All of the actors had been assine lines which they had to memorize excatly. The play was going to be taped so that critics could examin it on vidio. After the performance, people were humming the play's major mellody. Most said their favorate scene concerned the man in the bear disgise who snatched the barbicue chicken from the camper's grill. He looked very natureal.

TESTING

A. Read each sentence. Write the number of the sentence and **a** or **b** to indicate whether the underlined word is spelled correctly or incorrectly.

1. Their <u>vakation</u> was relaxing and fun. 　(a) correct 　(b) incorrect

2. We had great chicken at the <u>barbique</u>. 　(a) correct 　(b) incorrect

3. We know <u>excactly</u> how to get to the park from here. 　(a) correct 　(b) incorrect

4. Our <u>sceam</u> will work if everyone agrees. 　(a) correct 　(b) incorrect

5. The doctor wants to <u>examine</u> Sally's injury. 　(a) correct 　(b) incorrect

6. My little sister can sometimes be very <u>stubborn</u>. 　(a) correct 　(b) incorrect

7. There is a <u>method</u> to learning to play the piano. 　(a) correct 　(b) incorrect

8. The museum had an <u>exibit</u> of a local artist's work. 　(a) correct 　(b) incorrect

9. A <u>possitive</u> attitude can improve your whole day. 　(a) correct 　(b) incorrect

10. The <u>vidoe</u> recording of our school play is kept in the library. 　(a) correct 　(b) incorrect

B. Read each group of words. Write the number of the group and **a**, **b**, or **c** to indicate the word in each group that is spelled correctly.

1. (a) favorite
   (b) favorate
   (c) favorit

2. (a) melodi
   (b) mellody
   (c) melody

3. (a) asign
   (b) assign
   (c) assine

4. (a) natral
   (b) natureal
   (c) natural

5. (a) divelop
   (b) develope
   (c) develop

6. (a) disguise
   (b) disgise
   (c) disguis

7. (a) aproach
   (b) approach
   (c) approch

8. (a) contribut
   (b) contribute
   (c) conttribute

9. (a) costumer
   (b) costumer
   (c) customer

10. (a) opportunity
    (b) oportunity
    (c) oppertunity

CHALLENGE

A. Write the four spelling words that can only be used as nouns.

B. Write the four spelling words that can only be used as verbs.

C. Write the six spelling words that can be used as nouns or verbs.

LANGUAGE TO GO

A. The Spoken Word Give a **Book Talk** about one
of your favorite books. Your goal is to persuade
other students to read it.

Pretend you are the book's main character. Tell
about yourself and the other characters in the
book. Explain your relationship to the other
characters and how you feel about them. Try to
build suspense as you describe the plot or some of
the action, but do not give away the ending.
Finally, tell why you think your book should be
read by others.

B. The Written Word Aileen Fisher has written
many poems and articles. Here is her advice on
how to become a writer:

How does a writer go about becoming a
writer? Where does the inspiration come from?
From all around you. From the people you
know, the sights you see, the things you do and
remember, and particularly from the way you
feel. Open yourself to whatever means the
most to you, and ideas will flow in.

How do you get started? By doing, by
practicing, just as you learn to throw a Frisbee
or play a musical instrument. You don't start
out being a writer. You build up to it. You
practice.

Choose an experience which means something to
you—perhaps a pleasant memory, a special friend, or
an embarrassing moment—and write about it. Use
verbs to show action, nouns to name people, places,
and things, and adjectives to provide description.
Use the spelling words when you can.

1. proof
2. teaspoon
3. tablespoon
4. approve
5. routine
6. through
7. fluid
8. assume
9. introduce
10. intrude
11. conclude
12. aptitude
13. goodness
14. understood
15. neighborhood
16. could've
17. would've
18. should've
19. bulletin
20. cushion

Target Skill

The o͞o sound you hear in **proof**.
The o͝o sound you hear in **goodness**.

A. Write the spelling words that have the o͞o sound spelled **oo**. Circle the letters that make that sound.

B. Write the spelling words that have the o͞o sound spelled **ou**. Circle the letters that make that sound.

C. Write the spelling words that have the o͞o sound spelled with the **vowel-consonant-e** pattern.

D. Write the spelling words that have the o͞o sound in an **open syllable.** Circle the letters that make that sound.

E. Write the spelling words that have the o͝o sound spelled **oo**. Circle the letters that make that sound.

F. Write the spelling words that have the o͝o sound spelled **ou**. Circle the letters that make that sound.

G. Write the spelling words that have the o͝o sound spelled **u**. Circle the letter that makes that sound.

WORD STUDY

A. Structure Unscramble the letters to find the spelling words. Write the words you discover.

1. **ifuld**
2. **shonuci**
3. **reunito**
4. **pvearpo**
5. **slopenboat**
6. **putaited**

B. Dictionary When something contracts, it grows smaller in size. That's what happens with contractions. They are the result of combining two words into one by omitting some of the letters. An apostrophe is used to show the omission. Write the spelling words that are contractions for the underlined words.

1. You <u>could have</u> held the door open.
2. We <u>would have</u> congratulated their team.
3. That man <u>should have</u> said, "Excuse me."

C. Structure When verbs end in a silent **e,** drop the **e** before adding **ed** or **ing.** Write these spelling words with their **ing** and **ed** endings.

1. **assume**
2. **introduce**
3. **intrude**
4. **conclude**

D. Proofreading Find the misspelled words in this paragraph. Write the words correctly.

Threw our community bullitin, Chef Fidelia's favorite recipes appear each week. Her crowded naborhood restaurant is proff that she is a great cook. The goodnes of each dish is apparent to all. It is understud that she uses the best china and sterling silver taespoons and forks.

WORD SENSE

proof
teaspoon
tablespoon
approve
routine
through
fluid
assume
introduce
intrude
conclude
aptitude
goodness
understood
neighborhood
could've
would've
should've
bulletin
cushion

A. A declarative sentence begins with a capital letter and ends with a period. Write the missing spelling words. Then write the paragraph correctly.

our school is like a ___1___. it is important to ___2___ new friends to your classmates and teachers speak clearly so that you can be ___3___. do not ___4___ on a private conversation Make sure you apologize if you cut ___5___ a crowd of people listen quietly while waiting for a speaker to end or ___6___ a speech if you have an ___7___ for a certain subject, volunteer to be a tutor.

B. Write the spelling word that fits in the category.

1. announcement, news report, __?__
2. evidence, guarantee, __?__
3. pillow, buffer, __?__
4. water, liquid, __?__
5. system, schedule, __?__
6. kindness, thoughtfulness, __?__

C. Write the spelling words that match the definitions.

1. Small spoon commonly used for eating.
2. To regard favorably.
3. To take for granted.
4. Large spoon for serving food.
5. Ought to have.

WORDSCAPES: The Writing Connection

A. A sentence is a group of words that expresses a complete thought. A sentence fragment represents part of a complete thought. Rewrite the paragraph, turning the sentence fragments into complete sentences. Remember, every sentence must contain a subject and a verb.

Good manners began. in prehistoric times. when strangers met. they held out their hands. As proof that they were friendly and weren't holding weapons, and that's how the handshake. Got started now it is routine for people. To shake hands when they are introduced or are approving business deals. through the years good manners have made life. easier for everyone.

Who, me? Trouble? Let's be friends.

Content Words

declarative
interrogative
exclamatory
imperative
fragment

ceramics
pewter
pottery
kiln
glaze

B. Write the Language Arts Word that identifies each sentence or phrase.

1. Proper manners are easy to learn.
2. Come home immediately.
3. Why would such a small boy have such a large dog?
4. The bright blue sky.
5. Watch out for that car!

C. Use the Fine Arts Words to complete the paragraph.

The art of making ___1___ is called ___2___. Porcelain is a very fine clay to which a ___3___ is applied before the object is fired in a ___4___. Porcelain dishes and ___5___ candlesticks can make a simple meal an occasion.

1. niece
2. grief
3. thief
4. yield
5. shield
6. siege
7. shriek
8. relief
9. achieve
10. mischief
11. fierce
12. ceiling
13. receive
14. receipt
15. conceit
16. reign
17. sleigh
18. seize
19. leisure
20. weird

Target Skill
Words with the **ie** or the **ei** spelling pattern.

In their **leisure** some people enjoy mock jousting tournaments. They **achieve** victories by spearing rings.

A. Write the spelling words that have the long **e** sound spelled **ie**.

B. Write the spelling word that has the short **i** sound spelled **ie**.

C. Write the spelling words that have the long **e** sound spelled **ei**.

D. Write the spelling words that have the long **a** sound spelled **ei**.

E. Write the spelling words that have the same vowel sound you hear in **pierce**.

> Use **i** before **e**, except after **c** or when sounded as **a**, as in **neighbor** and **weigh**!

F. Write the three spelling words that are exceptions to this spelling rule.

WORD STUDY

A. Proofreading Find the misspelled words
in these sentences. Write the spelling
words correctly.

The queen's rein ran smoothly until the
winter of 1524 when barbarians attempted
to sieze the castle. The seige lasted for
months and caused the queen much greif.
One morning her golden crown was
mysteriously missing. The only clue was
that her neice had heard a shreik during the
night. The queen commanded, "Bring me
the villain! Whoever rescues my crown will
recieve a jewel-studded sheild!" Each knight
strutted to his horse with an air of conciet as
he imagined himself capturing the theif.

B. Structure Three words in each row follow the same
spelling pattern. Write the word that is different.

1. field, sleigh, shield, wield
2. receive, mischief, conceit, receipt
3. reign, neighborhood, receipt, sleigh
4. ceiling, grief, siege, shriek
5. leisure, conceit, seize, fierce

C. Dictionary Write the spelling words for the dictionary
respellings.

   1. /lē′ zhər/   2. /wîrd/   3. /yēld/   4. /ə chēv′/   5. /rĭ lēf′/

D. Dictionary Write the spelling word you would find
between these guide words.

1. reliable | relieve
2. weight | welcome
3. legend | lemon
4. ache | acquaint

WORD SENSE

niece
grief
thief
yield
shield
siege
shriek
relief
achieve
mischief
fierce
ceiling
receive
receipt
conceit
reign
sleigh
seize
leisure
weird

A. Write the spelling words that rhyme with the underlined words.

1. I <u>feared</u> I looked rather ___?___ .
2. It was ___?___ that caused Ann's <u>defeat</u>.
3. The drugstore ___?___ dropped at Jill's <u>feet</u>.
4. The boards did <u>creak</u> and Jim did ___?___ .

B. Complete the analogies. Write the spelling words.

1. **Brother** is to **sister** as **nephew** is to ___?___ .
2. **Delight** is to **joy** as **sorrow** is to ___?___ .
3. **House** is to **roof** as **room** is to ___?___ .

C. Write the spelling words missing from this paragraph. You will need to write one in the past tense and capitalize one word.

When Knight Valor met the __1__ , he shouted, "__2__ , you scoundrel!" After a scuffle, Valor __3__ the capture of the __4__ robber and the crown. He rode back in triumph in a horse-driven __5__ . "What a __6__ !" the queen exclaimed. "The __7__ is over! From now on, Valor is to __8__ new jewels for his __9__ each year of my __10__ ."

D. A sentence may be declarative, exclamatory, imperative, or interrogative. Write the spelling words missing from the sentences below. Then write what type of sentence each is.

1. Now ___?___ the opportunity.
2. Our playful puppy is full of ___?___ .
3. How I enjoy my ___?___ time!

38

The following story is based on **The Knights of the Silver Shield** by Raymond MacDonald Alden.

Cruel giants dwelt in the dark forest, but knights lived in a castle nearby. Each knight received a magic silver shield. At first, the shields were dull, but as the knights began to do noble deeds, the shields grew brighter. If the knight was lazy or cowardly, the shield grew duller. When a knight won a victory or completed a difficult task, a golden star appeared in the shield's center. One day the giants began to battle the knights. Sir Roland, the youngest knight, was told to stay behind and guard the castle.

A. Finish the story of the adventures of Sir Roland, who earns his golden star. Use the spelling words when you can.

Content Words

pigment
tapestry
etching
mural
hue

diplomat
protect
quota
rumor
enlist

B. Use the Fine Arts Words to complete the sentences.

1. A castle wall might be decorated by a painted __?__ .
2. A woven __?__ can be used to cover a stone wall.
3. An __?__ is a design made from a metal plate.
4. **Color** is a synonym for __?__ .
5. Chlorophyll is the __?__ that makes plants green.

C. Use the Social Studies Words in these sentences.

The queen needed someone to be a __1__ . News had come that the enemy was advancing. It was the queen's desire to see young men __2__ in her army to __3__ the kingdom, if indeed this __4__ was true. Lord Chauncy met the queen's __5__ of one thousand men in a fortnight.

1. carbon
2. carton
3. carpenter
4. partner
5. insert
6. concern
7. dirty
8. circular
9. confirm
10. mortar
11. territory
12. authority
13. adore
14. ignore
15. therefore
16. foreman
17. curfew
18. curtain
19. furnace
20. purchase

Target Skill

The **r**-controlled vowel sounds you hear in **partner, curtain, mortar,** and **therefore.**

A. Write the spelling words that have the /är/ sound spelled **ar.** Circle the letters that make the sound.

B. Write the spelling words that have the /ûr/ sound spelled **er.** Circle the letters that make the sound.

C. Write the spelling words that have the /ûr/ sound spelled **ir.** Circle the letters that make the sound.

D. Write the spelling words that have the /ûr/ sound spelled **ur.** Circle the letters that make the sound.

E. Write the spelling word that has the /âr/ sound spelled **er.** Circle the letters that make the sound.

F. Write the spelling words that have the /ôr/ sound spelled **or.** Circle the letters that make the sound.

WORD STUDY

A. Dictionary Write the spelling words that are the base words for the words below. Write the part of speech after each spelling word. Use your spelling dictionary.

1. adoration, n.
2. confirmation, n.
3. ignorance, n.
4. partnership, n.

B. Vocabulary Write the spelling words that answer the questions in these interrogative sentences.

1. What kind of paper is used to make copies?
2. What do you call a cardboard milk container?
3. What law requires that young people be home by nine o'clock?
4. What is the mixture of cement, sand, and water that builders use?
5. What pattern of motion does a pinwheel have?

C. Structure Write the spelling words in the plural form to finish the sentences. The plural of most nouns is formed by adding **s.** Two of the words below end in **y** preceded by a consonant. Form the plurals of these words by changing the **y** to **i** and adding **es.**

1. It makes no sense to use **curtain** in a yurt because it is a tent without windows.
2. Instead of **furnace,** the Innuit use lamps to heat their snowhouses.
3. Few **purchase** are required to build a grass house.
4. Birds are like **carpenter,** making their nests from twigs.
5. Native Americans fought to protect their **territory.**
6. Architects are **authority** in designing modern houses.

D. Proofreading Write the spelling words correctly.

In India the two parts of a houseboat are first constructed on land. The construction forman, therefor, must instruct the crew to insurt the house into the boat. There is no need to be conserned with durty smudges on the boat because the water will wash them away.

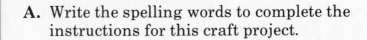

WORD SENSE

carbon
carton
carpenter
partner
insert
concern
dirty
circular
confirm
mortar
territory
authority
adore
ignore
therefore
foreman
curfew
curtain
furnace
purchase

A. Write the spelling words to complete the instructions for this craft project.

First, __1__ a piece of flexible cardboard that can be rolled and glued into a tube for the base of a __2__ grass house. You can cut out a window and __3__ a small __4__ made out of a scrap of material. If you are working with a __5__ , she can __6__ herself with collecting dry grass while you are constructing the frame. Make sure the grass is not __7__ before you glue it to the roof and base of your house.

B. Write the spelling word that belongs to each set.

1. heater, radiator, boiler, __?__
2. nitrogen, calcium, oxygen, __?__
3. love, cherish, admire, __?__
4. box, package, crate, __?__
5. verify, prove, justify, __?__
6. builder, woodworker, cabinetmaker, __?__
7. area, region, zone, __?__

C. Write the spelling word for each definition.

1. Person in charge of a group of workers.
2. A bowl used to hold substances while they are being crushed.
3. An order requiring people to retire from the streets at a certain time.
4. For that reason.
5. To disregard.
6. An accepted source of information.

WORDSCAPES: The Writing Connection

Pueblos once built their homes into the sides of very steep cliffs. Sandstone block and mud mortar were used to construct the walls. Several families lived in one building, each in its own small apartment-like space. Long ladders were used to get into these homes. In case of attack, the ladders could be pulled inside.

A. As you can see from the photographs, today's apartment buildings are something like the cliff dwellings. How are the two similar? How are they different? Write descriptive sentences that compare cliff dwelling to apartment life. Use the spelling words when you can.

Content Words

castanets
chimes
marimba
percussion
timpani

nitrogen
carbon dioxide
water vapor
pollution
environment

B. Write the Fine Arts Words that match the clues.

1. Musical sound produced by bells.
2. Large xylophone.
3. Sound created by striking objects.
4. Spanish dancer's instrument.
5. Kettledrums.

C. Use the Science Words to complete the sentences.

The effects of __1__ can be seen in our __2__ . Car fumes mix with __3__ to produce acid rain. Acid rain destroys the balance of __4__ and oxygen. Carbon dioxide, oxygen, and __5__ are elements of air.

43

1. legal
2. rival
3. central
4. neutral
5. rational
6. material
7. partial
8. typical
9. practical
10. label
11. cruel
12. tunnel
13. channel
14. talent
15. absent
16. turbulent
17. distant
18. instant
19. ignorant
20. unpleasant

Target Skill

The **schwa** sound in unstressed syllables, as in **legal** and **absent**.

Bridge and tunnel views of the Chesapeake Bay Bridge-Tunnel.

The building of underground and underwater **channels** involves **talent** in engineering and **practical** construction skills. The oldest known manmade **tunnel** was built under the river of Babylon in a **distant** age, some 4,000 years ago. The Chesapeake Bay Bridge-**Tunnel,** which runs over and under **turbulent** waters, was completed in 1964. It is a seventeen-mile span that has no **rival.**

A. Write the spelling words that have the /ə/ + l spelled **al.**

B. Write the spelling words that have the /ə/ + l spelled **el.**

C. Write the spelling words that have the /ən/ + t spelled **ent.**

D. Write the spelling words that have the /ən/ + t spelled **ant.**

WORD STUDY

A. Dictionary When you pronounce a word, you emphasize one syllable over any others. With a symbol called a **stress mark,** the dictionary indicates which syllable to emphasize. Write the spelling words ending in /ən/ + t that are pronounced with the stress on the first syllable. Note: The /ə/ usually appears in an unstressed syllable.

B. Structure The letters in each spelling word are scrambled. Write the spelling words correctly.

1. hanncel   2. bella   3. yapilct

4. rimaalte   5. nelnut

C. Vocabulary Adjectives are words used to describe nouns. From the spelling words, find the adjective that belongs in each sentence. Write the spelling words. Notice how each sentence becomes more defined when the adjective is added.

Building the Holland Tunnel in the 1920s was a ___1___ and nearly inhuman task. Each day ___2___ progress was made toward the goal. Finally, in what is known as the "hole through," the two ___3___ digging crews from opposite sides met in the ___4___ area of the tunnel.

The ___5___ odor of gas fumes caused by cars and the introduction of certain substances into the tunnel caused ___6___ problems. Eighty-four large fans were used to maintain the ___7___ quality of the air. Once, when the ceiling began to leak heavily, the ___8___ choice was made to evacuate the tunnel. Today it is not ___9___ to drive dangerous chemicals through the tunnel.

WORD SENSE

legal
rival
central
neutral
rational
material
partial
typical
practical
label
cruel
tunnel
channel
talent
absent
turbulent
distant
instant
ignorant
unpleasant

A. The words underlined are synonyms for spelling words. The spelling words that fit are all "spelling demons," or words often misspelled. Write the spelling words.

A truck filled with thick, black molasses rumbled down the road into the Holland Tunnel. The driver was <u>unaware</u> of the fact that the tank was leaking and that the sticky <u>substance</u> was draining out of the truck. When motorists noticed the strange stuff on the road, their <u>characteristic</u> response was to step on the brakes, even though this was not <u>useful</u> due to heavy traffic. Luckily, no accidents resulted.

B. Write the spelling word that completes the analogy.

1. **Misuse** is to **use** as **illegal** is to ___?___.
2. **Friend** is to **companion** as **enemy** is to ___?___.
3. **Calm** is to **tranquil** as **impartial** is to ___?___.
4. **Build** is to **bridge** as **dig** is to ___?___.
5. **Far** is to **distant** as **main** is to ___?___.
6. **Kind** is to **mercy** as ___?___ is to **pain**.
7. **Some** is to **all** as ___?___ is to **complete**.

C. Write the missing spelling words in this paragraph.

The waves in the ___1___ became ___2___ as the storm progressed. We counted on the ___3___ of our captain to get us through this ___4___ section of our voyage. We decided the ___5___ thing to do would be to put on our life jackets and wait for the ___6___ storm to cease. I read the directions on the ___7___ of my jacket aloud. Even though my appetite seemed ___8___, I sipped on a cup of tea. Then, in an ___9___, the storm was over.

46

Every paragraph has a **main idea** which is stated in the **topic sentence.** The other sentences in the paragraph support or develop that central idea.

A. Look at the picture on this page. What is the main idea of the picture? Write a topic sentence expressing this central idea. Several things are happening in the picture. Which of these details support your topic sentence? Write several sentences that develop the main idea.

Content Words

computation
estimation
difference
trillion
rounding

boundary
local
real estate
settlement
subdivide

B. Use the Math Words to complete the sentences.

When an engineer bids on a project, he gives an __1__ of the cost. There must not be a large __2__ between his estimate and actual costs. In making the __3__ of expenses, he may use a computer. He may give an estimate by __4__ off the numbers to the nearest hundred. No project has yet cost $1,000,000,000,000, or one __5__ dollars.

C. Write the Social Studies Words that match the definitions.

1. An edge, limit, or dividing line.
2. Of a particular place.
3. Land and anything on it.
4. The act or process of settling.
5. To divide into smaller parts.

47

1. skyward
2. upward
3. inward
4. outward
5. downward
6. afterward
7. homeward
8. eastward
9. barely
10. directly
11. certainly
12. loosely
13. scarcely
14. completely
15. finally
16. ideally
17. carefully
18. additionally
19. possibly
20. especially

Target Skill

Words that end in **ward** and **ly**, such as **downward** and **finally**.

There is **scarcely** an area of the world that has not been **completely** mapped. Maps exist of everything from the stars to the ocean floor, from air currents to cities. Airline pilots and ship captains **especially** depend on maps. Travelers **certainly** study road maps **carefully**. Before they look **skyward**, stargazers often pinpoint constellations on a map.

A. Write the words that end in **ward**.

B. Write the words that end with the vowel **e** + **ly**.

C. Write the word that drops the **le** from the base word before **ly** is added.

D. Write the words that end in a **consonant** + **ly**.

Spelling Hint

The suffixes **ward** and **ly** can often be added to base words to form adverbs.

WORD STUDY

A. Dictionary First write the part of speech of each base word below. Then add the **ward** or **ly** ending to form an adverb which is a spelling word. Write each new word. Follow this example:

final, adj.   finally

1. sky __?__   3. certain __?__   5. additional __?__
2. after __?__   4. scarce __?__   6. especial __?__

B. Proofreading Write the spelling words correctly.

Follow Route 94 estwerd. You will see a golf course on your right, bearly a mile before you have to turn. The road will then slope upword. Proceed carefuly—the road is rough. Turn right and follow the dirt road completly around the lake. When you finaly reach the campsite, our blue tent will be directlly to your left.

C. Structure The spelling words have been mixed up. Write the spelling words correctly.

1. downly   2. lyout   4. inpossi
   idealward   looseward   wardbly
                    3. wardhome

D. Vocabulary The vowels are missing in the spelling words. Write the spelling words correctly.

Orienteering is, __ d __ __ ll __ , done outside on a warm day. In this race, competitors must follow directions c __ mpl __ t __ l __ and c __ r __ f __ ll __ , using a map and a compass. To follow the course, a player must know __ __ stw __ rd, westward, southward, and northward directions.

49

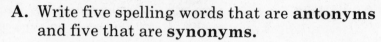

skyward

upward

inward

outward

downward

afterward

homeward

eastward

barely

directly

certainly

loosely

scarcely

completely

finally

ideally

carefully

additionally

possibly

especially

A. Write five spelling words that are **antonyms** and five that are **synonyms**.

Write the antonyms for:

1. upward
2. impossibly
3. westward
4. tightly
5. doubtfully

Write the synonyms for:

6. scarcely
7. cautiously
8. immediately
9. lastly
10. entirely

B. The suffix **ward** forms adjectives and adverbs and means "direction toward." The suffix **ly** forms adverbs and means "in a specific manner." Write the spelling word that matches each direction.

1. In the **direction toward** in.
2. In a scarce **manner.**
3. In the **direction toward** home.
4. In an ideal **manner.**
5. In a **direction toward** up.

C. Write the missing spelling words.

At the start of a voyage, sailors were __1__ bound. Looking __2__ at night, they used the stars to direct their ship's course. Sea charts, __3__ , were important in navigation. When the compass was invented, it was an __4__ helpful tool.

When you give directions, it is important to give them in sequence. For example, you might say, "First walk to the end of this street. Next, turn left." Such words as **first, second, now, then, directly, afterward, before, eastward, westward, homeward,** and **finally** help to organize directions. Referring to familiar sights, such as street names, signs, stoplights, the names of stores, or the colors of buildings, helps to make directions clear.

A. Draw a map of your local neighborhood. Select a place on the map where you want someone to go. Write directions to that place starting at your own home. Use the spelling words when you can.

Content Words

outback
paddock
grazing
drought
mutton

Celsius
exponent
scientific notation
Fahrenheit
squared

B. Write the Social Studies Words to complete the paragraph.

During a long hot summer in Australia, the ___1___ becomes very dry. This dry spell, or ___2___ , can be severe. Visitors often see sheep ___3___ on grass in a ___4___ . Meat from these sheep is called ___5___ .

C. Write the Math Words to complete the sentences below.

1. The temperature scale that registers the freezing point of water at 0° is called ___?___ .
2. The ___?___ of a number shows how many times the base number is to be multiplied by itself.
3. A method of writing numbers in terms of powers of ten is called ___?___ .
4. The temperature scale that registers freezing at 32° is called ___?___ .
5. When a number is ___?___ , it is multiplied by itself.

WORD CLUES AND STUDY

A. Write the spelling words that place the primary stress on the first syllable.

B. Write the spelling words that have one syllable.

C. Write the spelling words that end in **ly**.

D. Write the spelling words that end in silent **e**.

E. Write the spelling words that end in **al**. Then write the abbreviation for the part of speech of each of these words. Now write each word again, adding the **ly** ending. Write the part of speech of each new word. Ex. **final, adj.— finally, adv.**

F. Write the spelling words that are verbs. Write each two more times adding the **ed** and **ing** endings.

FURTHER PRACTICE AND ENRICHMENT

A. The jumbled words are spelling demons. Write the spelling words correctly.

1. guthhro
2. ingantor
3. fismiche
4. yifllan
5. carluric
6. notarc

B. Creative Writing Suppose you and your friends have decided to start a business doing odd jobs for people in your **neighborhood**—jobs such as leaf raking, dog washing, or lawn mowing. Write a **circular** advertising your new service, using this checklist. Use the spelling words when you can.

1. Give your business a catchy name.

2. Use complete sentences to describe each service.

3. Include the hours that you are available for work and the cost of purchasing your services.

4. Proofread your circular carefully for proper punctuation and spelling.

C. Proofreading Write the spelling words correctly. An **s** has been added to two spelling words. Rewrite the paragraph using the proper punctuation and capitalization.

Carla, mr Noogle's neice, designed three bullitins with funny pictures to interduce people to our naborbood service we had to perchase some matierals but we'll certenly make that money back. the picture i especialy like shows Allen, covered with soap bubbles, washing Ms pardo's seventy-five pound sheepdog, while Ms Pardo enjoys her liesure time. Our service is finaly launched.

TESTING

A. Read each sentence. Write the number of the sentence and **a** or **b** to indicate whether the underlined word is spelled correctly or incorrectly.

1. She peered <u>through</u> the fence.
   (a) correct (b) incorrect

2. The <u>bullitin</u> was posted on the wall.
   (a) correct (b) incorrect

3. Please <u>interduce</u> me to Salina.
   (a) correct (b) incorrect

4. The park in our <u>neigborhood</u> is big.
   (a) correct (b) incorrect

5. Jane is my father's <u>niece</u> and my cousin.
   (a) correct (b) incorrect

6. You will <u>recieve</u> the package today.
   (a) correct (b) incorrect

7. Watch this kitten get into <u>mischeif</u>.
   (a) correct (b) incorrect

8. We enjoy our <u>liesure</u> time.
   (a) correct (b) incorrect

9. The <u>carton</u> was filled with sponges.
   (a) correct (b) incorrect

10. A glass helps you draw a <u>circular</u> pattern.
    (a) correct (b) incorrect

B. Read each group of words. Write the number of the group and **a, b,** or **c** to indicate which word is spelled correctly.

1. (a) therefor
   (b) therefore
   (c) therfore

2. (a) perchase
   (b) purchas
   (c) purchase

3. (a) ignorant
   (b) ignorent
   (c) ignornt

4. (a) matieral
   (b) matirial
   (c) material

5. (a) tipical
   (b) typical
   (c) tipycal

6. (a) practical
   (b) practicle
   (c) practial

7. (a) certenly
   (b) curtainly
   (c) certainly

8. (a) especialy
   (b) especially
   (c) especally

9. (a) finally
   (b) finely
   (c) finaly

10. (a) afterwerd
    (b) afterwood
    (c) afterward

CHALLENGE _____

A. Write the spelling words based on these roots.

1. From two Latin words: **intro,** meaning "within," and **ducere,** meaning "to lead."

2. From Latin: **licére,** meaning "to be permitted."

3. From Old French: **meschief,** meaning "calamity."

B. Write the spelling words that are synonyms for:

1. vicinity
2. accept
3. uneducated
4. confidently

LANGUAGE TO GO

A. The Written Word In a novel called **Where the Lilies Bloom,** by Vera and Bill Cleaver, the teenage heroine, Mary Call, is forced to rely on her own abilities and resources to support her family after her father becomes ill. An idea starts to form in her mind, which in time becomes a means of income for the family.

" With the excitement in me beating hard I . . . read about . . . the medicine plants that grow wild in the green Appalachia—plants which Mr. Connell, the storekeeper, would gladly buy. . . . I gathered them, my family, around me to tell them about the big change that was going to take place in our lives."

Imagine that you, like Mary Call, wanted to begin a project to improve your life. What skills could you draw on? Write a personal description of your strengths and abilities. What are you good at? What do you need to improve? Start your essay with, "I am the type of person who . . ."

B. The Spoken Word Have you ever given directions on how to go from one place to another or how to do a specific task? If so, you know that giving a clear explanation involves expressing your thoughts in a step-by-step order. Choose one of the "how-to" topics below for an oral report. Be sure to explain the procedure for accomplishing the project in a step-by-step pattern. Use such spelling words as **finally, especially, therefore,** and **afterward.**

1. How to make a sandwich
2. How to wash a dog
3. How to ride a bike
4. How to clean your room
5. How to wash a car
6. How to fly a kite

1. faint
2. former
3. fashion
4. fulfill
5. golf
6. shelf
7. baffle
8. traffic
9. effort
10. difficult
11. offer
12. officer
13. suffix
14. phone
15. photo
16. phrase
17. physician
18. orphan
19. sophomore
20. triumph

Target Skill

The **f** sound you hear in **faint** and in **phone**.

LONG-DISTANCE FRIENDSHIP

Dear Editor,
I have a close friend who lives in Vermont. We go there for vacation every summer, but this year we're not going. I'm trying to keep in touch with her, but I don't think it will work. What can I do?
Robyn K., New Jersey

It is **difficult** to keep a long-distance friendship going, but maybe these friends could make an **effort** to **phone** each other regularly. If you were a magazine editor, replying to this "Letter to the Editor," what advice would you **offer?**

A. Write the spelling words that have the f sound spelled **f.**

B. Write the spelling words that have the f sound spelled **ff.**

C. Write the spelling words that have the f sound spelled **ph.**

WORD STUDY

A. Structure To form the possessive of a singular noun, you add an apostrophe and **s**—Laura's shelf. To form the possessive of a plural noun that ends in **s,** you simply add an apostrophe—students' efforts. Write the spelling words below in the singular and plural possessive forms.

Example: **photo's subject, photos' subjects**

	Singular Possessive		Plural Possessive	
1. officer	___?___	uniform	___?___	uniforms
2. phone	___?___	color	___?___	colors
3. sophomore	___?___	book	___?___	books
4. orphan	___?___	room	___?___	rooms
5. physician	___?___	duty	___?___	duties

B. Proofreading Write the spelling words correctly.

Karen felt fant as she came off the basketball court after a diffacult game. Her team had fulfiled their goal of having a winning season. The fraze she kept remembering was, "Success takes efort." The playing style of the Raiders, which had bafled the Nighthawks for half the game, ofered Coach Temple the opportunity to watch her athletes work as a team and eventually triumff.

C. Dictionary Write the spelling word for each dictionary respelling. Circle the letter or letters that spell the **f** sound.

1. /fôr′ mər/   3. /shĕlf/   5. /făsh′ ən/   7. /fō′ tō/
2. /gŏlf/   4. /trăf′ ĭk/   6. /sŭf′ ĭks/

faint
former
fashion
fulfill
golf
shelf
baffle
traffic
effort
difficult
offer
officer
suffix
phone
photo
phrase
physician
orphan
sophomore
triumph

A. Write the spelling word that matches the etymology or word origin.

1. From Greek **sophos,** meaning wise, and **moros,** meaning foolish.
2. From Latin the prefix **sub,** meaning secondary, and **figere,** meaning to fix.
3. From Old French **fisque,** meaning medical.
4. From Greek **orphanos,** without parents.
5. From Old English **ful,** meaning full, and **fyllan,** meaning to fill.

B. Proofreading marks show corrections to be made:

⊙ means insert a period. ≡ under a letter or
ℐ means take out. word means
∧ means insert. capitalize.

Write the spelling words similar in meaning to the underlined words. Add **ed** to one word. Rewrite the paragraph correctly.

Ted became angry because Norm, his <u>sports</u> partner, did not <u>give</u> advice on how to play a better game⊙The more ted tried, ℐto the more <u>mixed-up</u> he got. Ted made no <u>attempt</u> to be friendly. he knew he was making it <u>very hard</u> for Norm, but he didn't know how to <u>express</u> his frustrations.

C. Write the spelling words that match the clues.

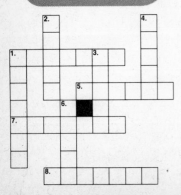

ACROSS	DOWN
1. victory	1. ___?___ jam
5. occurring earlier	2. pass out
7. ___?___ model	3. ___?___ album
8. police ___?___	4. ___?___ call
	6. cupboard ___?___

WORDSCAPES: The Writing Connection

A. When you listen to someone talking on the telephone, you hear only half of the conversation, but you can guess what the other person is saying. Here are the words of one speaker. Write the other half of the conversation. Use correct punctuation and quotation marks. Use the spelling words when you can.

Delores: "Why were you late yesterday?"
Patty:
Delores: "Are you feeling better now?"
Patty:
Delores: "I'm taking a photography class tonight. Would you like to come with me?"
Patty:
Delores: "Oh, that's right. Well, I hope the tournament goes well. I'll call you tomorrow."

Content Words

film
lens
photograph
shutterbug
tripod

amendment
candidate
nominate
patriot
suffrage

B. Use the Fine Arts Words to complete the paragraph.

Diana is a __1__ who never misses an opportunity to take a __2__ . She carefully loads the camera with __3__ , attaches the camera securely to the __4__ , and makes sure that the __5__ is facing the subject.

C. Write the Social Studies Words that complete the paragraph. You will need to add **s** to one word.

The right to vote, which is called __1__ , was fought for dearly by women __2__ before 1920. The nineteenth __3__ provided women with an opportunity to __4__ the __5__ of their choice.

59

1. amaze
2. freeze
3. magazine
4. phase
5. arise
6. tease
7. pause
8. browse
9. cruise
10. optimism
11. pessimism
12. husband
13. visitor
14. scissors
15. usual
16. casual
17. visual
18. vision
19. television
20. conclusion

Target Skill

The **z** sound you hear in **arise**.
The **zh** sound you hear in **usual**.

Visions

Sometimes I need to
Go out in nature to bring
My happiness back.

—Sonny Gonzales, Texas

A. Write the spelling words that have the **z** sound spelled by **z**.

B. Write the spelling words that have the **z** sound spelled by **s** followed by a silent **e**.

C. Write the spelling words that have the **z** sound spelled by **s** in the third syllable.

D. Write the spelling words with two or three syllables that have the **z** sound in the first syllable.

E. Write the spelling words that have the **zh** sound followed by **ual**.

F. Write the spelling words that have the **zh** sound followed by **ion**.

WORD STUDY

A. Proofreading In the journal entry, some words are misspelled. Write the spelling words correctly (**d** has been added to two of the words).

November 14, 1986

    This Saturday, as usal, Julio came over to my house. We spent a casul afternoon watching telavison and making collages out of magizine pictures that we cut out with sissors. I was amased at how many colorful photographs we found. I teazed Julio when he taped a paper mustache to his lip. He looked like a miniature version of my sister's huzband, who is Julio's brother.
I held up a mirror, and we both
started laughing at the vison we saw.
My mother's concluson is that we
are going through a silly fase.
Julio went home when my parents'
vistor came for dinner.

B. Structure Verbs that do not add **d** or **ed** to form the past tense are called irregular verbs. Write the two spelling words that are irregular verbs.

C. Vocabulary The dictionary gives more than one definition for most words. Write the spelling words that match the second definitions given below.

1. In music, a hold.
2. To feed on leaves, bark, young shoots, and twigs.
3. The belief that our world is the best of all possible worlds.
4. To run a vehicle at the speed that is most efficient.
5. The belief that evil in the world outweighs good.
6. Capable of being seen by the eye; visible.

WORD SENSE

amaze
freeze
magazine
phase
arise
tease
pause
browse
cruise
optimism
pessimism
husband
visitor
scissors
usual
casual
visual
vision
television
conclusion

A. The root **tele** means distance in Greek. The word **vision** comes from the Latin word **videre,** which means to see. Write the spelling word that stems from these roots.

B. Write the spelling words that complete the analogies.

1. **Scare** is to **shock** as **surprise** is to ___?___ .
2. **Chose** is to **choose** as **froze** is to ___?___ .
3. **Won** is to **win** as **arose** is to ___?___ .
4. **Budge** is to **move** as **pester** is to ___?___ .
5. **Hearing** is to **auditory** as **seeing** is to ___?___ .
6. **Airplane** is to **fly** as **ship** is to ___?___ .

C. Write the spelling words that complete the categories.

1. periodical, journal, publication, ___?___
2. brother, uncle, nephew, ___?___
3. staplers, paper clips, erasers, ___?___
4. sight, opticals, observation, ___?___
5. delay, break, rest, ___?___
6. guest, caller, company, ___?___
7. hopelessness, gloom, doubt, ___?___
8. scan, skim, glance through, ___?___
9. part, stage, aspect, ___?___

D. Write the spelling words that are antonyms for the words below.

1. pessimism	3. beginning
2. deliberate	4. uncommon

> Dreamy-eyed I watch
> Television superstars.
> Maybe I'll be one.

This poem reflects the experiences that some people have while watching television. Though television is often unrealistic, real people sometimes think their lives should be like those portrayed.

A. The poem is written in a form called haiku. Haiku is a type of Japanese poetry that has three lines. The first line has five syllables, the second line seven syllables, and the third line five syllables. See if you can write haiku about who you are or who you want to be. Try to use one or two spelling words.

Content Words

multiplier
multiplicand
multiples
factoring
divisibility

excel
ceremony
national
citizenship
patriotism

B. Use the Math Words to complete the sentences.

1. The __?__ of a number can be determined by __?__ .
2. The number by which the __?__ is multiplied is called the __?__ .
3. Four and six are __?__ of two.

C. Use the Social Studies Words to complete the sentences.

A special __1__ is held to grant immigrants __2__ in the United States. People who __3__ at learning languages generally adjust most easily to their new life. Many quickly develop an understanding of __4__ customs and a sense of __5__ and pride.

1. *directed*
2. *directing*
3. *resulted*
4. *resulting*
5. *profited*
6. *profiting*
7. *obtained*
8. *obtaining*
9. *complained*
10. *complaining*
11. *remained*
12. *remaining*
13. *differed*
14. *differing*
15. *admitted*
16. *admitting*
17. *permitted*
18. *permitting*
19. *excelled*
20. *excelling*

The Quarrel
by Eleanor Farjeon

I quarreled with my brother,
I don't know what about,
One thing led to another
And somehow we fell out.
The start of it was slight,
The end of it was strong,
He said he was right,
I knew he was wrong!

We hated one another.
The afternoon turned black.
Then suddenly my brother
Thumped me on the back,
And said, "Oh, come along!
We can't go on all night—
I was in the wrong."
So he was in the right.

A. Write the spelling words in which the base word does not change when you add **ed.**

B. Write the spelling words in which you double the final consonant before adding **ed.**

C. Write the spelling words in which the base word does not change when you add **ing.**

D. Write the spelling words in which you double the final consonant before adding **ing.**

WORD STUDY

A. Structure Write the spelling words in the past tense by adding **ed** to the underlined words.

Grandma and I made plans to go on a picnic. I <u>obtain</u> a big basket from the attic which Mom <u>permit</u> me to use for this special occasion. Grandma <u>admit</u> that egg salad sandwiches were her favorite. She <u>direct</u> me as I peeled the hard-boiled eggs and chopped the celery. Our efforts <u>result</u> in some fantastic sandwiches. Tink, my dog, <u>remain</u> at the door and <u>complain</u> with yips and barks as Grandma and I rode our bikes toward the park.

B. Dictionary The dictionary does not include an individual entry for every form of a word. To find a word with an **ed** or **ing** ending, look up the base word. Write the spelling words that you can make from these base words.

1. profit ___?___ ___?___
2. complain ___?___ ___?___
3. remain ___?___ ___?___
4. differ ___?___ ___?___
5. admit ___?___ ___?___
6. permit ___?___ ___?___
7. excel ___?___ ___?___

C. Proofreading The **ing** form of a verb can be used with the present, past, or future tense. This paragraph is written in the past tense. Write the spelling words correctly.

Several years ago Mr. Finn was directting the softball team when his son Ian hit a grand slam, resultting in a home run. Apparently Ian was profitting from practicing so much with his father. Ian was obtainning a reputation as a star batter. Even though he and his father spent a great deal of time differing over batting styles, they were exceling as a student and coach team.

WORD SENSE

directed
directing
resulted
resulting
profited
profiting
obtained
obtaining
complained
complaining
remained
remaining
differed
differing
admitted
admitting
permitted
permitting
excelled
excelling

A. A root is a word part that cannot stand alone. It becomes a word when it is joined to a prefix (added before the root) or a suffix (added after the root). Prefixes add meaning. The prefix **ob** means "toward," **re** means "again" or "back," and **ex** means "out of" or "beyond." Write the spelling words that have these prefixes.

ob	re	ex

1. __?__   3. __?__   5. __?__   7. __?__

2. __?__   4. __?__   6. __?__   8. __?__

B. Write the spelling words that complete the paragraph. Use each word only once.

Because of an earache, my brother __1__ all night, so I was __2__ to sleep on the couch. In the morning I __3__ to my dad that I was tired. Mom __4__ some medicine for earaches and __5__ Sam in how to use it properly. __6__ Sam in how to do anything was difficult because he could barely hear! Sam ended up __7__ me to give him his medicine.

C. Write the spelling words that complete these sentences written in the future tense.

1. Businesses will be __?__ from tourists.
2. People will start __?__ if the tickets are sold out.
3. In the debate, the political opponents will be __?__ on every issue.
4. Colleges will soon be __?__ students.

WORDSCAPES: The Writing Connection

Poems are often written to communicate feelings. Everyone has quarreled at some time with a brother, sister, or friend. Little differences can explode into huge arguments. And there never seems to be a good solution when you're feeling angry.

The Quarrel by Eleanor Farjeon is a good example of a family argument. The rhyming pattern in the poem shows which syllables are stressed. In each set of four lines, the last words in the first and third lines rhyme and the last words in the second and fourth lines rhyme.

A. Write a poem about an experience you've had with someone in your family which made you feel angry, happy, sad, silly, great, or nervous. See if you can make the last words in every other line rhyme. Use the spelling words when you can.

Content Words

Caribbean
coral
lagoon
sunset
tropics

crater
lunar
meteorite
module
terrain

B. Write the Social Studies Words that complete the paragraph. You will need to add **s** to one of the words.

The __1__ Sea has __2__ reefs and deep blue __3__ . Watching a __4__ in the __5__ is like watching a field of wild orange poppies bloom before your eyes.

C. Write the Science Words that complete the paragraph. You will need to add **s** to one of the words.

The __1__ made a safe __2__ landing. Soon after they left Earth, the astronauts had watched a burning __3__ fly through the inky black space. Now they noticed that the __4__ of the moon was covered with __5__ of different sizes.

1. knob
2. kneel
3. knack
4. knowledge
5. aisle
6. isle
7. debt
8. tomb
9. numb
10. crumb
11. plumber
12. palm
13. salmon
14. almond
15. hymn
16. solemn
17. autumn
18. column
19. cupboard
20. handkerchief

Target Skill

Words with more consonant letters than consonant sounds as in **knowledge.**

Somber days turn up
Old memories of a time when
Life was different and
Even the weather was
Much brighter and
Newer

— Barbara Rogers

A. Write the spelling words that have a silent **k.**

B. Write the spelling words that have a silent **s.**

C. Write the spelling words that have a silent **b.**

D. Write the spelling words that have a silent **l.**

E. Write the spelling words that have a silent **n.**

F. Write the spelling word that has a silent **p** and the spelling word that has a silent **d.**

WORD STUDY

A. Proofreading Some of the words in the paragraphs are misspelled. Write the spelling words correctly.

At school Christa realized she had lost the hankerchief her grandmother had embroidered by hand. Chan had a nack for finding lost items, so Christa asked him to neel down and look under the classroom cuboard. They peered down the ailes between the desks, too, but found nothing.

As Christa walked home on that crisp autum day, she knew she must tell her father. A num feeling settled over her. As she reached for the door nob, her pam felt slippery. With a solem face she told her dad about the loss. He smiled and handed her the missing treasure. He had found it behind the colum of shrubs along the sidewalk after she had left for school.

B. Dictionary Write the spelling words that match the dictionary respellings. Circle the silent letter in each word you write.

1. /dĕt/   2. /tōōm/   3. /krŭm/   4. /hĭm/

C. Structure In a special code, the numbers 21-46 represent the letters of the alphabet. The number 21 is A, 22 is B, and so on. Write the spelling words that are shown in coded form. Circle the one word that is miscoded. Write that spelling word correctly.

1. 29, 39, 32, 25

2. 36, 32, 41, 33, 22, 25, 38

3. 39, 21, 32, 33, 34, 35

4. 21, 32, 33, 35, 34, 24

5. 31, 34, 35, 43, 32, 25, 24, 27, 25

WORD SENSE

knob
kneel
knack
knowledge
aisle
isle
debt
tomb
numb
crumb
plumber
palm
salmon
almond
hymn
solemn
autumn
column
cupboard
handkerchief

A. Write the spelling words that complete the mystery clues. Then solve the mystery.

In December Mrs. Calder called a detective she had read about in a newspaper __1__ . He found her missing ring wrapped in a __2__ inside a jeweler's __3__ . The jeweler said, in a __4__ manner, "A man in a work uniform with a wrench in his pocket sold the ring to me." In the __5__ Ted Calder had lost his job as a __6__ for the Faucet Fix-It Co.

B. Write the spelling words that fit.

1. When you rest on your knees you __?__ .
2. A rounded handle can be called a __?__ .
3. Because he trained a yak, we say he has a __?__ with a yak.
4. All <u>knowing</u> occurs at this <u>ledge</u>. __?__
5. This fish is pink. __?__
6. A hairless part of a hand is the __?__ .
7. From the crust you get a __?__ .

C. Write and capitalize the spelling words that complete the headlines.

1. **Overdue** __?__ **Paid**
2. **The** __?__ **of Ancient Mummies Discovered**
3. **Frigid Weather Can Turn Fingers** __?__
4. __?__ **Nuts Found To Be Source of Calcium**

D. **Homophones** are words which sound the same but differ in spelling and meaning. Write the **homophones** for these words.

1. him __?__   2. I'll __?__ , __?__

WORDSCAPES: The Writing Connection

An acrostic poem is a poem in which the first letter of each line forms a word or message. On the first page of this unit, an acrostic poem describes the word **solemn.** Note that the words do not have to rhyme in an acrostic poem.

A. Choose a spelling word and write an acrostic poem that in some way expresses or describes the meaning of that word.

Content Words

broadcast
columnist
expert
journalist
literate

calorie
dietitian
metabolism
nourish
nutrition

B. Write the Language Arts Words that complete the sentences.

1. If you can read and write, you are ___?___ .
2. If you publish the news, you are a ___?___ .
3. If you are knowledgeable about a certain subject, you are an ___?___ .
4. If you write a magazine column, you are a ___?___ .
5. The transmission of a television program is a ___?___ .

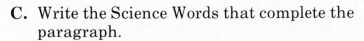

C. Write the Science Words that complete the paragraph.

A __1__ studies foods to learn what will best __2__ the human body. She also determines an individual's rate of __3__ to see how fast the energy from one __4__ is burned. With this information she can provide a patient with the kind of __5__ he or she needs.

1. banner
2. manner
3. connect
4. announce
5. innocent
6. error
7. mirror
8. horrible
9. terrible
10. accident
11. occasion
12. assist
13. issue
14. tissue
15. express
16. impress
17. recess
18. process
19. success
20. possess

Target Skill

Double consonant letters you see in words such as **manner, mirror,** and **success.**

Opinions

When I am with friends, I am always scared they might disagree with my ideas. I'm afraid they might say my opinion is stupid or something. Can you give me some ideas to prevent that?

Gwenael E., Quebec

Look in the **mirror.** Who are you? Do you **possess** opinions that you believe in strongly? How will people know who you are unless you **express** those opinions?

A. Write the spelling words that have **nn** in them.

B. Write the spelling words that have **rr** in them.

C. Write the spelling words that have **ss** in them.

D. Write the spelling words that have **cc** in them.

WORD STUDY

A. Structure Study the underlined letters in each sentence. Combine the letters to make spelling words.

I'm sorry the sound of my music bothers you. I'll put on some soothing records soon. I have many new records. I like every record. Relaxing pieces are easy to select. So just cancel your plans and listen. I'll take care of this selection while you sit down. I can listen to the music you don't like another time.

B. Vocabulary If a singular noun ends in **s,** you add **es** to make it plural. Write the spelling words in the paragraph, making each plural.

The process _ _ involved in printing school newspapers are numerous. Some papers are success _ _ and others are flops. The planning required must often take place during recess _ _ and on weekends.

C. Dictionary The dictionary usually gives more than one definition for each entry. Look up the definitions of these underlined spelling words. Decide which definition of each word is intended in the sentence. Write each spelling word.

1. Our soccer team had a <u>banner</u> year.
2. The operator will <u>connect</u> you with the main desk.
3. Marilyn <u>announced</u> the hockey game on the radio.
4. The <u>horrible</u> noise made us shiver with fright.
5. The <u>terrible</u> pollution made it unpleasant to go outside.
6. I stepped on the dog's tail by <u>accident</u>.
7. The <u>occasion</u> did not call for a formal introduction.
8. Belinda likes to <u>impress</u> everyone with her bird calls.
9. The tracing paper was thin <u>tissue</u> .
10. People's faces often <u>mirror</u> their moods.

WORD SENSE

banner
manner
connect
announce
innocent
error
mirror
horrible
terrible
accident
occasion
assist
issue
tissue
express
impress
recess
process
success
possess

A. Write the spelling words with the double consonants shown in the paragraph. You will need to put one verb in the past tense. Write the part of speech for each spelling word.

When the bell rang for _ _ _ _ ss, Jorge dropped his lunch tray as everyone pushed by him and raced outside. Terry used her _ _ ss _ _ to _ ss _ _ _ in cleaning up the mess. Our principal said the event reminded him of an _ _ _ _ _ ss train about to derail. After this _ cc _ _ _ _ _ in the lunch room, the principal _ ss _ _ _ new lunch room rules. Now, in the _ _ _ _ _ ss of leaving, we must proceed in an orderly _ _ nn _ _ .

B. Write the spelling words that are antonyms for the words in the **banners.**

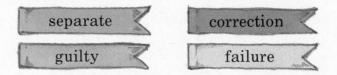

separate   correction

guilty   failure

C. Write the spelling word that completes each analogy.

1. **Know** is to **understand** as **own** is to ___?___ .
2. **Pattern** is to **mold** as **influence** is to ___?___ .
3. **Echo** is to **surface** as **image** is to ___?___ .
4. **Yell** is to **scream** as **proclaim** is to ___?___ .
5. **Sign** is to **poster** as **flag** is to ___?___ .
6. **Anniversary** is to **event** as **birthday** is to ___?___ .
7. **Horrifying** is to **horrible** as **terrifying** is to ___?___ .

74

WORDSCAPES: The Writing Connection

Opinions and feelings are not always easy to express. It is especially difficult when you're worried about how other people will react to what you have to say. Yet it is important to speak up for what you believe. Can you disagree with another person and still be friends? If someone criticizes your ideas, does it mean your ideas are worthless?

A. Write a response to Gwenael's letter on the first page of this unit. Include answers to the questions above. Use the spelling words when you can.

Content Words

collect
insure
nonrenewal
policy
provision

amplitude
decibel
loudness
receiver
reverberate

B. Write the Social Studies Words that complete the paragraph. You will need to add **s** to two words.

An insurance agency ___1___ payments from every person that it ___2___ . This is a ___3___ of the written contract, or ___4___ , which covers the person against loss. Sometimes a ___5___ clause will be part of a policy, to protect the insurance company against risk.

C. Write the Science Words that complete the paragraph. You will need to add **s** to two words.

Inside the ___1___ of a telephone is a thin piece of wire mesh, which ___2___ every time a sound wave passes through it. This small wire mesh is used to increase the ___3___ of a sound wave. This, in turn, increases the ___4___ of the sound, which is measured in ___5___ .

Amplitude is the distance between the highest and lowest point of a sound wave. When the amplitude increases, so does the loudness of the sound.

75

REVIEW

WORD CLUES AND STUDY

A. Write the spelling words that have the **f** sound.

B. Write the spelling words that have the **z** sound.

C. Write the spelling words that have the **zh** sound.

D. Write the spelling words that have double consonants.

E. Write the spelling words that have silent letters.

FURTHER PRACTICE AND ENRICHMENT

A. Write the spelling words that stem from these origins.

1. From Latin **concludere,** meaning **to end.**

2. From Latin **com,** meaning **with,** + **plangere,** meaning **to lament.**

3. From Latin **ad,** meaning **to,** + **mittere,** meaning **to send.**

4. From Latin **optimus,** meaning **best.**

5. From Latin **ex,** meaning **out,** + **fortis,** meaning **strong.**

6. From Latin **dirigere,** meaning **to give direction to.**

7. From Latin **com,** meaning **together,** + **nectere,** meaning **to bind.**

B. Creative Writing Mandy was a beautiful pointer dog who lived in the suburbs with Pete and Ann Martin. When the Martins moved to a nearby city, Mandy had no place to run. They found a good home for her on the Stevens farm 300 miles away.

Within a month George Stevens called to tell Ann and Pete that Mandy had run away. They searched for her everywhere, but she could not be found.

Several weeks later, the Martins heard a scratching noise at the door. Ann hurried to open it. "Mandy!" she shouted. Mandy, covered with mud, thin and quivering, jumped on Ann and licked her. "Oh, Mandy," said Ann, hugging her thin, exhausted dog, "I'll never let you go away again."

How did Mandy get home? How did she find the Martins? How did she travel 300 miles? Write your conclusion to the story.

C. Proofreading Proofread the conclusion you have written to Mandy's story. Ask yourself these questions:

1. Does your conclusion complete the story? Is your ending satisfying to you as a reader?

2. Have you placed your sentences in logical order? Is each a complete sentence?

3. Have you used proper punctuation and grammar? Are all the words spelled correctly?

TESTING

A. Read each sentence carefully. Write the number of the sentence. If one of the underlined words is misspelled, write its letter. If neither word is misspelled, write the letter **c**.

1. ⓐ ⓑ ⓒ The <u>moment</u> the bell rings, <u>recess</u> is over.
   　　　　　a　　　　　　　　　　b

2. ⓐ ⓑ ⓒ This was a very <u>special</u> <u>occassion</u>.
   　　　　　　　　　　　a　　　　b

3. ⓐ ⓑ ⓒ The bride and groom <u>marched</u> down the <u>isle</u>.
   　　　　　　　　　　　　　a　　　　　　　b

4. ⓐ ⓑ ⓒ Jan cut out the <u>pattern</u> with these <u>sissors</u>.
   　　　　　　　　　　a　　　　　　　b

5. ⓐ ⓑ ⓒ If you wish to <u>fulfill</u> your <u>goal</u>, you must work at it.
   　　　　　　　　　　a　　　b

6. ⓐ ⓑ ⓒ The <u>results</u> of your <u>efort</u> will be noticed.
   　　　　　a　　　　　　b

7. ⓐ ⓑ ⓒ Our family <u>phisician</u> is a <u>pleasant</u> man.
   　　　　　　　　　a　　　　　b

8. ⓐ ⓑ ⓒ Rachel is a <u>sophmore</u> in high <u>school</u>.
   　　　　　　　　　a　　　　　　b

9. ⓐ ⓑ ⓒ Her <u>optimism</u> helps everyone to maintain a <u>positive</u> outlook.
   　　　　　a　　　　　　　　　　　　　　　　b

10. ⓐ ⓑ ⓒ Stop <u>complaining</u> about your <u>problems</u>.
   　　　　　　a　　　　　　　b

B. Read each group of words. Write the number of the group and **a, b,** or **c** to indicate the word in each group that is spelled correctly.

1. ⓐ posses　　3. ⓐ handkerchief　5. ⓐ column　　7. ⓐ difered　　9. ⓐ usal
   ⓑ possess　　　ⓑ hankerchief　　ⓑ colum　　　ⓑ differed　　ⓑ usual
   ⓒ posess　　　ⓒ handkercheif　ⓒ colume　　ⓒ diffred　　ⓒ usuall

2. ⓐ conect　　4. ⓐ knowlege　　6. ⓐ admitting　8. ⓐ directted　10. ⓐ conclusion
   ⓑ connect　　　ⓑ knoledge　　ⓑ admiteng　ⓑ derected　　ⓑ conclution
   ⓒ connekt　　　ⓒ knowledge　ⓒ addmitting　ⓒ directed　　ⓒ conclucion

CHALLENGE

Write the spelling word that summarizes each underlined group of words.

I don't like <u>expressing how annoyed I feel</u> about my brother and sister, but sometimes I just have to. On <u>some particular days</u>, they seem to make an <u>eager attempt</u> to bother me. My <u>most common</u> response is to get really mad and tell them to leave me alone. I guess I'm supposed to <u>have within me</u> a great deal of patience because I'm older. Sometimes I'd like to take a <u>long break</u> from being older than my brother and sister.

LANGUAGE TO GO

A. **The Written Word** This poem, written by a student, describes how people mask their feelings because they think that others expect them to be happy.

Feelings
by Siobhan McCarthy, Age 12

Outside people are happy and glad;
Inside people are frustrated and sad.
The body is a mask of feelings inside.
The soul is a place where feelings can hide.
Feelings come from the heart and the soul.
The face on the outside may just be a role
That someone is acting, just being polite,
But their eyes never show any joy or delight.
Feelings express inner thoughts from our mind;
Show these emotions, don't lock them inside.

Write your own poem based on feelings. You may use a rhyming pattern like the one in the poem above, write haiku, or choose another poetry form.

B. **The Spoken Word** Here is a chance for you to become a parent. Act out the parts in this script. You decide how to end the story.

Parent: "I told you to clean your room."
Penny: "Ah, Dad, I don't want to do it now. Besides, Jason never has to clean his room!"
Parent: "Jason is only four. You should set a good example as his older sister."
Penny: "Well, I'm tired of being older. I always have to do more than he does."
Parent: "I know, but that's part of growing up. Don't you want to be a grown-up someday?"
Penny: "Yes, I guess so—someday—but now I just want to go outside."
Parent:
Penny:

1. favorable
2. profitable
3. acceptable
4. approachable
5. available
6. changeable
7. capable
8. probable
9. notable
10. adorable
11. valuable
12. edible
13. legible
14. sensible
15. visible
16. invisible
17. flexible
18. forcible
19. reversible
20. responsible

Target Skill

The suffixes **able** and **ible**, as in **favorable** and **visible**.

If you are **capable** of saving money, it is **probable** that you can say no to yourself when you want to spend all your **available** money. Saying no today can help you to reach your goals tomorrow. If you say no to small things, and save the money instead, you will be able to afford something really **valuable** and special in the future.

A. Write the spelling words in which the spelling of the base words does not change when you add the suffix **able** or **ible**.

B. Write the spelling words in which you drop the silent **e** from the base words before you add the suffix **able** or **ible**.

C. Write the spelling words in which you add **able** or **ible** to word roots.

A. Structure Use addition and subtraction to write the spelling words. Add prefixes and suffixes to the root or base words. In some cases, you will need to subtract a silent **e**.

1. note – e + able = ___?___ .
2. adore – e + able = ___?___ .
3. value – e + able = ___?___ .
4. sense – e + ible = ___?___ .
5. in + vis + ible = ___?___ .
6. force – e + ible = ___?___ .
7. re + verse – e + ible = ___?___ .
8. re + sponse – e + ible = ___?___ .

B. Vocabulary The negative prefixes **un, in, il** and **im** have been added to the ten spelling words in this Word Search puzzle. Write the spelling words that are the **opposites** of the words you find.

```
x o u m q r e n b p c f u
u i n v a l u a b l e g n
i n c a p a b l e e i j f
i l h c w a q u f k n s a
u n a v a i l a b l e h v
v i n v i s i b l e d m o
a z g d m p v r e j i d r
i b e g j g m t l d b k a
u n a c c e p t a b l e b
l f b p x c o n s v e t l
i i l l e g i b l e i x e
s o e i m p r o b a b l e
```

C. Proofreading Read the paragraph and write the misspelled spelling words correctly.

    It is important to keep a ledgible and accurate account of your savings. You may find that it is profetible to open a savings account at a bank. Most bankers are approachible. Otherwise, you might use a piggybank or ask your parents to be responsable for your savings. You can be flexable about how you save money. The point is to find a sensable method that works for you.

WORD SENSE

favorable
profitable
acceptable
approachable
available
changeable
capable
probable
notable
adorable
valuable
edible
legible
sensible
visible
invisible
flexible
forcible
reversible
responsible

A. The suffixes **able** and **ible** are used to form adjectives. The suffix adds the meaning **capable** or **worthy** to the base word or word root. Write the spelling words that fit the definitions.

1. Capable of being seen.
2. Capable of bending repeatedly.
3. Worthy of notice.
4. Capable of being eaten.
5. Not capable of being seen.
6. Capable of being read.

B. Write the spelling words that best fit in the following sentences.

1. Some jackets and sleeping bags are ___?___ .
2. Puppies and kittens are ___?___ .
3. Eating pizza with your hands is both ___?___ and ___?___ as good manners.
4. It is likely, or ___?___ , that there will be traffic at rush hour.
5. Dogs that are friendly and wagging their tails are usually ___?___ .
6. **Forceful** means **strong** or **effective,** but ___?___ means **applying physical force.**

C. Write the spelling words that complete the paragraph. One syllable from each word is printed on the line.

Kerri knows she is <u>cap</u>_____ of saving enough money to buy a watch. Jimmy the Jeweler has several types <u>a</u>_____. The one Kerri really likes has a _____<u>able</u> wristband. A watch is a _____<u>u</u>_____ possession for a girl who has a busy schedule. She feels it will be especially _____<u>it</u>_____ when her after-school job begins. Kerri's sense of responsibility has made a <u>fa</u>_____ impression on her parents.

82

Report writing involves many steps. The first step is to select a topic. Narrow your topic to a limited subject that you can cover completely in your report.

The next step is to research the topic. Start by locating books and articles on your subject. Use index cards to record any information you find. Write each idea or subheading you will cover in your report on a separate card. When you locate information on that specific subject, write it in your own words on the card. Be sure to note the title of the book or article, the author's name, and the relevant page numbers for each piece of information.

A. Choose a topic that interests you. Research the topic and write the information you will use on index cards. Remember to stick to a specific topic as you gather the facts.

Content Words

corrupt
demonstrate
defend
indict
verdict

debate
disagreement
logical
opinion
panelist

B. The Social Studies Words and the Language Arts Words have all been used in a single paragraph. Write the words that belong in the blanks. You will need to add **s** to three of the nouns.

The grand jury determines whether or not to __1__ officials who are accused of being __2__ . Lawyers __3__ their clients, and attempt to __4__ through evidence and testimony that their clients are not guilty. The jurors __5__ the issues that have been discussed during a trial. All jury __6__ must form __7__ , and make __8__ decisions based on their experiences as jurors. They must solve any major __9__ among themselves before the jury's __10__ is delivered.

1. irregular
2. irrational
3. irresistible
4. antisocial
5. antifreeze
6. illegal
7. illogical
8. illiterate
9. illegible
10. nonprofit
11. nonfat
12. nonreturnable
13. misread
14. misbehave
15. misinform
16. mislead
17. misplace
18. misuse
19. mistrust
20. misfortune

Target Skill

Negative prefixes.

Starting a Collection

I. Purposes
   A. **Nonprofit** hobby
   B. Profit-making business

II. Additions
   A. Locating sources
   B. Rejecting **irregular** items

III. Problems
   A. Dishonest "experts" who
      mislead and **misinform**
   B. **Misplaced** objects

A. Write the spelling words that begin with the prefix **ir.**

B. Write the spelling words that begin with the prefix **anti.**

C. Write the spelling words that begin with the prefix **il.**

D. Write the spelling words that begin with the prefix **non.**

E. Write the spelling words that begin with the prefix **mis.**

WORD STUDY

A. Vocabulary The prefixes **ir, il,** and **non** mean **not.** When you add **ir, il,** or **non** to the beginning of a word, the word then means the opposite of its original meaning. The prefix **mis** means **bad** or **badly**; add **mis** to behave, and you get **misbehave.**

Write the spelling words that match these directions.

1. not + rational
2. not + legal
3. not + literate
4. not + profit
5. badly + read
6. badly + behave
7. badly + lead
8. badly + use

B. Dictionary Look at the base words of the spelling words and their parts of speech. Add the prefix (and suffix if necessary) to each base word to form the spelling word, and write the new word's part of speech.

1. logic, n.
2. trust, n. or v.
3. fortune, n.
4. return, n. or v.
5. place, n. or v.
6. fat, n. or adj.
7. freeze, v.

C. Proofreading In this paragraph about a coin collector, or numismatist, the base words of the spelling words are underlined. Write the spelling words that belong in their place. One is in the past tense.

For Ryan, the numismatist, coin collecting is an <u>resistible</u> pursuit. Some people claim that it is a solitary hobby, and therefore <u>social</u>, but Ryan claims that this is not so. Ryan spends a great deal of time with other numismatists comparing the <u>regular</u> markings on some of their older coins. Because some of the lettering on these coins is <u>legible</u>, he frequently consults with others who have similar coins. Ryan believes that many people are <u>informed</u> about his hobby.

WORD SENSE

irregular
irrational
irresistible
antisocial
antifreeze
illegal
illogical
illiterate
illegible
nonprofit
nonfat
nonreturnable
misread
misbehave
misinform
mislead
misplace
misuse
mistrust
misfortune

A. Write the spelling words that complete the paragraph on collecting stamps.

    Because stamps rarely come in __1__ shapes, they can be easily placed in special albums, so collectors don't __2__ their stamps. The cancellation mark on a stamped envelope may make the stamp's words __3__. It is __4__ to reuse a cancelled stamp; the U.S. Post Office, a __5__ institution, does not tolerate this __6__ of stamps.

B. Write the spelling words that complete the analogies. Write each word only once.

1. **Reasonable** is to **unreasonable** as **logical** is to __?__.
2. **High** is to **low** as **literate** is to __?__.
3. **Little** is to **none** as **lowfat** is to __?__.
4. **Accept** is to **unacceptable** as **return** is to __?__.
5. **Summer** is to **coolant** as **winter** is to __?__.
6. **Outgoing** is to **timid** as **friendly** is to __?__.
7. **Strong** is to **powerful** as **magnetic** is to __?__.
8. **Simplify** is to **confuse** as **sensible** is to __?__.

C. Write the spelling words that can replace the phrases below.

1. Lead in the wrong direction.
2. To give wrong information.
3. Bad luck.
4. Behave poorly.
5. Read inaccurately.
6. To be wary of.

Once you have selected a topic for a report, you should prepare an outline. An outline provides an opportunity to preview your report before you've actually written it. It can help you decide what you will cover and in what order the information will appear.

A. Decide on at least three main headings to use in writing about the topic you have chosen. Then decide in what order you want the headings to appear. For each heading, select at least two subheadings that will add supporting facts and details. Write the headings and subheadings in the proper order. There is a sample of an outline on page 84.

Content Words

appositive
grammar
linking verb
modifier
tense

capacity
dimensions
mass
volume
velocity

B. The underlined words in these sentences are examples of the Language Arts Words. Write the words that match the underlined clues.

1. Jill, a sixth grader, will be twelve in April.
2. She laughed, laugh, will laugh all the way home.
3. He is feeling lighthearted today.
4. I only want advice. I want only advice.
5. All of the above.

C. Use the Math Words to complete the paragraph.

The astronauts noticed the increase in the __1__ of the space ship as they left Earth's atmosphere. The ship, carrying four astronauts, was at full __2__ . The __3__ of the interior were no greater than those of a full-size van. Although the __4__ of air in the capsule was adequate, each astronaut carried an emergency oxygen tank. They observed that their weight changed as a result of the change in gravitational pull, but that their __5__ did not.

1. *passage*
2. *postage*
3. *bandage*
4. *garage*
5. *garbage*
6. *courage*
7. *advantage*
8. *mileage*
9. *marriage*
10. *carriage*
11. *development*
12. *equipment*
13. *appointment*
14. *assignment*
15. *excitement*
16. *advancement*
17. *measurement*
18. *document*
19. *experiment*
20. *instrument*

Target Skill

Suffix endings **age** and **ment** used to form such nouns as **postage** and **experiment**.

Equestrian Questions

1. Riding **equipment** includes:
   a. bridle b. mare c. pinto

2. Which has the **advantage** of being the smallest horse?
   a. mustang b. Belgian c. Shetland

3. The unit of **measurement** used to determine a horse's height is:
   a. hand b. foot c. finger

A. Write the spelling words that have **age** added to a base word.

B. Write the spelling words that have **age** added to a root.

C. Write the spelling words that have **ment** added to a base word.

D. Write the spelling words that have **ment** added to a root.

E. Circle the consonant clusters in the spelling words you have written.

WORD STUDY

A. Vocabulary When the suffixes **age** and **ment** are added to a base word or root, they form nouns. Use the spelling dictionary to look up the suffix definitions. Then write the spelling words that match these clues.

1. The collective term for stamps.
2. The collective term for kitchen wastes.
3. The collective term for distance covered.
4. The process of conducting a test.
5. The result of moving ahead.
6. The means or tool by which something is done.
7. The process of determining dimensions.
8. The result of setting a time for a meeting.

B. Proofreading Write the spelling words that are misspelled in the paragraph.

    After their marrige Mr. and Mrs. Henry bought an old run-down estate where they could raise horses. It included a mansion, a barn, a garge, and even a carrage house. When Kevin got up enough currage to ask for a part-time job, they hired him. First, he cleaned all the garbige out of the old barn, but his major assinment was to groom and exercise the horses and clean their equippment. He was even asked to change the bandge on a lame horse named Dancer. Kevin loved the excitment of riding every day after school. In the next developement of his job, he will help train the horses.

C. Dictionary Write the spelling words that you would find between these pairs of guide words.

1. part | paste
2. mild | milk
3. expel | eye
4. possum | potato
5. count | cover
6. advance | adverb
7. ink | itch
8. do | dog

WORD SENSE

passage
postage
bandage
garage
garbage
courage
advantage
mileage
marriage
carriage
development
equipment
appointment
assignment
excitement
advancement
measurement
document
experiment
instrument

A. Write the spelling words that complete the paragraph.

Kelly wrapped the __1__ around Jasper's sore leg and tried to find the __2__ to ask the veterinarian if Jasper could ever jump again. Kelly was worried because she had read a __3__ in a trainer's manual which said that the __4__ of a leg problem may end a horse's jumping career.

As Kelly waited for her __5__ with the vet, she daydreamed about the __6__ and thrill of riding. The vet arrived and gave Kelly the __7__ of hand-walking Jasper so he could rest his leg. Kelly kept Jasper, with his bridle and other __8__, in a confined area near her family's __9__. When the vet later visited them, she said, "Your support gave Jasper an __10__, Kelly. His leg is nearly healed!"

B. Each word group relates in some way to one spelling word. Write the spelling words that match the clues.

1. trumpet, guitar, violin, __?__
2. letter, envelope, address, __?__
3. improvement, promotion, progress, __?__
4. gasoline, tires, distance, __?__
5. theory, evidence, formula, __?__
6. peelings, trash, leftovers, __?__
7. inch, mile, quart, __?__
8. certificate, license, diploma, __?__

C. Write the missing spelling words. Then circle the letter that represents the **y** in the base form of each spelling word.

After their __1__, the couple rode in a __2__ drawn by black Belgian horses.

90

WORDSCAPES: The Writing Connection

An **introduction** is a beginning, a brief description of what is to follow. In the introduction to a report, you tell your readers what you plan to cover. You also try to catch your readers' attention. An interesting piece of information or a stimulating question will make your readers curious and keep them reading.

A. Write an introduction to a report on a topic you have chosen. Write a topic sentence and at least three other sentences that both describe the major areas you will cover and arouse a reader's curiosity. Use the spelling words when you can.

Content Words

automation
horsepower
hydraulic
machinery
mechanize

agriculture
arable
famine
irrigate
scarcity

B. Write the Social Studies Words that match the definitions.

1. A term for machines as a group.
2. To equip with machines.
3. The automatic operation of a system.
4. Powered by a liquid under pressure.
5. A unit of power that will raise a one-pound weight 550 feet in one second.

C. Write the Science Words in the paragraph below. You will need to add **s** to one of the words.

As a nation's population increases, the availability of ___1___ land decreases. The construction of new buildings and roadways also adds to a possible ___2___ of land in the future. Today, efforts are being made in the area of ___3___ to teach people how to ___4___ their land and maintain rich soil. Such planning can help to prevent a major ___5___ .

1. wonderful
2. successful
3. eventful
4. doubtful
5. forgetful
6. delightful
7. dutiful
8. pitiful
9. fanciful
10. fearless
11. fruitless
12. priceless
13. tireless
14. senseless
15. worthless
16. thoughtless
17. tiresome
18. lonesome
19. wholesome
20. worrisome

Target Skill

The suffixes **ful**, **less** and **some** in such words as **wonderful**, **priceless**, and **wholesome**.

Barry was a **priceless** dog who rescued many people lost in the snowy Swiss Alps. **Fearless** and **tireless,** this **dutiful** animal explored the snow-covered mountain regions until he found the missing hikers. His **wonderful** sense of smell helped to make his rescue missions **successful.** Do you know what breed of dog Barry was?*

A. Write the spelling words that end in the suffix **ful.**

B. Write the spelling words that end in the suffix **less.**

C. Write the spelling words that end in the suffix **some.**

*Barry was a Saint Bernard.

WORD STUDY

A. Structure The syllables of six base words are scrambled in the nonsense words below. Write six spelling words by unscrambling the syllables and adding the suffix **ful** to each base word. To make two of the spelling words, you will need to change a **y** to an **i** before adding the suffix.

ventderywonpite   fansucgetcycessfor

B. Proofreading Use the proofreading skills you have learned in previous units to revise this paragraph about a hearing dog. First write the spelling words correctly. Then write the paragraph correctly.

skippy is a german shepherd puppy who seems tirless to his owner, linda. Linda was in a worrysome situation before skippy came along. You see, linda is deaf. skippy is a priseless pup who hears for linda. It is frutless to try to surprise linda because skippy will always warn her. skippy was trained to be feerless in the face of dangerous situations. Linda will never be thotless when it comes to making sure her puppy gets a wholsome meal every day. skippy will never become lonsome as long as linda is there. linda thinks skippy is the most delighful pet she's ever owned.

C. Vocabulary Write the spelling word that matches each definition.

1. Without worth.

2. Without sense.

3. Without tiring.

4. Causing tiredness.

5. Filled with a sense of duty.

6. Filled with doubt.

WORD SENSE

wonderful
successful
eventful
doubtful
forgetful
delightful
dutiful
pitiful
fanciful
fearless
fruitless
priceless
tireless
senseless
worthless
thoughtless
tiresome
lonesome
wholesome
worrisome

A. Write the spelling words that complete the paragraph. The first letter of each spelling word is printed to help you.

 Hamsters make w 1 pets. These four-ounce creatures enjoy a diet of such w 2 foods as dandelion leaves and fruit. It is d 3 that you will find caring for a hamster difficult. All a hamster needs is a wire cage and an exercise wheel. You might think the small cage would become t 4 , but a hamster will find ways to make each day e 5 . As long as you play with your hamster, it will not become l 6 . You will enjoy many d 7 hours with this pocket-sized pet.

B. Write the spelling word that could replace each underlined word.

 Unlike dogs, cats are <u>useless</u> in guarding property. Nevertheless, they are <u>invaluable</u> to their owners, who prize these pets for their warmth and affection. A <u>responsible</u> pet owner is never <u>neglectful</u> when it comes time to have the cat vaccinated against feline distemper. A sick cat is a <u>pathetic</u> and <u>anxiety-causing</u> pet. If your cat has a temperature of 101.5°F, it's <u>foolish</u> for you to worry, because that is a cat's normal temperature.

C. Write the spelling word that completes each group.

1. courageous, brave, ?
2. imaginative, unreal, ?
3. unproductive, unsuccessful, ?
4. inconsiderate, unthinking, ?
5. energetic, vigorous, ?
6. prosperous, profitable, ?

WORDSCAPES: The Writing Connection

The writing of a report gives you the opportunity to present your ideas on a particular subject or issue. It is important not to confuse fact with opinion. You can, however, use facts to support your views.

A report should follow a logical order, which is already determined if you have written an outline. Sequence words and phrases, such as **after, as soon as,** and **finally,** help to link different ideas together.

A. Write a report on a selected topic. Write several complete paragraphs that cover specific areas of research. Include interesting details to support your point of view. Use the spelling words when you can.

Content Words

astronomy
constellation
galaxy
nebula
stellar

czar
peasant
serf
steppes
tyrant

B. Write the scrambled Science Words correctly.

In <u>amostrony</u> class we observed the <u>tellars</u> skies, studying each major <u>cellostantion</u> in the Milky Way <u>laxyga</u>. We also saw a large <u>bulaen</u>.

C. Write the Social Studies Words that fit the clues.

1. Steps are not a natural feature of the plains called the __?__ .
2. A tyrannosaur would make a __?__ of a ruler.
3. A land-bound __?__ seldom saw the ocean's surf.
4. A Russian king was called a __?__ , which rhymes with **car.**
5. The life of a __?__ was often unpleasant.

WORDS AND CLUES

1. checkbook
2. bookstore
3. background
4. throughout
5. campsite
6. campfire
7. overcast
8. skyscraper
9. everybody
10. thunderstorm
11. weatherproof
12. grown-up
13. passer-by
14. cross-country
15. sister-in-law
16. self-addressed
17. wrist watch
18. all right
19. bill of sale
20. post office

Target Skill

Compound words, such as **bookstore, all right,** and **self-addressed.** A compound word is formed from two or more words to make a new word or word group.

All day the sky was **overcast** and windy. I thought of the **skyscrapers** back in the city as I looked at the tall pine trees swaying in the wind. I looked at my **wrist watch** out of habit, and realized it would soon be time to look for a **campsite.** Can you guess what happened next?

A. Write each spelling word that unites two words (**camp** and **fire**) into one single word (**campfire**) called a **closed compound.**

B. Write each spelling word that joins words (**grown** and **up**) by a hyphen (**grown-up**) and is called a **hyphenated compound.**

C. Write the spelling words that consist of separate words (**post** and **office**) that are placed in a word group (**post office**) called an **open compound.**

WORD STUDY

A. Proofreading A pronoun is a word used in place of a noun or noun phrase. Each sentence below contains at least one pronoun, as well as one or two misspelled spelling words. For each sentence, write the spelling word(s) correctly and then write the pronouns contained in the sentence. One spelling word is a pronoun. Circle that word after you write it.

We were planning a cross country bicycle trip that would take thirty-eight days. First I sent selfaddressed envelopes with requests for camping guides to the tourist centers of the states we would visit. Then we went to a book store to locate a publication on camping. Dad used his check book to pay for a book. Every-body thought a grownup like my dad would rather drive a car than pedal a bike on his vacation, but not my dad!

Finally, we were ready, and it was alright to inform friends of our departure. Mom called her sister in law to say we'd leave on Saturday. Saturday morning we pedaled out of the city, leaving the sky-scrapers behind.

B. Structure The underlined part of each compound word below is also part of a spelling word. Write each spelling word.

1. <u>back</u>fire
2. <u>watch</u>dog
3. <u>out</u>side
4. good-<u>by</u>

5. right-<u>hand</u>
6. <u>bill</u> of fare
7. <u>postpone</u>
8. <u>proofread</u>

C. Vocabulary Write the spelling word that, if used, would make the sentence shorter. Write the new sentences.

1. The site we chose to set up camp was protected by trees.
2. There was a gray cast over the entire sky.
3. The storm raged with thunder.
4. The fire at our camp went out during the night.

WORD SENSE

checkbook
bookstore
background
throughout
campsite
campfire
overcast
skyscraper
everybody
thunderstorm
weatherproof
grown-up
passer-by
cross-country
sister-in-law
self-addressed
wrist watch
all right
bill of sale
post office

A. Make a spelling word by matching a word in one column with a word in the other column.

1. book   office
2. watch   up
3. addressed   check
4. book   wrist
5. post   self
6. grown   store

B. Write the plural form of the spelling words that fits these definitions.

1. Buildings that are so tall they look like they are touching the sky.
2. A term for women related by marriage.
3. Receipts that show what was sold.
4. People who pass by.

C. A preposition is a word that shows the relationship between its object and some other word in the sentence. The words **on, in, after,** and **with** are examples of prepositions. Write the missing spelling words and the prepositions you find in each sentence. Circle the one spelling word that is a preposition.

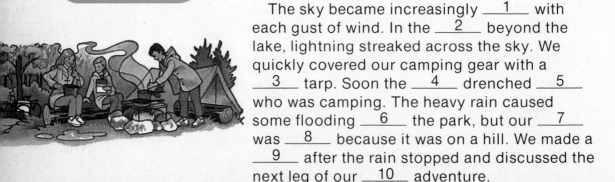

The sky became increasingly __1__ with each gust of wind. In the __2__ beyond the lake, lightning streaked across the sky. We quickly covered our camping gear with a __3__ tarp. Soon the __4__ drenched __5__ who was camping. The heavy rain caused some flooding __6__ the park, but our __7__ was __8__ because it was on a hill. We made a __9__ after the rain stopped and discussed the next leg of our __10__ adventure.

WORDSCAPES: The Writing Connection

A **conclusion** ties together all of the information in a report by describing the result or impact of the facts stated. The conclusion reminds readers of your point of view and may also provide them with a question to think about after reading your report. The conclusion is not the place for new information.

A. Choose a writing activity for which you can write a concluding paragraph. Write a conclusion that ties information together, expresses your point of view, and offers a provocative question.

Content Words

   caravan
oasis
turban
sultan
traveler

   medium
reflect
refract
spectrum
wavelength

B. Write the Social Studies Words that complete the paragraph. You will need to add **s** to two of the words.

In days gone by, a __1__ from Persia sent a small __2__ of nomads in search of a new temporary home. They wore __3__ to protect their heads from the desert's scorching sun. By midday, the __4__ had found a fertile __5__ .

C. Write the Science Words that fit the facts about a rainbow's formation. Add **ed** to two of the words.

Light waves are __1__ or bent as they pass through a fine mist of water. Raindrops are often fine enough to create a __2__ through which all the colors that make up sunlight can be seen. The water acts as a prism and separates the light into the light's __3__ . The colors you see __4__ in the sky are different because they each have a different __5__ .

A. Write the spelling words that end in **able** or **ible**.

B. Write the spelling words that begin with prefixes.

C. Write the spelling words that end in **age** or **ment**.

D. Write the spelling words that end in **ful, less,** or **some**.

E. Write the spelling words that are compound words.

FURTHER PRACTICE AND ENRICHMENT

A. Proofreading Some words in these book titles are misspelled. Write the spelling words correctly.

1. **Improve Your Running Milage**
2. **Secret Docuement #27**
3. **What Everbody Should Know About Money**
4. **Essential Camping Equippment**
5. **Recycling Nonreturnible Items**
6. **Valueable Tips for Coin Collectors**
7. **A Succesful Training Program for Dogs**
8. **Horses Thoughout the Ages**

B. Most of the spelling words are adjectives. Choose an adjective from the spelling words to modify or describe a noun of your choice. **Valuable decision** is an example. Repeat this activity with five different adjectives and nouns. Use your spelling dictionary if you need help.

C. Creative Writing A first-person narrative is a recounting of events using **pronouns** such as **I, me,** and **my.** Put yourself in the picture! Write a fictional first-person narrative that describes your adventures in the new place you see in the drawing.

D. Proofreading Check your written work for errors in spelling and grammar. As you reread your narrative, ask these questions:

1. Are the sentences placed in logical order?
2. Have you chosen words that describe exactly what you imagined that you did, saw, or experienced? Do the words capture the reader's interest?
3. Is the paragraph punctuated correctly?
4. Have you used the first person throughout?
5. Are all the words spelled correctly?

TESTING

A. Read each sentence. Write the number of the sentence and **a** or **b** to indicate whether the underlined word is spelled correctly or incorrectly.

1. An <u>aceptable</u> meal is often a balanced meal.   (a) correct   (b) incorrect
2. I had an <u>irresistible</u> urge to listen to my record.   (a) correct   (b) incorrect
3. This is a <u>valuable</u> piece of jewelry.   (a) correct   (b) incorrect
4. The weather is very <u>changable</u> during the spring.   (a) correct   (b) incorrect
5. Many immigrants who may seem to be <u>iliterate</u> actually can read their native language.   (a) correct   (b) incorrect
6. Tom is <u>responsable</u> for bringing corn to our picnic.   (a) correct   (b) incorrect
7. Many aluminum cans are <u>nonreturnable</u>.   (a) correct   (b) incorrect
8. My cat looked <u>pityful</u> when he broke his leg.   (a) correct   (b) incorrect
9. When I <u>misbehave</u>, my father gets upset.   (a) correct   (b) incorrect
10. At recess, <u>everybody</u> likes to run around.   (a) correct   (b) incorrect

B. Read each group of words. Write the number of the group and **a, b,** or **c** to indicate the word in each group that is spelled correctly.

1. (a) throught   (b) thrughout   (c) throughout
2. (a) thoughtless   (b) thoghtless   (c) thuoghtless
3. (a) all-right   (b) all right   (c) alright
4. (a) wholsome   (b) holesome   (c) wholesome
5. (a) self-addressed   (b) self addressed   (c) self-adressed
6. (a) marriage   (b) merriage   (c) mariage
7. (a) docuement   (b) document   (c) dokument
8. (a) sucessful   (b) succeful   (c) successful
9. (a) equipment   (b) equiptment   (c) equipement
10. (a) miliage   (b) milege   (c) mileage

CHALLENGE

Use the list of affixes to create new words from the spelling words. Write the new words by dropping affixes from the spelling words and adding new ones. You may use your spelling dictionary if you need help.

Prefixes	Suffixes
un- in- ex-	-tion or -ion -ive -ant

LANGUAGE TO GO

A. **The Written Word** Reading is a wonderful way to occupy your free time and to enliven your interest in other places. A book entitled **The Mexican Story,** by author May McNeer, offers a combination of short reports and stories that presents an overall picture of Mexico and her people. This is how the book begins:

> Mexico is a long triangle, pointing to South America. In the north it is a wide land, with many miles of cactus country . . . but in the south the country narrows as it meets the Central American states.

Write a paragraph that might come next in the book. The library has research materials in which you can find facts about Mexico. You may wish to write about that country's vegetation, climate, or traditions.

B. **The Spoken Word** Choose a report that you have written or another writing assignment that you have completed to prepare for an oral report.

When you make an oral report, your voice, your appearance, and your attitude are all on display. Try to be relaxed and natural. Don't fidget. Pronounce your words slowly and clearly, and speak loudly enough so that everyone can hear you. Vary your voice to express interest, excitement, and other feelings. To make the best impression, stand up straight and look at your audience. It helps to memorize most of your report.

Before you make your report, practice alone by talking into a tape recorder. Listen to see how you can improve your performance. You will gain confidence from practice.

1. immediate
2. accurate
3. approximate
4. delicate
5. moderate
6. desperate
7. ultimate
8. desolate
9. fortunate
10. unfortunate
11. momentary
12. secondary
13. honorary
14. necessary
15. temporary
16. ordinary
17. solitary
18. voluntary
19. customary
20. imaginary

Target Skill

The suffixes **ate** and **ary** that form adjectives, in words such as **accurate** and **imaginary.**

Anom Irawan, a Balinese boy, takes a deep breath. He will, **momentarily,** whirl into a series of strong, quick dancing movements. At age eleven Anom holds an **honored** position in his society because he is an experienced Baris dancer. This dance requires great concentration, **accurate** movements, and complete muscle control. It has been the **customary** festival dance on the Indonesian island of Bali for hundreds of years.

A. Write the spelling words that end with the suffix **ate.**

B. Write the spelling words that end with the suffix **ary.**

C. Write the spelling words that have these smaller words in them: late, rate, mate, tuna, moment, second, honor, and custom.

WORD STUDY

A. Structure These words are spelling demons in their most commonly misspelled forms. Write them correctly.

1. **desparate** 2. **temperary** 3. **desalate** 4. **volentary**

B. Dictionary Some words have both primary and secondary stress marks, showing how much emphasis to place on syllables when a word is spoken. Unmarked syllables receive the least stress; syllables with primary stress marks receive the most stress; syllables with secondary stress marks receive an intermediate level of stress.

Unscramble the syllables and write the spelling words correctly. Then look up the pronunciation of these words as adjectives. Circle each syllable with a secondary stress in one color, and each syllable with a primary stress in another color. Not every word has a secondary stress.

1. **iproxapmate**   3. **motarymen**   5. **ateermod**   7. **isolytar**
2. **tomycusar**   4. **delcatei**   6. **ondsecyar**   8. **nardiory**

C. Proofreading Write the misspelled spelling words correctly. Then rewrite the paragraphs correctly.

Ice skaters were fortuneate in 1817 when Joseph Merlin a belgian came up with a new idea He dreamed of an immaginery pair of skates that would work on any surface to make his idea work it was neccesary to replace ice-skate blades with wheels. His invention of roller skates became an imediate success

Roller-skating soon became the ultimit summer sport for ice skaters. An opera called *the prophet* even gave roller-skating an honerary position in the fine arts. In one performance in london, an unfortuneate girl skated right off the stage and landed in a big bass drum her stopping skills were obviously not very acurate.

WORD SENSE

immediate
accurate
approximate
delicate
moderate
desperate
ultimate
desolate
fortunate
unfortunate
momentary
secondary
honorary
necessary
temporary
ordinary
solitary
voluntary
customary
imaginary

A. Write all but one of the missing spelling words as adverbs by adding **ly** to the base words. When the base word ends in **y,** change the **y** to **i** before adding **ly.** The first letter of each spelling word is provided.

As a young child, Anom v __1__ and on his own tried to imitate, as a __2__ as he could, the dancers he had seen. He knew it would be n __3__ to take lessons if he truly wished to learn the dance. A Balinese teacher c __4__ works directly with the student, physically moving legs and arms, so that the student knows how it feels to perform correctly. Anom worked hard and, f __5__ , he quickly mastered the dance.

B. A **thesaurus** is used to find synonyms and antonyms. Write the spelling words that are synonyms or antonyms for the words below.

Synonyms	Antonyms
1. make believe	6. excessive
2. single	7. exact
3. brief	8. tough
4. direct	9. unusual
5. lesser	10. fortunate

C. Write the spelling word that completes each advertisement for dancers.

1. Apply now for __?__ work from May to September in summer stock.

2. Wanted: Ballerina to play princess lost in dismal, __?__ surroundings.

3. Here's your chance for the __?__ career in dance. Auditions at the Crouse Theater.

4. We are __?__ for experienced ballet performers. Contact Erma Chin at 555-0330.

WORDSCAPES: The Writing Connection

Analogies or comparisons are useful tools in writing clear, vivid description. Readers can almost see, smell, hear, taste, touch, or feel what the writer describes. One type of analogy is a metaphor, which compares unlike objects, people, or events. In a metaphor, such words as **like** and **as** are not used; the comparison is implied. A metaphor creates a vivid mental picture for the reader:

> The ballerinas became **delicate** flowers, waving gracefully on poised stems that stretched toward the warm sun.

In this example of metaphor, ballerinas are compared to flowers.

A. Write five of your own metaphors. Use the spelling words when you can.

Content Words

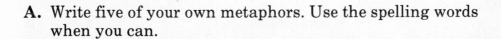

equivalent	consonant
invert	linguistics
proportion	unvoiced
ratio	vibrate
reciprocal	voiced

B. Write the missing Math Words. Add **s** to one word.

An equation which states that two __1__ are __2__ is called a __3__ . If you __4__ the fraction 1/3, the product is **3.** When the product of two numbers is 1, we call these numbers __5__ .

C. Write the Language Arts Words that complete the paragraph on the study of the spoken language.

The study of __1__ includes understanding how the vocal system works. The __2__ **g** causes the vocal cords to __3__ , which in turn produces a __4__ sound. The letter **h,** however, produces an __5__ sound.

1. midway
2. midsummer
3. underpass
4. undercover
5. underground
6. underneath
7. superstar
8. supervise
9. supersonic
10. subway
11. submarine
12. subtotal
13. intersect
14. interface
15. interact
16. interchange
17. interview
18. interstate
19. intrastate
20. intramural

Target Skill

The prefixes that indicate position, in words such as **midsummer, underpass, superstar, subway, interact,** and **intramural.**

What team sport is played and watched by more people throughout the world than any other?

Baseball superstar George Brett

A. Write the spelling words that begin with the prefix **mid.**

B. Write the spelling words that begin with the prefix **under.**

C. Write the spelling words that begin with the prefix **super.**

D. Write the spelling words that begin with the prefix **sub.**

E. Write the spelling words that begin with the prefix **inter.**

F. Write the spelling words that begin with the prefix **intra.**

WORD STUDY

A. Dictionary Write these spelling words in alphabetical order.

1. **intersect**   3. **supervise**   5. **interface**   7. **underground**
2. **underpass**   4. **subway**   6. **submarine**   8. **intrastate**

B. Proofreading The spelling words are misspelled in the sports facts below. Write the spelling words correctly.

1. Ice hockey is to team sports what the suppersonic jet is to aviation.

2. At a possible 100 miles per hour, the hockey puck travels faster than cars on interstat highways.

3. Team sports provide an excellent opportunity for people to inneract with each other.

4. Wally Walker, a pro basketball player, claims that every supperstar starts by learning the basics.

5. A friendly intrechange between players on rival teams sometimes occurs after a close game.

6. Biddy Basketball is included in many elementary intermural athletic programs.

7. Biddy Basketball players must stand underneth the five-foot six-inch marker to qualify.

8. Some goalkeepers can head a soccer ball middway down a field.

C. Structure Prefixes and bases are mismatched in the words below. Write the spelling words correctly.

1. **midtotal**   2. **intercover**   3. **underview**   4. **subsummer**

WORD SENSE

midway
midsummer
underpass
undercover
underground
underneath
superstar
supervise
supersonic
subway
submarine
subtotal
intersect
interface
interact
interchange
interview
interstate
intrastate
intramural

A. Each spelling word is a combination of a prefix and a base word. Write the spelling words that match these combinations.

1. middle-distance
2. beneath-protection
3. below-sea
4. below-land
5. between-switching
6. above-the speed of sound

B. The prefixes or base words of eight spelling words are given. Write the spelling words. You will need to add **ing** to one word. (Enjoy the underlined baseball idioms.)

The mid___1___ picnic was a <u>hit</u> with the road construction crew. The foreman super___2___ the project let them know <u>right off the bat</u> that he is pleased with their progress on the new ___3___pass. He claimed their success is due to teamwork: they ___4___act well together. Though they were <u>thrown a curve ball</u> when told that a proposed inter___5___ highway would ___6___sect the intra___7___ road, they all pitched in to do the work so the two roads could ___8___face.

C. Write the spelling words that fit the clues.

1. When you are standing ___?___ the net, it is hard to make a basket.

2. Pelé will always be this sport's ___?___ .

3. The high net and rotation of the players make this a popular ___?___ sport in schools.

4. An incomplete score can be called a ___?___. In what sport can the score be love?

5. After the Stanley Cup was awarded, every sportscaster wanted to ___?___ the winners.

Hockey superstar Wayne Gretzky holds Stanley Cup.

110

WORDSCAPES: The Writing Connection

Interviews are helpful in gathering up-to-date information. Questions, prepared ahead of time, should cover the five W's of journalism: who, what, where, when, and why. Good interview questions evoke more than a yes-or-no answer.

WHO?
WHAT?
WHERE?
WHEN?
WHY?

A. Choose a favorite sports figure and write an imaginary interview. Work with a partner or play both roles, interviewee and interviewer, yourself. Write at least five questions that include the five W's. Answer each question as you imagine the sports figure might.

Content Words

civilian
defense
endanger
military
protection

cirrus
cumulus
cumulonimbus
stratus
nimbostratus

B. Write the Social Studies Words that complete the paragraph below.

Through taxes, every United States citizen helps to support the nation's ___1___ . When threats of foreign invasion ___2___ our freedom, the armed forces prepare to provide ___3___ . A citizen not serving in the ___4___ is referred to as a ___5___ .

C. Write the Science Words that match each definition.

1. A low-altitude cloud, often resembling fog.

2. A high-altitude cloud composed of narrow bands.

3. A dense, white, fluffy cloud.

4. An extremely dense, vertical cloud with a hazy outline that may cause heavy rain or hail.

5. A low gray cloud that may cause snow or sleet.

1. mountainous
2. continuous
3. wondrous
4. fabulous
5. tremendous
6. nervous
7. jealous
8. various
9. furious
10. glorious
11. studious
12. industrious
13. curious
14. obvious
15. tedious
16. precious
17. cautious
18. nutritious
19. gorgeous
20. courageous

Target Skill

The suffix **ous** in words such as **tremendous, studious,** and **courageous.**

It was a **glorious** sun-filled winter day in Vermont. Amelia stood on her skis with **nervous** anticipation as she stared at the **gorgeous** snow-covered peaks. Finally, she pushed herself off **cautiously** with her poles and began skiing down the steep **mountainous** trail.

A. Write the spelling words in which **ous** is added to base words that end in **y.**

B. Write the spelling words in which **ous** is added to base words ending in **e.**

C. Write the spelling words in which **ous** is added to base words ending in a **consonant.**

D. Write the spelling words in which **ous** is added to a root.

WORD STUDY

A. Structure Follow the math and write the spelling words.

1. vary – y + i + ous = ___?___ .
2. study – y + i + ous = ___?___ .
3. fury – y + i + ous = ___?___ .
4. industry – y + i + ous = ___?___ .
5. glory – y + i + ous = ___?___ .

B. Proofreading The underlined spelling words are mixed up and misspelled in this passage on ski slope safety. Write the spelling words correctly and in the right order.

Most ski resorts rely on the <u>tedius</u> efforts of their brave ski patrol to insure the safety of the skiers. Each ski patrol person must train in high <u>continueus</u> areas and in all weather conditions. They are trained to be <u>nerveous</u> when moving injured skiers. They are a <u>curragous</u> help to <u>tremendus</u> skiers who need encouragement.

Helping those in need is a <u>mountianous</u> challenge throughout the ski season. Yet, it never becomes <u>fabulus</u> or boring. Most people on the ski patrol show an <u>causous</u> enthusiasm for their job. They tell some <u>obveus</u> tales of incredibly daring rescue missions.

C. Dictionary Each letter in this code stands for the letter that comes immediately before it in the alphabet. For example, **b** stands for **a, c** stands for **b** and so on. Write the words that are represented by the code.

1. xpoespvt
2. hpshfpvt
3. kfbmpvt
4. ovusjujpvt
5. dvsjpvt
6. qsfdjpvt

WORD SENSE

mountainous
continuous
wondrous
fabulous
tremendous
nervous
jealous
various
furious
glorious
studious
industrious
curious
obvious
tedious
precious
cautious
nutritious
gorgeous
courageous

A. The spelling words are adjectives. Write those that belong in this paragraph in their adverbial forms by adding **ly** to each. The first letter of each missing word is provided.

    For children in the Arctic, wintertime is t ___1___ exciting. Winter sports are o ___2___ very popular. They use a c ___3___ shaped sled called the "one-legged." This ski-like chair sled is used c ___4___ throughout the long winter.
    A river overflow makes skating exciting. An overflow occurs when water backs up and pours out of cracks in the ice, creating a g ___5___ smooth skating surface as it freezes.

B. Write the spelling word that fits each definition. Then circle the base word. Finally, write each base word.

1. Characterized by high elevation.
2. Full of intense anger.
3. Full of diligence.
4. Devoted to study.
5. Full of bravery.
6. Of the nerves.
7. Full of wonder.
8. Of diverse kinds.

C. Write the spelling word which stems from each of these origins.

1. From Latin **fabula,** meaning fable.
2. From Latin **cautio,** meaning taking care.
3. From Latin **taedium,** meaning weariness.
4. From Latin **pretium,** meaning price.
5. From Middle English **gorgayse,** meaning elegant.
6. From Latin **nutrire,** meaning to feed.

114

WORDSCAPES: The Writing Connection

A **simile,** like a metaphor, is a comparative figurative phrase that describes an event, person, or object. A simile, however, always uses the words **like** or **as** in the comparison. Phrases such as **as strong as an ox** or **as cool as a cucumber** are overworked similes that have become **clichés.** To revise them, you might say **as strong as a weight lifter** or **as cool as an ice cube.**

A. Make up five of your own similes or revised clichés. For example, you might write **as wondrous as a dream come true.** Invent one simile to describe your favorite winter sport. Write a paragraph of persuasion in which you use this simile, as you attempt to convince a classmate to try this sport.

Content Words

derrick	congruent
petroleum	linear
pipeline	parallel
platform	perpendicular
tanker	transversal

B. Write the Social Studies Words which complete the paragraph. You will need to add **s** to one word.

The large drill was placed in the ___1___ , and the operation began. As the engineers watched, black crude oil spurted up and splashed down on the ___2___ around them. Once oil was discovered, several ___3___ were filled daily with ___4___ . The construction of a new ___5___ will provide work for many people.

C. Write the Math Words which match the pictures.

1. = ___?___ line.

2. = ___?___ figure.

3. = ___?___ lines.

4. _____ = ___?___ lines.

5. = ___?___ line segments.

1. victory
2. jewelry
3. different
4. probably
5. restaurant
6. athlete
7. similar
8. pigeon
9. bargain
10. villain
11. captain
12. bureau
13. amateur
14. surely
15. muscle
16. rhythm
17. appreciate
18. license
19. sauce
20. perspire

Target Skill

Words that are often misspelled such as **restaurant, muscle,** and **license.**

Elizabeth Cull performs **rhythmic** gymnastics. It is a sport that combines ballet, baton twirling, acrobatics, juggling, and synchronized exercise—all rolled into one.

Elizabeth believes that you really have to love a sport to become an expert. "Everyone wants to do the tricky stunts," she says, "but it's the **athletes** who can 'grin and bear' the boredom of repetition who win **victories** and gold medals."

A. Write the spelling words that end in **y.**

B. Write the spelling words that end in a silent **e.**

C. Write the spelling words that end in a **consonant.**

D. Write the spelling word that ends in the letters **eau** (pronounced ō).

WORD STUDY

A. **Proofreading** The spelling words in this activity are spelling demons. Write the misspelled spelling words correctly. The most common misspelling of each word is used. After you write the spelling words, circle the part of each word that makes it a spelling problem.

1. Some gymnasts perform routines to the rythm of music.
2. Most coaches do not allow gymnasts to wear jewelery while practicing.
3. Rhythmic gymnasts perform with five diffrent pieces of equipment—a silk ribbon, a rubber ball, a pair of clubs, a jump rope, and a large hoop.
4. Any amater who wants to become professional in a sport must practice daily.
5. The vaulting horse is probly the best apparatus from which to do a running handspring.
6. Although gymnasts may prespire and feel nervous, their movements must be controlled and smooth.
7. An athelete must have confidence to succeed.
8. The 16-foot-long, four-inch-wide balance beam requires a gymnast to have excellent musle control.

B. **Dictionary** Words are often misspelled because their pronunciation differs from their spelling. From these dictionary respellings, pronounce each word and write the spelling word. Then circle that part of each word that is represented by the letter(s) underlined in the respelling.

1. /sôs/	5. /lǐ′ səns/
2. /vǐl′ ən/	6. /rěs′ tər ənt/
3. /sǐm′ əl ər/	7. /bâr′ gǐn/
4. /byoor′ ō/	8. /pǐj′ ən/

C. **Structure** The letters of the spelling words are scrambled in the sentence. Write the spelling words.

The patcain of the team will ruelsy preaceatip the covirty award.

WORD SENSE

victory
jewelry
different
probably
restaurant
athlete
similar
pigeon
bargain
villain
captain
bureau
amateur
surely
muscle
rhythm
appreciate
license
sauce
perspire

A. Write the spelling words that fit the paragraph. Add **s** to two of the words.

Gymnastics dates back to 2000 B.C. when Egyptian __1__ used their bodies to form human pyramids and perform balancing stunts. Although today's gymnastics events are somewhat __2__ to those of ancient Egypt, the sport has expanded. There are events for __3__ gymnasts as well as professional competitors. The __4__ pieces of equipment include the vaulting horse, balance beam, and uneven parallel bars. When a gymnast's hands or feet __5__ , chalk helps to keep them dry. The __6__ in the legs, arms, and stomach are very important to a gymnast.

B. Write the spelling words which complete the analogies.

1. **Carefully** is to **cautiously** as **definitely** is to __?__ .
2. **Flour** is to **bread** as **tomato** is to __?__ .
3. **Doubtfully** is to **certainly** as **unlikely** is to __?__ .
4. **Movie** is to **theater** as **meal** is to __?__ .
5. **Airplane** is to **pilot** as **ship** is to __?__ .
6. **Food** is to **savor** as **music** is to __?__ .
7. **Hammers** are to **tools** as **rings** are to __?__ .
8. **Price** is to **discount** as **sale** is to __?__ .

C. Write these forms of the spelling words.

1. The plural possessive of rhythm.
2. The possessive of villain.
3. The plural of victory.
4. The possessive of bureau.
5. The plural of license.
6. The plural possessive of pigeon.

118

WORDSCAPES: The Writing Connection

In **expository** (or explanatory) **writing,** writers may explain what something is, how it works, or how it is made; or they may tell about some event, describing what happened and why. This type of writing is informative and based on facts. Some examples of expository topics include: how to lace and tie an athletic shoe, how points are scored in volleyball, what a lob is in tennis. Most newspaper articles incorporate expository writing.

A. Write an expository article about a sports-related topic. Use the spelling words when you can.

Content Words

heritage	digestive
kinsman	enzyme
mores	liver
taboo	pancreas
tribe	saliva

B. Write the scrambled Social Studies Words correctly.

1. A male relative is a <u>maskinn</u>.

2. When several villages share a common ancestry, language, culture, and name, the result is a <u>brite</u>.

3. The customs accepted by a particular social group are considered this group's <u>romes</u>.

4. When a society forbids the use or even the mention of something, that subject or object is <u>tooba</u>.

5. Our <u>gearithe</u> is passed on through the generations.

C. Write the Science Words that complete the sentences. You will need to add **s** to one word.

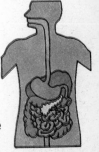

The ___1___ juices such as ___2___ and stomach ___3___ help break down food. The ___4___ also produces digestive juices. The ___5___ transfers nutrients into the blood.

119

1. action
2. direction
3. invention
4. suggestion
5. information
6. consideration
7. location
8. operation
9. population
10. completion
11. introduction
12. position
13. condition
14. attention
15. satisfaction
16. discussion
17. expression
18. tension
19. decision
20. permission

Target Skill

Suffix endings in words such as **action**, **introduction**, and **information**.

A. Write the words that add the suffix **ion** to the base word without changing the base word.

B. Write the words that add the suffix **ation** to the base word.

C. Write the words that drop the final **e** from the base word before adding the **ion** suffix.

D. Write the words that change or drop the final letter of the base word before adding the suffix **tion.**

E. Write the words that stem from these Latin words: **positio** (place); **condicio** (stipulation); **satisfacere** (to satisfy).

F. Write the words in which the final letter(s) of the base words are changed to **s** or **ss** before the suffix **ion** is added.

WORD STUDY

A. Proofreading Write the misspelled spelling words correctly. You will need to add **s** to two of the words.

SUPER SURFER'S SUGGESTIONS

To prepare beginners for the real thing, Lee Kravitz, a surfboarding instructor, gives them a basic introdution to surfing while they are still on shore. First, he offers sugestions on selecting a board, followed by a discusion about surfing safety. The drill on dry land includes learning the correct foot postions for standing and balancing. Finally, Mr. Kravitz pushes students in the direcion of a good wave. The decission to ride a wave is ultimately up to the surfer. There is great satifaction in riding all the way to the shore.

B. Structure When the suffix **ion** is added to verb roots or bases, nouns are formed. Follow the directions and write the spelling words.

1. act + ion = ___?___ .
2. locate – e + ion = ___?___ .
3. populate – e + ion = ___?___ .
4. tense – e + ion = ___?___ .
5. express + ion = ___?___ .
6. permit – t + ss + ion = ___?___ .
7. attend – d + t + ion = ___?___ .

C. Dictionary By changing affixes, you can sometimes form several words from one stem. **Act, action, active, inactive, actor,** and **activity,** for example, all come from the same root. Write the part of speech of each word below. Then subtract and add affixes to create a spelling word. Write the spelling word and its part of speech.
Ex. permissible, adj., permission, n.

1. inventive
2. misinform
3. inconsiderate
4. operational
5. complement
6. unconditional

WORD SENSE

action

direction

invention

suggestion

information

consideration

location

operation

population

completion

introduction

position

condition

attention

satisfaction

discussion

expression

tension

decision

permission

A. Write a spelling word to replace each underlined phrase.

1. Keep the <u>rope taut</u> between boat and skier.
2. Lynne Cox enjoys the <u>pleasurable feeling</u> of being an accomplished swimmer.
3. The <u>commonly used phrase</u> "hot dogger" refers to a surfer doing gymnastics.
4. "Hang ten" means the <u>movement or process</u> of hooking one's toes over the surfboard.
5. The wind surfer is a recent <u>new device</u>.

B. Write the spelling words which stem from these Latin word origins.

1. **Dirigere,** meaning to give direction to.
2. **Suggerere,** meaning to carry up.
3. **Informare,** meaning to inform.
4. **Locus,** meaning place.
5. **Opus,** meaning work.
6. **Populus,** meaning the people.
7. **Complere,** meaning to fill out.
8. **Discutere,** meaning to discuss.
9. **Introducere,** meaning to bring in.

C. Write the scrambled spelling words correctly. Add **s** to two of the words.

Dangerous sharks and ice-cold waters are important sitercoinanods for Lynne Cox when she is about to begin a long-distance swim. Though stormy weather noncidtios have kept Lynne out of the water, she holds the tipsonio of being the first person in the world to swim the icy Straits of Magellan. On one long-distance swim, Lynne's tenatnoti was drawn to sixty dolphins swimming near her. They seemed to give her merponissi to swim with them. Their playfulness helped her make the cidesoni to finish the swim.

WORDSCAPES: The Writing Connection

Expository and figurative writing are both used in advertising. In addition, advertising uses special techniques to try to persuade you to buy something. When a famous athlete is paid to support a product, for example, the technique is called an endorsement. Advertising also makes claims stressing the popularity of a product or maintaining that it is healthy.

Surfers Do Better on LIGHTWEIGHT

A. Write a magazine advertisement for a sports product such as water skis, a swimming cap, a bicycling helmet, or protective clothing. Use your imagination!

Content Words

decagon
parallelogram
quadrilateral
rhombus
trapezoid

accord
ally
blockade
regional
sanction

B. Write the Math Words that match the clues. Each word can be used only once.

1. A ___?___ is a figure with four sides.
2. A ___?___ is a quadrilateral whose opposite sides are parallel.
3. A ___?___ is a parallelogram with equal sides.
4. A ___?___ is a quadrilateral with only one pair of parallel sides.
5. A ___?___ has ten angles and ten sides.

C. Write the Social Studies Words that complete the analogies.

1. **Foe** is to **friend** as **enemy** is to ___?___ .

2. **Discord** is to **harmony** as **conflict** is to ___?___ .

3. **Municipal** is to **statewide** as **local** is to ___?___ .

4. **Highway** is to **roadblock** as **harbor** is to ___?___ .

5. **Approval** is to **permission** as **endorsement** is to ___?___ .

123

WORD CLUES AND STUDY

Greg Lemond, winner of the 1986 *Tour de France*.

A. Write the spelling words that have prefixes that indicate position. These prefixes are **under, super, inter,** and **intra.**

B. Write the spelling words in which the spelling of the base word does not change when the suffix is added.

C. Write the spelling words that drop an **e** before the suffix is added.

D. Write the spelling words in which the spelling of the base word changes when the suffix is added.

E. Look at the spelling words and see how many smaller words you can find within each word. There are at least fifty. Write the spelling words and then write the smaller words under each spelling word.

FURTHER PRACTICE AND ENRICHMENT

A. Write the spelling words that can be used to replace these expressions.

1. Happening right now.
2. Very lucky.
3. Lasting for a short time.
4. Oversee.
5. Most likely.
6. Never-ending.
7. Absolutely essential.
8. Sports contestant.
9. Legal permission.
10. Extremely large.

B. Creative Writing Write imaginative dictionary entries for the following nonsense sports expressions. For each one, write the part of speech, and invent a daffy definition and word origin. Place the entries in alphabetical order.

1. water hockey
2. cold dogger
3. gymswimnast
4. sled skier

C. Editing Some of the spelling words in this passage are misspelled. Write the misspelled words correctly. Then rewrite the paragraph correctly.

Anyone can go fly a kite. you don't have to be an athelete or obtain a special lisence to enjoy kite flying. At first youll probly experience some difficulties making your kite do what you want it to. Once youve mastered the technique, youll get imediate results. here are some sugestions.

For kite flying, its nessery to choose a windy day. holding the the kite in your right hand, start running and thrust the kite into the wind with treemendous force. allow a continous line of string to unwind from the spool. If the kite starts to dive, due to a temperary lack of wind, the excess string must be quickly wound up quickly. for safety reasons, do not stand underneth power lines and trees.

TESTING

A. Read each sentence carefully. Write the number of the sentence. If one of the underlined words is misspelled, write its letter. If neither word is misspelled, write the letter **c.**

1. ⓐ ⓑ ⓒ A <u>reporter</u> often has to <u>interveiw</u> people.
                 a   b

2. ⓐ ⓑ ⓒ We saw a small grey kitten <u>underneath</u> the <u>porch</u>.
                                       a   b

3. ⓐ ⓑ ⓒ Schools <u>organize</u> <u>intermural</u> sports for students.
                     a   b

4. ⓐ ⓑ ⓒ I feel <u>fortunate</u> to have a good <u>friend</u>.
                a   b

5. ⓐ ⓑ ⓒ There is a <u>tremendous</u> racket during <u>recess</u>.
                 a   b

6. ⓐ ⓑ ⓒ Charles expected an <u>imediate</u> <u>answer</u>.
                         a   b

7. ⓐ ⓑ ⓒ The coach will <u>supervise</u> soccer <u>practice</u>.
                  a   b

8. ⓐ ⓑ ⓒ The <u>continuous</u> yellow line down the center of the narrow country
               a
   road <u>meant</u> "No Passing."
       b

9. ⓐ ⓑ ⓒ The power <u>failure</u> caused a <u>temperary</u> blackout.
                a   b

10. ⓐ ⓑ ⓒ An <u>industryous</u> student is <u>usually</u> organized.
               a   b

B. Read each group of words. Write the number of the group and **a, b,** or **c** to indicate the word in the group that is spelled correctly.

1. ⓐ completion
   ⓑ compltion
   ⓒ complesion

2. ⓐ sugestion
   ⓑ sugesstion
   ⓒ suggestion

3. ⓐ couragous
   ⓑ currageous
   ⓒ courageous

4. ⓐ license
   ⓑ lisence
   ⓒ lisense

5. ⓐ decision
   ⓑ decission
   ⓒ desision

6. ⓐ diffrent
   ⓑ different
   ⓒ differant

7. ⓐ expression
   ⓑ exppresion
   ⓒ expresion

8. ⓐ probably
   ⓑ probly
   ⓒ probaly

9. ⓐ athlet
   ⓑ athlete
   ⓒ athelete

10. ⓐ nessery
    ⓑ necessary
    ⓒ nessary

CHALLENGE

Write the spelling words that complete the categories.

1. fortuitous, felicitous, ___?___
2. diligent, assiduous, ___?___
3. incessant, interminable, ___?___
4. indispensable, essential, ___?___
5. administer, regulate, ___?___
6. disparate, diverse, ___?___
7. gargantuan, colossal, ___?___
8. verbalization, utterance, ___?___
9. resolution, judgment, ___?___

LANGUAGE TO GO

A. **The Written Word** In "Young Man in a Hurry," author Joseph N. Farley writes about a long-distance runner. Here's a paragraph adapted from his article, which first appeared in the magazine **Accent on Youth:**

> James William Bowles has logged well over forty thousand miles in his years as a long-distance runner . . . that's about one and a half times around the world! James is five feet six inches tall and weighs 125 pounds. He explains, "I was too small for football and basketball. I wasn't big enough to make the baseball team; and I was too slow for sprints. For a while I thought I was going to be a full-time spectator." It wasn't until the school track coach suggested long-distance running that Jim really thought about becoming an athlete.

Notice how the author uses factual information, a direct quotation, and related material to capture the reader's interest. Write a short factual magazine article on one of these topics: 1) the development of an athlete; 2) what happened at a particular sporting event that you witnessed; 3) an "expert's" advice on choosing equipment for a particular sport. (Interview someone you know who plays the sport and quote this person in your article.) Use the spelling words when you can.

B. **The Spoken Word** Give an oral report and demonstration on how to play a particular game or sport. Do not use actual equipment for your demonstration, but explain with words and gestures. Some possible topics include: Techniques in Pitching Baseball, Keeping Score in Tennis, How to Dribble a Basketball. Choose a topic related to a sport you enjoy.

1. engineer
2. volunteer
3. comedian
4. guardian
5. custodian
6. librarian
7. musician
8. electrician
9. tenant
10. merchant
11. servant
12. applicant
13. assistant
14. attendant
15. participant
16. lieutenant
17. agent
18. resident
19. opponent
20. superintendent

Target Skill

The suffixes **eer**, **ian**, **ant**, and **ent** in words such as **engineer**, **librarian**, **assistant**, and **resident**.

"Learn what you can about as many different subjects as you can so you'll have a balanced view of the world." This advice is from Buckminster Fuller, a famous **engineer.**

First, learn about yourself. What are your abilities and interests? Discover what "success" means to you, and create your own career goals. Be a **participant** in life. New vocations are born as our awareness of the world expands.

A. Write the spelling words that end in the suffix **eer.**

B. Write the spelling words that end in the suffix **ian.**

C. Write the spelling words that end in the suffix **ant.**

D. Write the spelling words that end in the suffix **ent.**

WORD STUDY

A. Structure The base words for some of the spelling words end in **y.** Write the spelling words formed from these bases:

> 1. comedy   2. custody   3. library   4. apply

B. Vocabulary The spelling words are scrambled in the sentences. Write the spelling words correctly.

1. An <u>nenigere</u> enjoys learning about how things work.
2. A <u>tenorluve</u> contributes his time free of charge.
3. An <u>elniticreac</u> is skilled at installing, maintaining, and repairing electrical circuitry.
4. A professional <u>nasimuci</u> devotes himself to his art.
5. Anyone who takes part in something is a <u>trappanciti</u>.
6. A <u>pendentersutin</u> intends to supervise.

C. Dictionary The suffixes **eer, ian, ant,** and **ent** all convey the meaning of **one who.** The origins or roots of ten of the spelling words are given below, along with their literal definitions. Write each of these spelling words. Then write their modern definitions. You may refer to the dictionary if you wish.

1. From Latin **opponere** (oppose): one who opposes.
2. From Latin **mercari** (to trade): one who trades.
3. From Old French **garder** (to guard): one who guards or protects.
4. From Latin **agere** (to do): one who does.
5. From Latin **ad** (near to) and **sistere** (to stand): one who stands near to.
6. From Latin **attendere** (to heed): one who pays heed to.
7. From Old French **tenir** (to hold): one who holds or occupies.
8. From Old French **lieu** (place) and **tenir** (to hold): one who holds the place of or acts in place of.
9. From Latin **re** (back) and **sedere** (to sit): one who sits back or stays.
10. From Old French **servir** (to serve): one who serves.

WORD SENSE

engineer
volunteer
comedian
guardian
custodian
librarian
musician
electrician
tenant
merchant
servant
applicant
assistant
attendant
participant
lieutenant
agent
resident
opponent
superintendent

A. Write the spelling words that match the job descriptions.

1. Wanted: a __?__ . Make people laugh.
2. Book lover needed to assist __?__ .
3. Band to hold auditions for __?__ .
4. Hospital seeks a __?__ to visit patients.
5. An __?__ needed to rewire building.
6. New school system looking for top administrator or school __?__ .

B. Write the spelling word that can be substituted for the underlined words.

Every person actively involved in the job search process can use assistance. Some adults register with a professional representative at an employment agency. You might talk to your guidance counselor or see a retail store owner if you have an interest in sales. A person with mechanical skills might consider a job as building caretaker or might become a bridge designer. Each person applying for a position must be qualified.

C. Write the spelling words that complete the analogies.

1. **Colleague** is to **teammate** as **competitor** is to __?__ .
2. **Head** is to **chief** as **parent** is to __?__ .
3. **Help** is to **helper** as **service** is to __?__ .
4. **Occupy** is to **occupant** as **reside** is to __?__ .
5. **Hive** is to **bee** as **tenement** is to __?__ .
6. **Skipper** is to **captain** as **aide** is to __?__ .
7. **Assist** is to **assistant** as **attend** is to __?__ .
8. **Colonel** is to **general** as **sergeant** is to __?__ .

WORDSCAPES: The Writing Connection

A family tree is a chart of a family's ancestry. It names several generations of family members on both the maternal (mother's) and paternal (father's) side.

A. To start your family tree, write your full name, birth date, and birthplace. Write the same information about your parents. Then ask your parents about their parents, and theirs, and theirs—for as many generations back as possible. Other relatives may also provide information. Draw a large tree with pairs of branches for each generation, and fill in your family's history. Spell all the names correctly. As you work on this project, ask your relatives to tell you family stories. Write them down for a family history book.

Content Words

collective
plural
possessive
proper
singular

finance
fiscal
partnership
invest
stockbroker

B. Write the appropriate Language Arts Word for each blank.

Family is a __1__ noun because it refers to a group as a whole. **Families** is a __2__ noun; it refers to more than one person, place, or thing. A __3__ noun, such as **family's,** shows ownership. **Child** is a __4__ noun, referring to a single person, place, or thing. A __5__ noun, such as **Murphy,** is a formal name.

C. Write the Social Studies Words which fit the blanks.

1. A business of two or more individuals is a __?__ .
2. A __?__ buys and sells stocks for a living.
3. A __?__ matter pertains to finances.
4. The study of money management is the study of __?__ .
5. When you commit money to gain profit, you __?__ .

131

1. clearance
2. appearance
3. attendance
4. performance
5. importance
6. inheritance
7. balance
8. instance
9. distance
10. ambulance
11. insurance
12. silence
13. absence
14. excellence
15. innocence
16. obedience
17. patience
18. residence
19. experience
20. sequence

Target Skill

The suffixes **ance** and **ence** in words such as **clearance, instance,** and **experience.**

A. Write the spelling words that end with the suffix **ance.**

B. Write the spelling words that end with the suffix **ence.**

Here is a sample form for a résumé, which you may follow to describe your own abilities and **performance.**

	Name
	Address
	Phone Number
	Grade
Writing Experience	List and briefly describe reports, compositions, journal entries, etc. that you have written.
Special Skills and Abilities	Describe your abilities and interpersonal skills. (Are you an excellent speller or proofreader? Is your work neat and accurate? Are you a good listener or leader? Cite your best qualities.)
Interests and Extracurricular Activities	List your interests, activities, and hobbies.
Work-related Experience	List any work you have done for family, friends, or teachers that shows your reliability.
Education	Name and address of school Grade average Favorite subjects

WORD STUDY

A. Dictionary The suffixes **ance** and **ence** form nouns. When these nouns are pronounced, the syllable containing the suffix is not stressed.

Write the part of speech for each word below. Then write the spelling word that is related to it. After writing the spelling words, circle three of them that are homophones for three of the words below. A homophone is a word that is pronounced like another word, but has a different spelling and meaning.

1. insure	3. ambulatory	6. experiment	9. innocents
2. distant	4. silent	7. patients	10. absent
	5. excellent	8. instants	

B. Structure The underlined words can be found in the spelling words that complete the sentences. Write the spelling words.

1. When we heard of the bargains, we <u>ran</u> to the ___?___ sale.
2. At <u>ten</u> o'clock, ___?___ was taken at the <u>dance</u>.
3. A dark <u>form</u> appeared during the ___?___ .
4. Can you maintain your ___?___ while holding a <u>lance</u>?
5. On which <u>side</u> of the street is your ___?___ ?
6. The antiques reminded Carla of <u>her</u> ___?___ .

C. Proofreading Each misspelled spelling word is preceded by an adjective. Write the adjective with the correctly spelled spelling word.

1. The famous economist made a formal apperance at our annual business dinner.
2. She stressed the ultimate importence of keeping up to date with national business trends.
3. Follow a logical secquence in planning the financial development of a business.
4. Strict obediance to standard accounting practices is essential to business success.

WORD SENSE

clearance
appearance
attendance
performance
importance
inheritance
balance
instance
distance
ambulance
insurance
silence
absence
excellence
innocence
obedience
patience
residence
experience
sequence

A. Write the missing spelling words, using the given syllables as clues. **Proper nouns** are always capitalized. Write the proper nouns correctly.

   Young jack kramer knows that his in____ of the family _sur____ business is a great opportunity. jack realizes the value and _por____ of every employee, and he insists on a good _ten____ record from each one. He understands that each worker contributes to the _cel____ of kramer insurance company. The staff appreciates jack's pa____ and fairness in evaluating their _per____.

B. Write the spelling words that belong in these interview questions. The first letter of each word is provided.

1. What past e_____ qualifies you for this job?

2. Tell me about your previous employment in s_____, starting with your first job.

3. Can you explain your long a_____ from your last job?

4. How far away is your current r_____ from R and B Vehicle Services?

5. Have you ever driven an a_____?

6. Are you comfortable driving a long d_____?

7. Can you describe an i_____ that shows your ability to think and act quickly?

C. Write the spelling words that complete the categories.

1. space, passage, ___?___   4. acceptance, compliance, ___?___

2. equalize, weigh, ___?___   5. stillness, quiet, ___?___

3. looks, sight, ___?___   6. blamelessness, purity, ___?___

134

A résumé summarizes your personal history and work experience and shows an employer how your abilities match the needs of the workplace.

A. Imagine that you are trying to get a writing job on the school newspaper and that the faculty advisor has requested a résumé from each applicant for the position. Using the format at the opening of this unit, write a résumé which demonstrates your best writing skills, describes your ability to work with others, and covers all of your qualifications for the job. Use the spelling words when you can.

Content Words

atom
electron
neutron
nucleus
proton

arc
chord
circumference
pi
radius

B. Write the Science Words that match the definitions.

1. A stable particle, smaller than an atom (subatomic), which has a positive charge.

2. A subatomic particle, with a negative charge, found surrounding the nucleus of an atom.

3. The smallest complete unit of an element.

4. An electrically neutral subatomic particle having about the same mass as a proton.

5. The central, positively charged core of an atom.

C. Write the Math Words that complete the paragraph.

The __1__ of a circle can be determined by multiplying __2__, or 3.14, times the __3__ squared. An __4__ is a part of a circle. A __5__ is a line segment joining two points on a circle.

1. aged
2. wound
3. compound
4. compact
5. contract
6. conduct
7. content
8. convert
9. convict
10. console
11. buffet
12. object
13. rebel
14. refuse
15. present
16. primer
17. progress
18. minute
19. extract
20. invalid

Target Skill

Homographs, such as **content/content.**
Homographs are words that are spelled the same but have different meanings, origins, or pronunciations.

The doctor **wound** a clean, protective bandage around the **wound** on her patient's leg. She then sat down at the computer **console** and sent a prescription to the pharmacist. To **console** the patient, the doctor said, "You should feel better soon."

A. Write the spelling words that end in the letter **d.**

B. Write the spelling words that start with **com** or **con.**

C. Write the spelling words that end in the letters **et** or **te.**

D. Write the spelling words that start with the letters **pr.**

E. Write the spelling words that start with the prefix **ob, re,** or **ex.**

WORD STUDY

A. Dictionary Write the spelling word for each dictionary respelling. Write the part of speech for each pronunciation. An example is provided.

> **Ex.** /rĭ bĕl′/, /rĕb′əl/ rebel v., rebel n.

1. /ā′jĭd/, /ājd/
2. /wo͞ond/, /wound/
3. /kŏm′ pound/, /kŏm pound′/
4. /bə fā′/, /bŭf′ ĭt/
5. /mĭn′ ĭt/, /mī no͞ot′/
6. /ĭk străkt′/, /ĕk′ străkt/

B. Proofreading Read the paragraph. Write the spelling words correctly. You will need to add **s** to two of the words. Rewrite the paragraph, spelling all words correctly and following the proofreading marks.

> # means to insert a space   ⟍ means to delete

The contant of the Hippocratic Oath influences the conduck of every student of medicine. it prescents doctors with a a set of principles, which they promise to obey. They contrack to work only for the progres and health of the sick and invilid. They refuce to perform any dangerous operations for which they are not trained. They also objekt to spreading rumors about patients. Such actions might injure, rather than consol, those under their care. hippocrates was the first doctor to rebell against the belief that magic could drive away disease His notes provided a common sense primmer of medical information for others to follow.

C. Vocabulary Write the spelling words that fit in these word groups.

1. conversion, convertible, ____?____
2. convince, conviction, ____?____
3. compactor, compactly, ____?____

WORD SENSE

aged
wound
compound
compact
contract
conduct
content
convert
convict
console
buffet
object
rebel
refuse
present
primer
progress
minute
extract
invalid

A. Write the missing spelling words with spaces between the syllables. Add accent marks to show proper stress.

1. The __?__ senior citizen walked with a child __?__ six and a half.
2. They'll __?__ the problems if they move prisoners from that __?__ .
3. When it was her turn to __?__ a school tour, the student's __?__ was commendable.
4. I will __?__ to dispose of their __?__ .
5. Will you __?__ the medal and the __?__ ?
6. This __?__ on painting suggests using a __?__ coat.
7. A __?__ speck of dust settled on the table only a __?__ after it was cleaned.
8. The jury will __?__ that woman if she's proven guilty, and she will become a __?__ .

B. Write the spelling words with spaces between the syllables to complete the paragraphs. Add stress marks to show which pronunciation is used.

There's no point in being a __1__ when it's time to visit the dentist. Any excuses I make for not going are __2__ . My dentist's receptionist sits at a computer __3__ to record the patients' checkup dates.

Because I signed a __4__ with my dentist to brush my teeth three times a day, I always carry a __5__ brush with me. After the supper __6__ , I brushed my teeth and __7__ floss around my finger. The __8__ of flossing is to remove plaque. Dentists sometimes have to __9__ a decayed tooth. I feel __10__ knowing I've made __11__ in keeping my teeth clean. I've become a __12__ to proper dental care; I want my teeth to last my entire life.

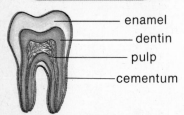

enamel
dentin
pulp
cementum

A healthy tooth is nourished by blood vessels and protected by a coat of enamel.

When you apply for a job, you send a cover letter with your résumé. The purpose of the letter is to introduce you to the person in charge of hiring. It briefly explains why you want a job and what makes you especially suited for it. In format, a cover letter is like any business letter.

A. Pretend that you are applying for a job as a dog walker or for some other job that you would like for which you are qualified. Write a cover letter introducing yourself as a responsible person. Describe just enough about your experience to encourage the reader to look at your résumé. Include a sentence that begins "As you can see from my résumé," and finish the sentence by describing why you would be the best choice for the job.

Content Words

discount	dermis
interest rate	epidermis
percent	complexion
percentage	hygiene
portion	dermatologist

B. Write the Math Words that match the clues.

1. section
2. reduced rate
3. fraction or ratio
4. %
5. charge for a loan

C. Write the Science Words that complete the paragraph. You will need to add **s** to one word.

Most ___1___ agree that proper ___2___ is the best way to keep your ___3___ healthy. The skin, the largest human organ, consists of layers. The ___4___, or outer layer, suffers the most wear and tear. The ___5___, the layer just below the epidermis, contains the structures that allow the skin to sweat.

139

1. graphic
2. photography
3. telegraph
4. paragraph
5. autograph
6. biographer
7. biology
8. thermal
9. thermostat
10. thermometer
11. diameter
12. barometer
13. speedometer
14. geometry
15. geology
16. geologist
17. geography
18. geographer
19. autobiographer
20. oceanographer

Target Skill

Words formed from combining Greek roots.

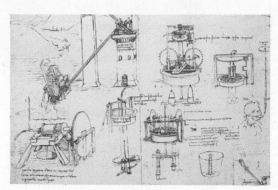

Centuries before the invention of contemporary machinery, Leonardo da Vinci conceived and drew modern devices.

The boy peered into the inky depths of the cave. His interest in **oceanography, biology,** and **geography** lured him inside. There he found the skeleton of an ancient fish—a discovery that told him the sea had once covered the land.

The young discoverer was Leonardo da Vinci, the great artist, scientist, and inventor, born in 1452.

A. Write the spelling words that stem from the Greek word **graphein** (to write).

B. Write the spelling words that stem from the Greek word **bios** (life).

C. Write the spelling words that stem from the Greek word **therme** (heat).

D. Write the spelling words that stem from the Greek word **metron** (measure).

E. Write the spelling words that stem from the Greek prefix **geo** (earth).

F. Write the spelling words that stem from the Greek word **autos** (self).

WORD STUDY

A. Proofreading Write the misspelled spelling words correctly. You will need to add **s** to one of the words.

The photagraphy of Dorothea Lange helped to change America. Her grafic portrayals of the hungry and homeless in the 1930s forced people everywhere to become aware of the hardships endured during the Great Depression. Dorothea's husband reported on the desperate needs of the migrant workers. Dorothea took pictures to illustrate particular paragrafs in these reports. Her photographs were seen by millions. A biografer named Milton Meltzer has written a book about her life.

Migrant Mother by Dorothea Lange

B. Vocabulary Write seven of the spelling words by combining roots. Match a root from Group A with a root from Group B. Use all of the roots.

A. tele bio dia baro therm thermo speedo

B. meter al meter graph meter logy stat

C. Vocabulary The Greek prefix **geo** means **earth.** Write the spelling words that are science and mathematics terms related to the history, structure, measurements, shapes, and features of earth.

D. Dictionary Read the Greek word origins and definitions below. Write the spelling words you can form from the roots.

1. **Therme** (heat) + **metron** (measure).
2. **Okeanos** (a great river encircling the earth) + **graphein** (to write).
3. **Autos** (self) + **graphe** (writing).
4. **Autos** (self) + **bios** (life) + **graphein** (to write).

WORD SENSE

graphic
photography
telegraph
paragraph
autograph
biographer
biology
thermal
thermostat
thermometer
diameter
barometer
speedometer
geometry
geology
geologist
geography
geographer
autobiographer
oceanographer

A. Write the spelling words that complete these sentences. Add **s** to two words. The first letter of each word is provided.

Jacques-Yves Cousteau is a famous o___1___ . He has studied the b___2___ of the ocean's animals and plants. Cousteau can be considered an a___3___ because he writes about his own experiences in his books about exploring the sea. The p___4___ in his books are filled with interesting information. His p___5___ of the undersea world is breathtakingly beautiful.

To protect themselves from the cold, oceanographers wear t___6___ body suits. A t___7___ below sea level allows divers to record changes in temperature.

With its hills and valleys, the g___8___ of the ocean floor resembles that of the land. By studying the ocean floor, g___9___ learn about the history and structure of earth.

B. Write the spelling words that match the clues. You may use the spelling dictionary to look up the definitions of the spelling words, and you may refer to the activities on page 140 for definitions of the Greek roots.

1. Shown in **writing** or **drawing.**
2. Identifying one's **self** through **writing.**
3. **Measuring through** a circle.
4. **Measuring pressure.**
5. **Measuring speed.**
6. **Earth measuring.**
7. Someone who describes the **earth** through **writing.**
8. **Heat stabilizer.**
9. Someone who tells a **life** history in **writing.**

Jacques-Yves Cousteau

142

WORDSCAPES: The Writing Connection

An **autobiography** is the story of a person's life. It can be written in a humorous or serious vein. It includes both factual information and opinion. Anecdotes about the writer's life make the autobiography interesting. An autobiography may end with the person's plans for the future, including career plans.

My Life

by
Linda Zimmer

A. Write your own autobiography in four paragraphs. Include an anecdote or two. In the first paragraph, tell about your family and your early life. In the second paragraph, describe yourself as a student. Describe your personality and interests in the third paragraph. In the final paragraph, discuss your future goals and plans.

Content Words

artery
bleed
emergency
pressure
tourniquet

bilingual
cabinet
parliament
premier
province

B. Write the Science Words that complete the first aid report. You will need to add **ing** to one word.

A __1__ is used in an __2__ when a major __3__ is cut and is __4__ heavily. The tourniquet is used to apply the right amount of __5__ to control loss of blood.

C. Write the missing Social Studies Words.

Ontario is a __1__ of Canada, as is British Columbia. A __2__ is the head of the government in each province except Quebec. Many people in Quebec are __3__ , speaking both French and English. The prime minister is Canada's chief executive. He appoints a __4__ of ministers to help him govern. Canada's legislative body is the __5__ .

143

1. *mph*
2. *rpm*
3. *bit*
4. *laser*
5. *sonar*
6. *scuba*
7. *A.M.*
8. *P.M.*
9. *VCR*
10. *PBS*
11. *BASIC*
12. *OPEC*
13. *SALT*
14. *POW*
15. *COD*
16. *DOB*
17. *CEO*
18. *IRA*
19. *CPU*
20. *IRS*

Target Skill

Abbreviations and **acronyms**, such as **mph** and **laser**. An **abbreviation** is a shortened form of a word or phrase. An **acronym** is a word formed by combining first letters or parts of a series of words.

A. Write the **acronyms** for these phrases.

1. binary digit
2. light amplification by stimulated emission of radiation
3. sound navigation ranging
4. self-contained underwater breathing apparatus
5. beginner's all-purpose symbolic instruction code

B. Write the **abbreviations** for these phrases.

1. miles per hour
2. revolutions per minute
3. ante meridiem
4. post meridiem
5. videocassette recorder
6. Public Broadcasting System
7. Organization of Petroleum Exporting Countries
8. Strategic Arms Limitations Talks
9. prisoner of war
10. cash on delivery
11. date of birth
12. chief executive officer
13. Individual Retirement Account
14. central processing unit
15. Internal Revenue Service

WORD STUDY

A. Vocabulary Read the paragraph and find the phrases which can be shortened into acronyms or abbreviations. Write them correctly in their shortened forms.

Computer technology has added its own vocabulary to the American language. Shortened forms of computer terms make them easier to say and remember. The smallest unit the central processing unit can store is a binary digit. Using beginner's all-purpose symbolic instruction code, a programmer can record information in the computer. Light amplification by stimulated emission of radiation printing is one means of getting computer information on paper. One by-product of the computer age is the videocassette recorder.

B. Dictionary Write the abbreviations correctly. Use the spelling dictionary.

1. **pbs**   3. **Rpm**   5. **S.a.l.t.**   7. **D.o.b.**   9. **ira**

2. **am**   4. **opec**   6. **pow**   8. **ceo**   10. **I.R.S.**

C. Proofreading Write the acronyms or abbreviations correctly. Circle the acronyms.

When the mail carrier came with my package, it was stamped C.o.d. I paid her and quickly opened the package, which contained my new skuba gear. I planned to use it on my first night dive. At 8 P.m. Terry and I put our suits and tanks in the car and drove to the harbor at 55 M.P.H. Once we were out on the water in the large motorboat, Terry used a soner device to find our exact diving location.

145

WORD SENSE

mph

rpm

bit

laser

sonar

scuba

A.M.

P.M.

VCR

PBS

BASIC

OPEC

SALT

POW

COD

DOB

CEO

IRA

CPU

IRS

A. Write the acronyms or abbreviations specifically related to each subject.

1. **Computers** (4 acronyms or abbreviations)
2. **Televison** (2 abbreviations)
3. **U.S. Business/Taxes** (3 abbreviations)
4. **Oceanographer's Equipment** (2 acronyms)

B. Write the acronyms and abbreviations that complete the paragraph.

Telecommunication makes it easier to stay on top of what is happening in the world. Due to advancements in __1__ technology, we are able to watch programs from distant parts of the world during the __2__ and __3__ hours. Light travels at a rate of 670,615,200 __4__ !   When delegates from the U.S. and U.S.S.R. met to negotiate the __5__ treaties, it was possible for the people of the world to know the results at once. And whenever the __6__ nations decide on new oil prices, this information is quickly sent throughout the world.

C. Write the word missing from each definition. Then find the abbreviations in the puzzle. Write each abbrevation.

ACROSS

1. __?__ on delivery.
2. prisoner of __?__ .
3. revolutions per __?__ .

DOWN

4. __?__ of birth.
5. Internal Revenue __?__ .

C	O	D	s	m
v	P	O	W	a
R	I	B	o	e
p	r	p	m	l
s	V	R	a	R
B	r	E	s	S

146

WORDSCAPES: The Writing Connection

Dreams to Sell
T.L. Beddoes

If there were dreams to sell,
 What would you buy?
Some cost a passing bell;
 Some a light sigh,
That shakes from Life's fresh crown
Only a rose-leaf down.

If there were dreams to sell,
Merry and sad to tell,
And the crier rang the bell,
 What would you buy?

A. Write a short composition about a dream or goal you have. In the first paragraph, explain what the dream means to you and why you want to pursue it. In the next paragraph, describe your plans for making your dream a reality. Finally, describe what you imagine it will feel like to accomplish your goal.

Content Words

avalanche
debris
delta
sediment
shale

debugging
flow chart
input
output
programming

B. Write the missing Social Studies Words.

1. After an ___?___ , there is a lot of ___?___ to clean up.

2. At the ___?___ of a river, ___?___ collects.

3. A rock composed of fine-grained sediments is ___?___ .

C. Write the Math Words that go with the clues below.

Providing the computer with a set of instructions for problem solving is called ___1___ . What you put into a system is ___2___ . What you get out of a system is ___3___ . Removing errors in programming is called ___4___ . A diagram showing the sequence of operations is a ___5___ .

147

WORD CLUES AND STUDY

A. Write the spelling words that indicate a person.

B. Write the spelling words that have two syllables.

C. Write the spelling words that have three syllables with an unaccented final syllable.

D. Write the acronyms and the abbreviations.

FURTHER PRACTICE AND ENRICHMENT

A. Proofreading Write the spelling words correctly.

When the mercury rises in the thermeter, signaling the start of summer, your patients with cool weather will be rewarded. Your vacation will provide new experiences to write about in your journal. You might write about a friend and become a biographr. If you travel, you will experiance firsthand the geografy of the land. Whatever your plans, you will soon say farewell to ratios and geomtry and hello to summer fun and maybe a summer job!

B. Write the spelling words that are missing from these sentences. Add **'s** to two words to make them possessive. Add **s** to three words to make the subjects and verbs of the sentences agree. The first letter of each spelling word is given.

1. We appreciated the v___?___ friendly manner.
2. Our school l___?___ suggests good books to read.
3. Many b___?___ write about sports heroes.
4. The conductor c___?___ the orchestra masterfully.
5. The l___?___ promotion to captain was a surprise.
6. Five a___?___ were interviewed for that job.

C. Creative Writing There are thousands of different types of jobs. Some of them are very unusual. For example, how would you like to be a dolphin trainer, a toothpaste tester, a decoy carver, or a trapeze artist? Choose any two jobs and write a paragraph about each job. Describe what you think your duties would be, what you would do each day, and what unusual situations you might face.

D. Editing Research the jobs you have written about in Activity C. Look for factual information and take notes. Compare your opinions to the facts you find. If something you have written in Activity C is inaccurate, correct it.

TESTING

A. Read each sentence. Write the number of the sentence and **a** or **b** to indicate whether the underlined word is spelled correctly or incorrectly.

1. My brother is a <u>volunteer</u> at the hospital.
   ⓐ correct   ⓑ incorrect

2. I gave my sister a <u>present</u> for her birthday.
   ⓐ correct   ⓑ incorrect

3. The army <u>leiutenant</u> stood at attention.
   ⓐ correct   ⓑ incorrect

4. The tired child didn't have any <u>patience</u> left.
   ⓐ correct   ⓑ incorrect

5. A job <u>aplicant</u> should be well-groomed.
   ⓐ correct   ⓑ incorrect

6. The <u>librarian</u> knows a great deal about books.
   ⓐ correct   ⓑ incorrect

7. Mathematics includes the study of <u>jeometry</u>.
   ⓐ correct   ⓑ incorrect

8. My school <u>attendence</u> record is perfect.
   ⓐ correct   ⓑ incorrect

9. Please <u>conduct</u> yourselves properly on the field.
   ⓐ correct   ⓑ incorrect

10. We are learning <u>basic</u> in computer science.
    ⓐ correct   ⓑ incorrect

B. Read each group of words. Write the number of the group and **a**, **b**, or **c** to indicate the word in the group that is spelled correctly.

1. ⓐ SCUBA
   ⓑ scuba
   ⓒ s.c.u.b.a.

2. ⓐ experience
   ⓑ experiance
   ⓒ experence

3. ⓐ performence
   ⓑ performance
   ⓒ preformance

4. ⓐ minite
   ⓑ minit
   ⓒ minute

5. ⓐ object
   ⓑ objec
   ⓒ objekt

6. ⓐ biograffer
   ⓑ bigraphre
   ⓒ biographer

7. ⓐ laser
   ⓑ l.a.s.e.r.
   ⓒ LASER

8. ⓐ geographee
   ⓑ geografy
   ⓒ geography

9. ⓐ rpm
   ⓑ R.P.M.
   ⓒ R.pm

10. ⓐ thremometer
    ⓑ thermometer
    ⓒ thermometre

CHALLENGE

Which of the spelling words are verbs? Which of the spelling words are formed from base words that are verbs? Write all of these verbs —spelling words and base words—in the past tense.

LANGUAGE TO GO

A. The Written Word Maria Augusta Trapp wrote her autobiography, telling about her experiences with the Trapp Family Singers. **The Sound of Music** is the movie version of her story. Here is the way she describes her first few days at her new job as governess.

> "I lived in a continual state of bewilderment. Nothing—nothing at all was familiar to me in this house. First, I had to get used to different people . . . . Besides the large family and the servants, which amounted to twenty persons, there was the spacious old house. So many rooms, hallways, corridors, bay windows, balconies, and in the rooms, so many quaint things I had never met before."

Choose a time from your own life—or imagine a time—when you had to change to fit a new place and new people. Describe how you did this. How did you go about getting to know your new surroundings? Write about that time, about the new place and people, and how you adjusted.

B. The Spoken Word Work as part of a group to prepare a panel discussion. Choose the leader of the group. This person will announce the topic to be discussed. He or she will then direct the conversation by asking questions. Each panel member should research one part of the topic. Use both facts and opinions to express the views of the group. Discuss one of the following topics:

1. How to get the most out of your summer.
2. Summer employment for students.
3. Things to do and see in your community.

Challenge Activities

adequate	elastic	container
ancestor	exclaim	complaint

A. Write the challenge word that fits each "Who or What Am I" statement.

1. I return to my normal shape after I'm stretched.

2. I may be enough or suitable, but I'm not of the best quality.

3. I am a statement expressing annoyance or unhappiness. Sign me "Gripe."

4. I am family. I was born before your grandparents.

5. I am used to hold something. Call me a box or a barrel.

B. Write the challenge words that complete this "vacation album" story.

A great-grandfather, one __1__ of mine, enjoyed spending his summer vacation at home. But he hated to live in his home in the winter. His landlord never provided __2__ heat for the house. My great-grandfather did not write the landlord a letter of __3__. He did not knock on the landlord's door to __4__ about how cold it was. He put one piece of coal into a __5__ and sent it to the landlord as a hint!

C. Pretend that you are the landlord mentioned in Activity B. Write a letter in response to the man who sent you a piece of coal. Tell what you think he should have done. Tell him how you plan to correct the situation. Use as many challenge words as possible.

Challenge Activities

definite	**velvet**	**appeal**
prevent	**cheetah**	**charity**

A. Write the challenge word that completes each analogy.

1. **Unclear** is to **exact** as **uncertain** is to ___?___ .
2. **Wild pig** is to **boar** as **wild cat** is to ___?___ .
3. **Stingy** is to **selfishness** as **generous** is to ___?___ .
4. **Metal** is to **steel** as **fabric** is to ___?___ .
5. **Answer** is to **ask** as **help** is to ___?___ .

B. Write the word that does not belong in each group. Then add a challenge word that does belong and write the complete group of new words.

1. stop   halt   ticket   check
2. ask   request   plea   offer
3. unkindness   good will   sympathy   brotherly love
4. precise   explain   exact   certain
5. tiger   leopard   dog   lion

C. Write a story about a musical event given at a zoo to raise money for your favorite charity. Use some of the challenge words in your story.

UNIT 3

Challenge Activities

categorize	hibernate	logic
glimpse	citrus	inhabit

A. Write a challenge word to answer the question. Put the word in a phrase if it makes more sense. Tell what you could do in the situation given.

1. You see a stack of books that is not arranged in any kind of order. What could you do with these books?

2. You are Sherlock Holmes explaining how you solved a mystery. What do you claim helped you to solve the mystery?

3. You are a bear who doesn't want to be active in the winter. What could you do?

4. You are in a crowded store. You think you see a friend of yours walk by, but you do not get a good look. What kind of a look were you able to get?

B. Write the challenge word that would be found on a dictionary page with each pair of guide words below.

1. cause | city
2. catchy | citizen
3. log | logrolling
4. glisten | hiccup
5. hibiscus | inhale
6. glimmer | hibachi

C. Write what the main character, Blob, might do in a science fiction story that takes place on a strange planet covered with fruit trees. Use as many challenge words as possible.

154

UNIT 4

Challenge Activities

focus	melodious	devote
commotion	Congress	monument

A. Write challenge words to complete the news story. One of these words should be capitalized.

A concert was held on the steps of the Lincoln Memorial. It was in honor of the brave men and women who __1__ their lives in service to their country. People from across the country, as well as members of __2__ , crowded around this historic __3__ . Police were standing by in case there was any __4__ , but the crowd was orderly. The band struck up a __5__ tune. Then the speeches began. The __6__ of the speeches was on national pride.

B. Write a challenge word that relates to each group of words.

1. Statue of Liberty Jefferson Memorial Mount Rushmore

2. camera eye attention

3. lawmakers legislators representatives

4. voice violin bird

C. Write a short report telling about an event that you would organize if you were the President of the United States. What would be the focus of the event? Who would be invited? Where would the event be held? Use some of the challenge words in your report.

UNIT 5

Challenge Activities

| confusion | strenuous | substance |
| continual | punishment | sculpture |

A. Complete this short story about a tour guide's first day on the job at the Statue of Liberty.

> "This is ___1___ work!" I thought to myself. All day long there is a ___2___ flow of sightseers. Surprisingly, things run quite smoothly. There is very little ___3___ . But standing on my feet all day is torture. My shoes take a lot of ___4___ . It's all worth it, however. The Lady is a marvelous piece of ___5___

B. Look at each base word in parentheses. To complete each sentence, write a challenge word that is the same part of speech as the abbreviation shown beside the base word. Then underline the suffix.

1. Should the (punish, n.) fit the crime?
2. What is the name of this huge (sculpt, n.)?
3. I lost my keys in all this (confuse, n.).
4. This month, it seemed as though I was on a (continue, adj.) diet of fresh fruit.

C. Write two tongue twisters. In the first, use words beginning with the letter **c,** and include two challenge words. Your tongue twister could be, for example, "Cam's cousin created continual confusion." In the second, use words beginning with the letter **s,** and include three challenge words.

156

| renewal | juvenile | supermarket |
| distribute | supreme | bulldozer |

A. Write an antonym for each word in the first column. Write a synonym for each word in the second column. Use challenge words.

1. adult
2. collect
3. cancellation

4. highest
5. tractor
6. self-service store

B. Read the sentences. Write a challenge word to replace the underlined word(s) in each sentence.

1. Mr. Moyer's lease was up last year. He went to the landlord to ask for <u>an extension</u>.
2. Miss Andrews was new in the neighborhood. She was looking for a <u>store where she could pick out her groceries</u>.
3. Steve loved his younger brother Eddie, but sometimes Eddie was too <u>young</u> to be included in Steve's activities.
4. There was a farm auction last week. The best <u>tractor for moving earth</u> was sold right away.
5. Our boss told us to divide the stacks of newspapers and <u>give</u> them <u>out</u>.

C. What could you say or do to show your good manners in each of the following situations? Write your answers using challenge words.

1. You accidentally bump your shopping cart into someone at the store.
2. You are walking past a construction site. You recognize one of the workers.
3. You forgot to renew your library card.
4. Your neighbor asks you to watch her small child for an hour.
5. Your teacher needs volunteers to give out notices for the school fair.

Challenge Activities

overview	fiendish	chiefly
surveillance	deceit	piercing

A. Write a challenge word to answer each question. Put the word in a phrase if it makes more sense.

1. What kind of noise or cry could penetrate the air?
2. What kind of wicked act could you expect in a mystery movie?
3. What do you call the practice of telling a falsehood in order to trick someone?
4. What might a speaker give in his or her speech to let the audience know the broad picture of a topic?
5. What do you call the close observation of a person under suspicion by the police?

B. Use challenge words to complete this list started by Detective R3.

__1__ of Contents of Detective Kit

One whistle with __2__ tone to use
only in emergencies
A pair of binoculars to use for __3__
A scary face disguise with __4__ grin
A shiny badge that is __5__ for show

C. Complete this science fiction story. Include as many challenge words as you can.

Detective R3 heard a chilling sound near the secret lab station. He quickly boarded his rocket car that had special equipment.

nursery	garment	dormitory
departure	porcelain	formation

A. Write a challenge word that relates to each row of words.

1. room   babies   cribs
2. rooms   school   beds
3. dress   shirt   sweater
4. good-by   takeoff   liftoff
5. china   earthenware   teacups
6. arrangement   order   organization

B. Read each job description. Then answer each question with a phrase that includes a challenge word.

1. I work in a college. My job is to supply fresh laundry to the rooms where the students sleep. Where do I spend my working hours?
2. I work in a factory. My job is to sew clothes that will be sold in stores. In which type of industry do I work?
3. I work outdoors where young trees and plants are raised for transplanting. Where do I work?
4. I work in a studio. I make fine cups and dishes out of clay. What is the material I often use in my work?

C. Follow the steps below to develop prewriting notes and then a paragraph. Use challenge words when you can.

1. Make a list of names for certain rooms in a home or other type of building.
2. Make a list of materials that could be used to make objects for inside or outside a home or other building.
3. Make a list of different land formations.
4. Use some of the words in your lists to describe a home or building. Begin your paragraph with this topic sentence: This dream home (building) is quite a departure from an ordinary home (building).

UNIT 10
Challenge Activities

hysterical	interval	jovial
cordial	frequent	inhabitant

A. Answer each "What would you be?" question with a challenge word.

1. What would you be if you were good-hearted and full of fun?
2. What would you be if you were unusually emotional or showing a lack of self-control?
3. What would you be if you lived in a certain town?
4. What would you be if you had a warm and friendly nature?
5. What would you be if you were a period of time between now and then?

B. Complete each sentence using the challenge words. After each word, tell whether it is used as a noun or an adjective in the sentence.

1. At each __?__ in the road was an __?__ of the town who was helping people evacuate the area during the emergency.
2. This police officer tried to be __?__ to drivers who became __?__ when they got stuck in __?__ traffic jams in the Midtown Tunnel.

C. Imagine that you are a smart and friendly mole. You like to have many guests over to your tunnel home. Write a fanciful story about one of the "down-to-earth" parties you gave. Use some of the challenge words in your story. If you'd prefer to be a rat or a chipmunk or some other animal, go right ahead and change the main character.

160

| frontward | politely | actively |
| practically | perfectly | vigorously |

A. Write a challenge word to complete each analogy.

1. **Back** is to **front** as **backward** is to ___?___ .
2. **Nearly** is to **closely** as **almost** is to ___?___ .
3. **Faultily** is to **imperfectly** as **ideally** is to ___?___ .
4. **Noisily** is to **quietly** as **rudely** is to ___?___ .
5. **Powerfully** is to **forcefully** as **strenuously** is to ___?___ .

B. Answer each question with a challenge word.

1. If you wanted a favor from your parents, how would you ask them?
2. If you went to a parade and you wanted to get a good view, which way would you move?
3. If someone offered you a free ticket to see and hear a famous rock star, how would you answer "Yes" or "No"?
4. If your teacher asked you if you had finished answering the questions in part B, what could your one-word answer be?
5. Which word tells how you answered these questions?

C. Complete each sentence with a challenge word.

1. Shake the bottle ___?___ to make sure the two liquids blend.
2. Move the chess piece ___?___ to advance two spaces.
3. Ask the operator ___?___ for the phone number of the nearest library.
4. Check the content, grammar, and punctuation to make sure you wrote your report ___?___ .
5. Your heart rate increases when you are ___?___ playing sports.
6. When you turn left at the barn, you'll know you are ___?___ at the farmhouse.

UNIT 13

Challenge Activities

finalist	tariff	offense
fantastic	sheriff	phobia

A. Write the challenge word that fits each definition.

1. a breaking of the law
2. a system of taxes on imports or exports
3. a person who takes part in a final competition
4. a deep, unreasonable fear of something
5. the chief law-enforcement official of a county
6. fanciful or imaginary

B. Complete each sentence with a challenge word.

1. If you get into trouble in this county, call the ___?___ .
2. Jay took part in the event as a ___?___ .
3. You can be fined or imprisoned for an ___?___ .
4. Their fear of riding on escalators may be a ___?___ .
5. Sandy's dream was strange and ___?___ .
6. On imported cars there is a high ___?___ .

C. A person could have several different feelings about a dream, a fear, or an incident. Write a sentence about more than one feeling someone might have in each situation below. Use the underlined challenge word or words in the sentence.

1. Someone becomes a <u>finalist</u> in a talent contest for the very first time.
2. The <u>sheriff</u> gives someone a ticket for a speeding <u>offense</u>.
3. Someone dreams that he or she has to pay a high <u>tariff</u> for the imported watch he or she bought.
4. The shapes someone sees in clouds are <u>fantastic</u>.
5. Someone has a <u>phobia</u> of heights but had to climb a ladder one day.

162

| drizzle | disaster | excursion |
| amusing | mayonnaise | pleasurable |

A. Complete this silly poem with a challenge word that rhymes with the underlined word above it.

Yesterday was quite <u>confusing</u>,
Though I found it rather ___1___ .
The sun was so hot, it began to <u>sizzle</u>.
Then from the clouds it began to ___2___ .
It poured and poured, faster and <u>faster</u>
Until there was almost a major ___3___ !
Then it happened. What a sight!
Everyone running to get a bite.
They ran for the jar they all thought so <u>treasurable</u>.
In it was something smooth and ___4___ .
Could it be? Could that explain their <u>ways</u>?
Surely they weren't eating all the ___5___ !

B. Write a challenge word you associate with each set of words.

1. joke   silly song   comics
2. salad dressing   sandwich spread   egg salad
3. ferryboat ride   field day   family hike
4. earthquake   forest fire   plane crash
5. cloud   sleet   light rain

C. Suppose all the children in your school enjoy eating hamburgers with lettuce, tomatoes, and low-fat mayonnaise. One day tragedy strikes—your school cafeteria runs out of mayonnaise! Write a humorous story about that day and how you and your friends went in search of more low-fat mayonnaise. Use some of the challenge words in your story.

163

discovered	satisfied	overlapped
discovering	satisfying	overlapping

A. Write the challenge word or words that were formed by the following rules.

1. + **ed** only
2. change **y** to **i** + **ed**
3. double final consonant + **ed**
4. + **ing** only
5. double final consonant + **ing**

B. Write the challenge word that can be used as a synonym for the group of words given below.

1. fulfilling, convincing, gratifying, ___?___
2. found, came upon, learned, ___?___
3. coincided partly, extended over, shingled, ___?___

C. Use the correct ending for each word in parentheses to complete the sentences. Write the challenge words.

1. He is (overlap) the wallpaper as he hangs it.
2. The teacher is not (satisfy) with our test results.
3. Scientists are (discover) new things every day.
4. Our schedules (overlap) yesterday.
5. Don't start (satisfy) your hunger with snacks now.
6. Who (discover) the Pacific Ocean in 1513?

D. Write a short report about the things a group of friends can do or share together. Mention the satisfactions or rewards that come from sharing experiences as a group. Use some of the challenge words.

164

Challenge Activities

rhinoceros   symptom   naphtha

rhubarb   subpoena   condemn

A. What do you associate with certain occupations? Answer each question below using a challenge word.

1. What might a pie baker use?

2. What might a lawyer send someone?

3. What might a dry cleaner use to get out stains?

4. What might a doctor check a patient for?

5. What might a zookeeper show off?

B. Decide what the challenge word is for each clue. Write the challenge word.

1. I am a liquid made from coal. I am used as fuel or as a spot remover.

2. I am a written summons to appear in a court of law.

3. I am part of a plant used for making sauces or pies.

4. I am what you do to someone or something you disapprove of strongly.

5. I am a change in the normal working of the body that shows sickness.

6. I am a large thick-skinned mammal with horns.

C. You are a newspaper reporter who wants to know everything and find out who is the busiest person in town. Use the cast of characters given in Activity A. Report your findings and your final decision. Give reasons for your decision. Use challenge words where you can.

quizzical   irritate   plummeted

rapport   possession   propeller

A. Choose a challenge word that is more exact than the underlined word in each sentence.

1. The two kites collided and <u>fell</u> to the ground.

2. A mechanic repaired the <u>fanlike</u> <u>device</u> on the boat.

3. The student had a <u>perplexed</u> expression on his face because he didn't understand the question.

4. Some soaps <u>bother</u> my skin.

5. My friend and I have a good <u>relationship</u> because we agree on many things.

6. Ellen has many books in her <u>holding</u>.

B. Write the challenge word that is suggested by the situation. Look for hidden clues in each statement.

1. "You and I get along," said one musician to another.

2. "You rub me the wrong way," said the dog to the flea.

3. "You can't move without oars," said the plane forcefully to the boat.

C. Choose a living being from the animal kingdom that you might like to be for a day. Then write a short story as if you were that animal. Mention the things you might value. For example, if you were a bird you might value nature, freedom, and communicating with other birds. Use some of the challenge words in your story.

breakable	perceptible	amiable
deductible	understandable	digestible

A. Think of a synonym for each verb below. Then add the suffix **able** or **ible** to the base of each synonym. Write the new adjective that is formed. Each answer should be a challenge word.

> 1. **smash** 2. **comprehend** 3. **subtract** 4. **consume**

B. Write a challenge word that relates to the words given.

1. **visible, discernible,** ___?___
2. **pleasant, agreeable,** ___?___

C. Write the challenge words that complete the paragraph.

   Amy wants to open her own savings account at a bank. She knows how to manage her money. The application form is easy to fill out. It is __1__ . The bank clerks are very helpful and __2__ . They'll explain to Amy that a service charge is added to her monthly statement. This __3__ charge would be subtracted from her savings each month. If there is any problem with Amy's account, the clerks will observe it quickly. Problems are very __4__ . The only thing they'll warn Amy about is not to bring her piggy bank with her. It is __5__ !

D. It's tax time! Imagine that you are an IRS official collecting taxes from people. How will you act with these people when they come to your office? What will you tell them? Write your answers using challenge words or forms of them. For example, you might use **digest** to mean **comprehend** rather than use the word **digestible.**

antidote	mispronounce	nondescript
misunderstand	nonchalant	nonproductive

A. The prefix **mis** can mean **wrongly.** The prefix **non** can mean **not.** Write your own definition of the following words:

misunderstand   mispronounce   nonproductive   nondescript

B. Read the first sentence. Complete the second sentence with a challenge word.

1. People take your meaning the wrong way. They ___?___ .

2. We passed a row of houses that had no particular style. They were ___?___ .

3. What the patient needs is something that will counteract the poison. The patient needs an ___?___ .

4. She was so casual that she didn't seem to have a care in the world. She was ___?___ .

5. This factory must be shut down because it hasn't yielded much in years. It is ___?___ .

6. I thought your name rhymed with **cane.** Did I ___?___ it?

C. You collect strange and funny mistakes in news stories. Give examples from your own "collection." Be as creative as you like. You could give an example of a word that a famous politician might have mispronounced. You could give an example of a business person's idea that was nonproductive. You could also tell about the time when a reporter, who was sent to cover a famous, colorful wedding, wrote that the guests and the wedding decorations were nondescript! Use challenge words or forms of them in your examples.

leverage   puzzlement   enrichment

breakage   detriment   compartment

A. What is your opinion about each issue below? Write your answer for one, using the challenge word in parentheses.

1. Does a horse or its rider have the advantage? Who is really in control? (leverage)

2. There is a sign by the stable that reads: "Ride at your own risk." Why is it there? What harm can there be? (detriment)

3. What might be rewarding or meaningful about being able to ride a horse? (enrichment)

4. There is some confusion about whether a horse is a smart or a dumb animal. Why do you think there is any question about it? (puzzlement)

B. Complete each analogy with a challenge word.

1. **Handicap** is to **disadvantage** as **benefit** is to ___?___ .

2. **Bewilder** is to **problem** as **confuse** is to ___?___ .

3. **Building** is to **construction** as **smashing** is to ___?___ .

4. **House** is to **room** as **toolbox** is to ___?___ .

5. **Help** is to **harm** as **well-being** is to ___?___ .

C. Imagine that you are a riding instructor. You love horses, but you want people to learn how to ride them correctly. Your greatest concern is that nobody gets hurt. Write an ad for horseback riding lessons. Use the challenge words. You may also use any of the ideas in Activity A.

UNIT 22 Challenge Activities

| faithful | forceful | troublesome |
| blameless | countless | speechless |

A. Use a challenge word to describe each of these pets.

1. Rex always waits at the door for me to come home, and then he brings me the newspaper.

2. Fluffy wasn't the cat who broke the dish. She is innocent.

3. Lora, the parrot, was surprised when the cat jumped on her birdcage. For once, she couldn't talk!

4. Duke is always up to some kind of mischief. This dog gives me more to worry about than all the others.

5. Twinkle is strong and full of drive. She protects her food from the other cats.

B. Write a synonym for each word in the first column. Write an antonym for each word in the second column. Use challenge words.

loyal	limited
powerful	talkative
difficult	guilty

C. Write five different descriptions of a dog or cat whose behavior could be associated with adjectives that are challenge words. Give clues. You may use Activity A as a guide. Then exchange papers with a partner to identify each other's descriptions.

170

Challenge Activities

videotape	**volleyball**	**hindsight**
bookmobile	**public school**	**weather-beaten**

A. Write each challenge word by matching a word in the first column with a word in the second column.

weather	school
hind	ball
book	sight
volley	tape
public	beaten
video	mobile

B. Answer each question with a challenge word.

1. What would you be watching if you were looking at a prerecorded TV show?
2. What would you be using to figure out past events that you didn't fully understand at the time?
3. What would you call wood or a house that is worn by exposure to the weather?
4. What would you be looking at if you saw a truck with book-lined shelves that is used as a traveling library?
5. What game would you be playing if you hit a ball back and forth across a net with your hands?
6. What place is supported by taxes and provides free education to children in a community?

C. Think of an ideal campsite. What would it look like? What things could you do at the camp? Write your description using challenge words. Then interview someone who has gone to camp. Review your paper. What things would you change using hindsight?

extemporary	dietary	immaculate
culinary	intricate	considerate

A. Write an adjective that completes each description. Use the challenge words.

1. I am not simple. I have a complicated pattern. I am an ___?___ design.

2. I don't like to plan things. I like to do and say ___?___ things.

3. I am thoughtful and ___?___ about other people's feelings.

4. I am a list of ___?___ rules that tell what foods to eat and how to prepare them for healthful living.

5. I always make sure that my clothes are clean, in good repair, and without wrinkles. My clothes are ___?___ .

6. I have studied many cookbooks and produced extraordinary meals. I possess ___?___ skills.

B. Write an adjective that describes the opposite kind of person or thing described below. Use the challenge words.

1. A person who does not take into account other people's feelings.

2. A room that is quite messy and dirty.

3. An uncomplicated story with no plot twists.

4. Dialogue in a play that is written and rehearsed in advance.

C. Complete this story about the life of a dancer. Use the challenge words in your story.

I love to dance, but the life of a professional dancer is not easy. For example, I must practice every day. I must watch my weight all the time.

172

midyear	interject	substandard
interfere	superpower	underlying

A. Prefixes and bases are mismatched in the challenge words below. Write these words correctly.

1. **sublying**
2. **midject**
3. **interpower**
4. **interyear**
5. **understandard**
6. **superfere**

B. Write the challenge word that would be found on a dictionary page with each pair of guide words below.

1. Superior, Lake | supper
2. intention | interim
3. subset | suburb
4. midst | migration
5. interior | intern
6. undergo | understand

C. Use a challenge word to replace the underlined combination that matches it in meaning.

1. This <u>higher nation</u> has many industries.
2. Shane got an A on his <u>middle-annual</u> exam.
3. In my opinion, this car is <u>below an acceptable level of quality</u>.
4. The <u>beneath-the-surface</u> reason for my lateness is that I overslept.

D. Imagine you are a sports announcer at an imaginary sports game of your choice. The team that all the experts expected would win the game is losing badly. What is going wrong? Explain why the team is losing so badly. Use challenge words in your explanation.

Challenge Activities

hideous	anxious	harmonious
monstrous	contagious	treacherous

A. Write the challenge word that fits both definitions.

1. a. agreeable; b. pleasing to the ear
2. a. very ugly; b. frightful
3. a. like a monster; b. huge
4. a. worried; b. eager
5. a. tending to spread from person to person, as in yawning; b. easily catching, as in a disease
6. a. disloyal; b. dangerous

B. Complete each sentence using a challenge word. Next to each challenge word write the letter **a** or **b** for the meaning given in Activity A that matches the use of the word in the sentence.

1. The feeling of excitement and anticipation spread like a ripple of __?__ laughter throughout the grandstand.
2. The cheerleaders sang a lovely, __?__ cheer.
3. One team mascot was __?__ in size.
4. The other team mascot was a person in a __?__ disguise.
5. The fans were __?__ about the outcome of the game.
6. The mountain road didn't cause the bus driver immediate alarm, but it turned out to be __?__ .

C. What do you know about ice hockey? How dangerous is it? How exciting is it for the players? Make up your own similes, using the challenge words to describe the game. For example, you can use your own version of "as happy as a clam" in this way: The players are as harmonious as clams.

sherbet	banquet	luncheon
guidance	naive	jeopardize

A. Write the challenge word that answers each question.

1. Suppose you were invited to eat lunch to celebrate the annual gymnastics contest. Would you go to a lunchon or a luncheon?

2. If you wanted to eat a frozen, fruit-flavored dessert, would you order a sherbet or a shebert?

3. For this special event, would the large meal be a banquet or a banqet?

4. If the star gymnast was an adult but thought like a child, would he or she be niave or naive?

5. Would the coach give the athletes guidance or giudance?

6. Would an accident jeopardize or jepardize an athlete's career?

B. Write the challenge word or words you associate with the following things.

1. three things associated with food
2. something associated with leadership
3. a word associated with risk
4. a word associated with a childlike quality

C. You are invited to a luncheon in honor of your favorite famous athlete. Write a testimonial, or a speech showing admiration, for your favorite athlete. Don't forget to thank the sponsors of the event for the food they have provided! Use challenge words in your testimonial.

connection	collection	donation
contribution	recession	explanation

A. Write the challenge words that fit each spelling rule below.

1. Add the suffix **ion** to the base word with no spelling change.

2. Drop **e** to add **ion** to the base word.
3. Change the base word before adding the suffix **ion**.

B. Write the noun for each verb below.
1. donate   4. contribute
2. connect   5. recess
3. explain   6. collect

C. Which two challenge words have similar meanings?

HELP SAVE OUR POOL

D. Suppose you and your classmates wanted to set up a fund to repair the old pool in the school gym so that the swimming team could use it. What plans would you make to raise the money? Include challenge words in your written plans.

| auctioneer | pediatrician | defendant |
| historian | vice president | contestant |

A. Write the challenge word that describes each of the following persons.

1. one who holds the second place in authority
2. one who is an expert in or writes about important past events
3. one who conducts a public sale of things to be sold for the most money offered
4. one who takes part in a game or race
5. one who specializes in the branch of medicine dealing with children and their diseases
6. one who is accused or sued in a court of law

B. Write the challenge words formed from the bases given below.

1. **defend**   2. **auction**   3. **contest**   4. **history**

C. Make headings for six columns by using the challenge words. List other people that each person listed might encounter in the course of a day. Some of your lists will probably be longer than others. Then select one list. Use some of the people as characters for a short play. What will your setting be? What names will you give your characters? What will they say? What will be the plot and the climax of your play? How will it end? After you have considered answers to these questions, write your play.

Challenge Activities

| admittance | annoyance | diligence |
| reluctance | existence | indifference |

A. Write the noun that is formed when **ance** or **ence** is added to each verb below. Next to each noun write its meaning.

   1. **annoy**
   2. **exist**
   3. **admit** + t
   4. prefix **in** (meaning "not") + **differ**

B. Write a challenge word for each meaning below.

   1. permission to enter
   2. feeling of irritation or impatience
   3. careful and steady effort
   4. unwillingness
   5. lack of interest or caring
   6. being; life

C. Some of the challenge words on this list have or imply positive meanings. Other words have or imply negative meanings. Choose the words that fall into the first category, and tell what they mean to you and what situations they suggest. Then do the same thing with the words that fall into the second category. Add other words and explanations of your own to each category.

| verses | cession | palate |
| versus | session | pallet |

A. Choose the correct homophone shown in parentheses to answer each set of questions. Write the appropriate challenge word for each.

1. a. What might a person sleep on? (palate, pallet)
   b. What part of the mouth do you use when you eat? (palate, pallet)

2. a. What might a poet write? (versus, verses)
   b. What is a synonym for **against**? (versus, verses)

3. a. What might you call a meeting or a period of lessons? (cession, session)
   b. What describes the act of giving up territory to another country? (cession, session)

B. Write the homophone that completes each sentence.

1. The biggest game of the school year is almost always the Reds ___?___ the Blues. (verses, versus)

2. The dentist looked at my mouth, especially the ___?___ . (pallet, palate)

3. We signed up for a ___?___ of swimming lessons. (cession, session)

4. Do you only like ___?___ that rhyme? (versus, verses)

C. Write a mixed-up message for one of the words in each pair of challenge words that are homophones. Then trade messages with a partner and correct the mistakes.

| bibliography | altimeter | biologist |
| lexicographer | telephoto | antibiotic |

A. Rearrange the word elements to form a word. Write the challenge word.

1. graph y biblio

2. lexico er graph

3. meter alti

4. log ist bio

5. bio tic anti

6. photo tele

B. Complete each sentence with a challenge word.

1. I put the ___?___ lens on my camera to get a good shot of some distant birds.

2. Penicillin is an ___?___ that doctors sometimes prescribe.

3. The pilot studied the measuring device called an ___?___ while the plane was in flight.

4. **Lexis** means **word,** and the person who writes a dictionary is called a ___?___ .

5. Our social studies books usually have a list of books, or a ___?___ , referring to the topic of the unit.

6. A person who studies living organisms is known as a ___?___ .

C. Use the information in Activity B to write a "Who or what am I" riddle for each challenge word. Add other words that are from Greek words or forms and write riddles for them, too.

UNIT 35

Challenge Activities

emcee	**Fortran**	**NASA**
R.S.V.P.	**COBOL**	**NATO**

A. An **acronym,** you will recall, is a word or name that is created by combining the first letters in a group of words. For example, **radar** is an acronym made from "**ra**dio **d**etection **a**nd **r**anging."

   Write the acronym for each group of words below. Use challenge words.

1. North Atlantic Treaty Organization
2. Common business-oriented language
3. National Aeronautics and Space Administration
4. Formula translation

B. A challenge word is used incorrectly in each sentence. Rewrite the sentences with the correct challenge words inserted.

1. The talent show was a huge success, and the NATO did a great job as the announcer.
2. At the end of the invitation, there was a request for a reply, or a COBOL.
3. The sign in front of the space research building read Fortran.
4. To solve the math problems, use the programming language called NATO.

C. Write an invitation for a fund-raising event for a space agency or an international organization. Use as many challenge words as possible in your invitation.

Pronunciation Key _____

The **pronunciation key** lists the symbols that represent the sounds in the respellings presented in your spelling dictionary. The sample words show, in boldface type, the letters that spell that sound.

ă	pat	l	lid, needle	*th*	this	
ā	pay	m	**mum**	ŭ	cut	
âr	care	n	**no**, sudden	ûr	urge, term, firm,
ä	father	ng	thing		word, heard
b	**bib**	ŏ	pot	v	valve
ch	**church**	ō	toe	w	with
d	**deed**	ô	caught, paw,	y	yes
ě	pet		for	z	zebra
ē	be	oi	noise	zh	vision, pleasure,
f	**fife, rough**	ŏŏ	took		garage
g	**gag**	ōō	boot	ə	about, item, pencil,
h	hat	ou	out		gallop, circus
hw	**which**	p	**pop**	ər	butter
ĭ	pit	r	roar		**Stress**
ī	**pie, by**	s	sauce		Primary stress ′
îr	**pier**	sh	**ship, dish**		af ter /af′tər/
j	**judge**	t	**tight, stopped**		Secondary stress ′
k	**kick, cat**	th	thin		af ter noon /af′tər noon′/

Using the Spelling Dictionary

The **spelling dictionary** provides information about syllabication, pronunciation, parts of speech, meanings, inflected forms, and word origins.

Use these sample entries to identify the parts of your spelling dictionary.

an•cient /ān′shənt/, *adj.* belonging to times long ago. *There are many ancient temples in Greece, Italy, and Egypt.* [Latin *ante*, before.]

ar•range /ə rānj′/, *v.* 1. to organize; put in order. *Everything is arranged for the party.* 2. to plan; prepare. *I can arrange to go tonight.* **ar•rang•es, ar•ranged, ar•rang•ing.**

- **Guide words** appear at the top of each page and indicate the entries that fall between them alphabetically. The guide words are the first and last words on that page of the dictionary.

- **Word entries** are listed in alphabetical order and are printed in boldface type. Dots are used to separate the syllables within each word. In this spelling dictionary, entry words include abbreviations and acronyms. (In some dictionaries, abbreviations are listed separately in a special section.)

- The **entry** is the word you look up and everything written about it.

- A **dictionary respelling** follows each word entry and provides the proper pronunciation. Dictionary symbols are presented in the **pronunciation key** and at the bottom of every second page. The key provides sample words that contain the sounds represented by the dictionary symbols. An accent mark following a boldface syllable shows that the syllable receives the greatest stress in pronunciation. A secondary accent follows a syllable in regular type when that syllable should receive some stress in pronunciation, but not as much stress as the boldface syllable.

- The abbreviation for the **part of speech** of each word follows the dictionary respelling. These abbreviations include:

n.	noun
adj.	adjective
pron.	pronoun
conj.	conjunction
v.	verb
adv.	adverb
prep.	preposition
interj.	interjection

If a word is used as more than one part of speech, the parts are listed and defined in the order of the most common usage.

- The **definitions** for the entry word are provided after each part of speech. When a word has more than one meaning, the definitions are numbered. Generally, the most common definition is presented first. A **sample sentence** is provided to show the correct usage of each meaning.

- If an entry is an **affix,** the definition shows whether the affix is a **prefix** or **suffix** and the meaning is given. Samples of words using the affix are also presented.

- If an entry word has a **homophone,** the spelling dictionary lists the homophone after the sample sentence. Your spelling dictionary shows homophones like this:

(Sounds like **due.**)

- **Inflected forms** of spelling words that slightly change the spelling of the base word, such as words that drop the final **e** or change the final **y** to **i** to add **s, es, ed,** or **ing,** are shown after the sample sentence. If a spelling word has a plural or verb form that is commonly considered irregular (**calf/calves, buy/bought**), the irregular form is presented as a separate entry. This entry provides the pronunciation for the word and directs the reader to the base word entry.

- The **etymology,** the history or origin of a word, is presented in brackets at the end of some entries. An etymology traces a word back to the language from which it came. The language is followed by the original word from which the entry word is derived. A definition for the original word is also provided.

A a

ab•bre•vi•a•tion /ə brē′ vē ā′shən/, *n.* a shortened form of a word; a syllable, letter or letters standing for a word or words. *Dr. is an abbreviation for Doctor.*

-able, a suffix used to form adjectives meaning: 1. capable of: *understandable.* 2. worthy of: *lovable.*

ab•sence /ăb′ səns/, *n.* 1. being away. *Ryan brought a note to excuse his absence.* 2. not having; lack: *an absence of interest.*

ab•sent /ăb′ sənt/, *adj.* away; not here. *Kate was absent on Monday but present on Tuesday.*

ac•cent /ăk′ sĕnt′/, *n.* 1. a mark (′) used to show stress. *A syllable with an accent is pronounced more strongly.* 2. a distinctive way of speaking: *a British accent.*
v. 1. to stress; emphasize. *Accent the first syllable.* 2. to add to; enhance. *Beth's pink scarf accents her white dress.*

ac•cept•able /ăk sĕp′tə bəl/, *adj.* agreeable; satisfactory. *Everyone at the meeting found the plan acceptable.* **ac•cept•a•bly,** *adv.*

ac•ci•dent /ăk′ sĭ dənt/, *n.* 1. a harmful or unexpected event. *Ali had an accident on his bike.* 2. something that occurs without being planned for. *The cure for the disease was discovered by accident.*

ac•cord /ə kôrd′/, *n.* agreement; harmony. *The nations were in accord on the issue of world hunger.*

ac•cu•rate /ăk′ yər ĭt/, *adj.* correct; without mistakes. *The witness's testimony was accurate and consistent with the evidence.*

ac•cuse /ə kyo͞oz′/, *v.* to blame for wrongdoing. *The police accused him of speeding and reckless driving.* **ac•cus•es, ac•cused, ac•cus•ing.**

a•chieve /ə chēv′/, *v.* to reach; accomplish. *If you wish to achieve success you must work hard.* **a•chieves, a•chieved, a•chiev•ing.**

ac•tion /ăk′ shən/, *n.* 1. a thing done; deed. *The firefighter was praised for her brave action.* 2. motion; movement. *Debbie likes action, but David prefers peace and quiet.*

a•cute /ə kyo͞ot′/, *adj.* 1. severe or sharp; intense: *acute pain.* 2. having fewer than 90 degrees. *A triangle must have at least two acute angles.*

ad•di•tion•al•ly /ə dĭsh′ ə nə lē/, *adv.* also; moreover; in addition. *Additionally, the movie has won international awards.*

ad•mit /ăd mĭt′/, *v.* 1. to let in. *If you don't have a ticket they can't admit you to the show.* 2. to acknowledge, confess. *The mayor admitted that she had not been aware of the problem.* **ad•mits, ad•mit•ted, ad•mit•ting** [Latin *admittere,* from *ad,* to + *mittere,* to send.]

ă pat/ā pay/âr care/ä father/ĕ pet/ ē be/ĭ pit/ī pie/îr pier/ŏ pot/ō toe/ ô paw, for/oi noise/ou out/o͝o took/ o͞o boot/ŭ cut/ûr urge/th thin/*th* this/ hw which/zh vision/ə about, item, pencil, gallop, circus

a•dor•a•ble /ə dôr′ə bəl/ or /ə dōr′-/, *adj.* lovable; charming. *The stuffed animals were cuddly and adorable.*

a•dore /ə dôr′ / or /- dōr′ /, *v.* to feel deep love and respect for. *The parents adored their new child.* **a•dores, a•dored, a•dor•ing.**

ad•vance /ăd văns′ /, *v.* to go forward. *Please advance to the front of the line.*
n. any forward movement; progress. *Medical research has made great advances.*

ad•vance•ment /ăd văns′ mənt/, *n.* improvement; progress; promotion. *They dedicated their new club to the advancement of poetry.*

ad•van•tage /ăd văn′tĭj/, *n.* 1. anything that helps bring about success. *That basketball player has the advantage of being tall.* 2. help; benefit; gain. *Studying is to your own advantage.*

af•ter•ward /ăf′tər wərd/, *adv.* later. *We'll do some shopping and have lunch afterward.*

-age, a suffix used to form nouns meaning: 1. a collective or general group: *baggage.* 2. state or condition of: *marriage.* 3. act of: *breakage.*

ag•ed /ā′ jĭd/, *adj.* 1. old; having lived long. *The aged man was having difficulty walking.* 2. /ājd/, having a certain age: *aged three.*

a•gent /ā′ jənt/, *n.* 1. a person or company whose business is to represent another: *an insurance agent.* 2. a substance that causes a certain action to begin. *Yeast is the agent that causes bread to rise.* [Latin *agens,* effective, from *agere,* to do.]

ag•ri•cul•ture /ăg′rĭ kŭl′chər/, *n.* farming; raising food and farm animals. *We all depend on agriculture for food.*

aisle /īl/, *n.* a passage between rows or seats. *The usher stood in the aisle.* (Sounds like **isle.**)

al•bum /ăl′ bəm/, *n.* 1. a book with blank pages on which photographs, stamps, etc., may be kept. *Will you sign my autograph album?* 2. a recording of several different pieces of music. *I like the title song on that album.*

all right /ôl′ rīt′ /, *adj.* satisfactory. *Your answer looks all right to me.*
adv. 1. yes; very well. *All right, I'll come home early.* 2. in a satisfactory way. *Is everything going all right?*

al•ly /ăl′ ī′ /, *n.* a person or country united with others for a specific purpose. *During World War II the United States and the Soviet Union were allies.* **al•lies.**

al•ma•nac /ôl′ mə năk′ /, *n.* a reference book published yearly. *A farmer may read an almanac to find out when to plant crops.*

al•mond /ä′ mənd/, *n.* the nut of the almond tree. *Toasted almonds make a good snack.*

A.M. or **a.m.,** an abbreviation meaning "in the morning." *My appointment is Tuesday at 10 A.M.* [Latin *ante meridiem,* before noon.]

am•a•teur /ăm′ ə tûr′ / or /-chŏŏr′ /, *n.* a person who participates in activities for fun, not money. *Even an amateur can become skillful with regular practice.*

a•maze /ə māz′ /, *v.* to surprise or astonish. *We were amazed at the acrobat's ability to do high jumps.* **a•maz•es, a•mazed, a•maz•ing.**

am•bu•lance /ăm′ byə ləns/, *n.* a vehicle for bringing people who are hurt or sick to the hospital. *An ambulance is equipped with special lights and a siren.*

a•mend•ment /ə měnd′ mənt/, *n.* a change in a law or bill. *An amendment to the Constitution gave women the right to vote.*

am•pli•tude /ăm′ plĭ tōōd′/ or /-tyōōd′/, *n.* the distance between the highest and lowest point of a wave. *As the amplitude of a sound wave increases, so does the loudness of the sound.*

-ance, a suffix used to form nouns meaning: 1. state or quality of: *resemblance.* 2. act of: *resistance.* 3. thing that: *conveyance.*

an•nounce /ə nouns′/, *v.* 1. to tell; make known; give notice. *Would the principal announce that school will be closing early?* 2. to provide commentary and deliver announcements on radio or TV. *The sportscaster announces the tennis match.* **an•nounc•es, an•nounced, an•nounc•ing.**

-ant, a suffix used with verbs: 1. to form adjectives meaning "having the quality of": *resistant.* 2. to form nouns meaning "person or thing that": *assistant.*

anti-, a prefix that means "against": *antiseptic.*

an•ti•freeze /ăn′ tĭ frēz′/, *n.* a liquid mixed with another liquid, to keep it from freezing. *Cars need antifreeze during the winter.*

an•ti•so•cial /ăn′ tē sō′ shəl/, *adj.* avoiding the company of others. *It is a mistake to assume that a shy person is deliberately antisocial.*

a•pos•tro•phe /ə pŏs′ trə fē/, *n.* a mark (') used: 1. to show that a letter or letters have been purposely left out of a word: *it'll, vou've.* 2. to show possession: *Jim's, girls'.*

ap•pear•ance /ə pîr′ əns/, *n.* 1. being seen by the public. *The TV star made a personal appearance at the shopping mall.* 2. the looks of a place or person. *New paint really improved the room's appearance.*

ap•pli•cant /ăp′ lĭ kənt/, *n.* a person applying for a job or position. *There were many applicants for the after-school job.*

ap•ply /ə plī′/, *v.* 1. to put on: *apply paint.* 2. to put to use. *We did an experiment to apply what we learned in science.* 3. to make a request. *She applied to join the Girl Scouts.* **ap•plies, ap•plied, ap•ply•ing.**

ap•point•ment /ə point′ mənt/, *n.* an arrangement to meet someone at a certain time. *I have a two o'clock appointment.*

ap•pos•i•tive /ə pŏz′ ĭ tĭv/, *n.* a noun or noun phrase placed next to another noun for further explanation or description. *In the sentence "Brian, Dan's brother, also came,"* the appositive is "Dan's brother."

ap•pre•ci•ate /ə prē′ shē āt′/, *v.* 1. to see the value of something. *The recital made us appreciate the pianist's hours of practice.* 2. to be thankful for. *I appreciate your help.* **ap•pre•ci•ates, ap•pre•ci•at•ed, ap•pre•ci•at•ing.**

ă pat/ā pay/âr care/ä father/ě pet/
ē be/ĭ pit/ī pie/îr pier/ŏ pot/ō toe/
ô paw, for/oi noise/ou out/ŏŏ took/
ōō boot/ŭ cut/ûr urge/th thin/*th* this/
hw which/zh vision/ə about, item, .
pencil, gallop, circus

ap•proach /ə prōch′/, *v.* to come near. *The deer ran away as we approached.*

ap•proach•a•ble /ə prō′ chə bəl/, *adj.* friendly; easy to approach. *The librarian's smile made her seem approachable.*

ap•prove /ə prōōv′/, *v.* 1. to give official consent to. *The board approved the plans for the new gym.* 2. to have a good opinion of. *Do you approve of his choice of colors?* **ap•proves, ap•proved, ap•prov•ing.**

ap•prox•i•mate /ə prŏk′ sə mĭt/, *adj.* nearly right; almost correct. *The architect gave them an approximate cost of the new house.*

ap•ti•tude /ăp′ tĭ tōōd′/ or /-tyōōd′/, *n.* a talent or ability for learning. *She had a natural aptitude for languages; she spoke French, German, and Italian.*

ar•a•ble /ăr′ ə bəl/, *adj.* able to be farmed or cultivated. *Rocky land is not arable.*

arc /ärk/, *n.* a curved line; a line that is part of a circle. *A rainbow forms an arc in the sky.*

a•rise /ə rīz′/, *v.* 1. to get up. *On school days we arise early.* 2. to appear; begin. *If any problems should arise, phone us at this number.* **a•ris•es, a•rose, a•ris•en, a•ris•ing.**

ar•ter•y /är′ tə rē/, *n.* any of the body's vessels that carry blood from the heart to all parts of the body. *Which artery carries blood to the brain?* **ar•ter•ies.**

-ary, a suffix used to form adjectives meaning "of" or "relating to": *honorary.*

as•sign /ə sīn′/, *v.* 1. to give out; distribute. *Our teacher assigns us homework every evening.* 2. to appoint to a position. *The teacher assigned him to be hall monitor this month.*

as•sign•ment /ə sīn′ mənt/, *n.* a thing assigned. *It took me three hours to complete my homework assignment.*

as•sist /ə sĭst′/, *v.* to help; aid. *I assisted Mother in preparing dinner.*

as•sis•tant /ə sĭs′ tənt/, *n.* a person who assists another; helper. *We need an assistant to help with the project.* [Latin *assistere*, to assist, from *ad-*, near to + *sistere*, to stand.]

as•so•ci•ate /ə sō′ shē āt′/, *v.* 1. to think of as related. *Most people associate tears with sadness, but many people cry when they are happy.* 2. to join as a friend. *Joy associates with her softball teammates regularly.* **as•so•ci•ates, as•so•ci•at•ed, as•so•ci•at•ing.** *n.* /ə sō′ shē ĭt/, a friend or fellow worker. *Mr. Ortiz is an associate of my father's.*

as•sume /ə sōōm′/, *v.* 1. to accept as true; take for granted. *People once assumed the earth was flat.* 2. to accept; take upon oneself. *Megan assumed the job of decorating the room.* **as•sumes, as•sumed, as•sum•ing.**

as•tron•o•my /ə strŏn′ ə mē/, *n.* the study of planets, stars, and other bodies in outer space. *Telescopes are used in astronomy.*

-ate, a suffix used: 1. to form adjectives meaning "having" or "characterized by": *fortunate.* 2. to form verbs meaning "to act upon": *renovate.*

ath•lete /ăth′ lēt′ /, *n.* a person who performs in competitive sports. *An athlete trains daily.*

-ation, a suffix used to form nouns meaning: 1. action or process: *consideration.* 2. the result of an action or process: *inflammation.*

at•las /ăt′ ləs/, *n.* a book of maps. *Our atlas has maps of all the major highways.* **at•las•es.**

at•om /ăt′ əm/, *n.* the smallest particle into which a chemical element can be divided. *Everything around us is made up of atoms.*

at•tend /ə těnd′ /, *v.* to go to; be present at. *Did you attend the last meeting?*

at•ten•dance /ə těn′ dəns/, *n.* 1. the act of being present. *His attendance at school has been perfect all year.* 2. the number of persons present. *During a losing streak attendance drops at baseball games.*

at•ten•dant /ə těn′ dənt/, *n.* a person who serves or waits on others. *There are always four attendants working at this gas station.*

at•ten•tion /ə těn′ shən/, *n.* 1. staying alert to what is happening. *Always pay attention in class.* 2. thoughtfulness; consideration. *Rhonda gave a lot of attention to her grandparents during their visit.*

at•tic /ăt′ ĭk/, *n.* a room just below the roof of a house. *We found a big box up in our attic.*

au•thor•i•ty /ə thôr′ ĭ tē/ or /-thŏr′ / or /-ō-/, *n.* 1. the right or power to control, command, or enforce. *Police officers have the authority to enforce laws.* 2. any source of correct information. *The encyclopedia is an authority on many different subjects.*

au•to•bi•og•ra•pher /ô′ tō bī ŏg′ rə fər/, *n.* a person who writes the story of his or her own life. *A good autobiographer must be honest and descriptive.*

au•to•bi•og•ra•phy /ô tō bī ŏg′ rə fē/, *n.* a person's life story told or written by himself or herself. *Helen Keller wrote an autobiography.* **au•to•bi•og•ra•phies.** [Greek *autos,* self + *bios,* life + *graphein* to write.]

au•to•graph /ô′ tə grăf′ /, *n.* anything written in a person's own handwriting, especially his or her name. *I collected the autographs of all the students in my class.*
v. to sign one's name. *She asked the pitcher to autograph her ball.* [Greek *autos,* self + *graphein,* to write.]

au•to•ma•tion /ô′ tə mā′ shən/, *n.* the automatic operation of a system, a process, or equipment. *Most factories rely heavily on automation.*

au•tumn /ô′ təm/, *n.* the season that comes after summer and before winter; fall. *In autumn, many leaves turn beautiful colors.*

a•vail•a•ble /ə vā′ lə bəl/, *adj.* able to be used or obtained. *The firefighters used all the available equipment.*

ă pat/ā pay/âr care/ä father/ĕ pet/
ē be/ĭ pit/ī pie/îr pier/ŏ pot/ō toe/
ô paw, for/oi noise/ou out/oŏ took/
ōō boot/ŭ cut/ûr urge/th thin/*th* this/
hw which/zh vision/ə about, item,
pencil, gallop, circus

av•a•lanche /ăv′ ə lănch′ /, *n.* 1. a large mass of snow sliding swiftly down a mountain. *The avalanche buried several trees.* 2. anything that comes on suddenly: *an avalanche of orders.*

B b

back•ground /băk′ ground′ /, *n.* the distant part of a picture or scene. *Mountains were painted in the background.*

baf•fle /băf′ əl/, *v.* to puzzle; bewilder. *The riddles baffled the students.* **baf•fles, baf•fled, baf•fling.**

bal•ance /băl′ əns/, *n.* 1. equality in weight or number. *Our teacher keeps a good balance between praise and criticism.* 2. a steady position. *I tripped and lost my balance.*
v. 1. to weigh or measure in or as in a balance. 2. to bring into a condition of balance.

bal•lad /băl′ əd/, *n.* a poem, often sung, that tells a simple story. *Many country and western songs are ballads.*

ban•dage /băn′ dĭj/, *n.* a strip of cloth used to cover a wound. *He put a bandage over the cut.* [French *bande,* band, strip.]

ban•ner /băn′ ər/, *n.* 1. a flag. *"The Star-Spangled Banner" is a song about the American flag.* 2. a piece of cloth with a picture, design, or writing on it. *The museum hung a banner for its new exhibit.*
adj. very good: *a banner season.*

bar•be•cue /bär′ bĭ kyōō′ /, *n.* a meal cooked over an open fire, especially outdoors. *They served hamburgers at the barbecue.*

bare•ly /bâr′ lē/, *adv.* hardly; scarcely. *We could barely see the cars because of the fog.*

bar•gain /bär′ gĭn/, *n.* 1. an agreement. *I made a bargain with Molly to rake the leaves if she would bag them.* 2. something with a low price. *He found a bargain at the sale.*
v. to try to agree on the terms of a deal. *The employer and employees bargained over the new contract.*

ba•rom•e•ter /bə rŏm′ ĭ tər/, *n.* an, instrument that measures air pressure. *A falling reading on a barometer can indicate worse weather to come.* [Greek *baros,* weight + *metron,* measure.]

BA•SIC /bā′ sĭk/, *n.* an acronym for a common computer-programming language. *We wrote a math program in BASIC.* [**B**eginner's **A**ll-purpose **S**ymbolic **I**nstruction **C**ode.,]

be•have /bĭ hāv′ /, *v.* 1. to act properly; to do the right things. *If you don't behave, you won't be invited again.* 2. to act; to conduct oneself. *How did the toddler behave at the movies?* **be•haves, be•haved, be•hav•ing.**

be•yond /bē ŏnd′ / or /bĭ yŏnd′ /, *prep.* in a place farther away than; past. *The grocery store is just beyond the park.*

bi•lin•gual /bī lĭng′ gwəl/, *adj.* able to speak two languages equally well. *Manuel is bilingual in Spanish and English.*

bill of sale /bĭl′ əv sāl′ /, *n.* a document stating that personal property has been transferred to a new owner. *The lawyers drew up a bill of sale for our old house.*

bi•og•ra•pher /bī ŏg′ rə fər/, *n.* a person who writes a life history of another person. *A good biographer does careful research.* [Greek *bios,* life + *graphein,* to write.]

bi•ol•ogy /bī ŏl′ ə jē/, *n.* the scientific study of living things. *Botany and zoology are two branches of biology.* [Greek *bios,* life + *logos,* word, speech.]

bit /bĭt/, *n.* an acronym for the smallest unit of storage in a computer; a tiny memory space that can contain one of two choices. *A byte is made up of eight bits.* [**B**inary dig**it**.]

bleed /blēd/, *v.* to lose blood. *Her knee began to bleed when she scraped it.* **bleeds, bled, bleed•ing.**

block•ade /blŏ kād′/, *n.* the closing off of an area. *During the Civil War, blockades were formed to prevent supplies from reaching the other army.*

book•store /bŏŏk′ stôr′ / or /-stôr′ /, *n.* a store where books are sold. *That bookstore has a good selection of books for children.*

bound•a•ry /boun′ də rē/, *n.* the ending line or edge of one thing and the beginning edge or line of another. *The fence marks the boundary of our property.* **bound•a•ries.**

broad•cast /brôd′ kăst′/, *v.* to send through the air by radio or TV. *The President's speech was broadcast last evening.* **broad•casts, broad•cast** or **broad•cast•ed, broad•cast•ing.** *n.* a radio or television program. *Many viewers watch the six o'clock news broadcast.*

bro•chure /brō shŏŏr′ /, *n.* a small booklet or pamphlet. *Zachary sent for a brochure on soccer camps.*

bronze /brŏnz/, *n.* an alloy of copper and tin or some other highly resistant metal. *The Olympic teams may win medals of gold, silver, or bronze.*

browse /brouz/, *v.* 1. to look at in a leisurely way; skim through. *Sam browsed through the magazines in the dentist's office.* 2. to feed on leaves. *Giraffes browse on tall trees.* **brows•es, browsed, brows•ing.**

budge /bŭj/, *v.* to move slightly. *The car wheels were stuck in the mud and did not budge.* **budg•es, budged, budg•ing.**

buf•fet¹ /bə fā′ / or /bŏŏ-/, *n.* a meal at which guests may serve themselves from food laid out on a table or sideboard. *After the meeting, we served a salad buffet.*

buf•fet² /bŭf′ ĭt/, *v.* to strike; knock about with force. *The wind buffeted the fragile flowers.*

bu•gle /byŏŏ′ gəl/, *n.* a brass instrument similar to a trumpet, used for military signals. *The soldiers woke up to a bugle call.*

bul•le•tin /bŏŏl′ ĭ tn/, *n.* 1. a short news report. *The television program was interrupted for a bulletin about the storm.* 2. a small magazine or newspaper. *The club puts out a bulletin twice a month.*

bu•reau /byŏŏr′ ō/, *n.* 1. a chest of drawers for holding clothing. *My socks are in the top drawer of the bureau.* 2. an office for a special kind of business. *We visited the passport bureau.*

ă pat/ā pay/âr care/ä father/ĕ pet/
ē be/ĭ pit/ī pie/îr pier/ŏ pot/ō toe/
ô paw, for/oi noise/ou out/ŏŏ took/
ŏŏ boot/ŭ cut/ûr urge/th thin/th this/
hw which/zh vision/ə about, item,
pencil, gallop, circus

C c

cab·i·net /kăb′ə nĭt/, *n.* 1. a piece of furniture in which things are stored on shelves: *a medicine cabinet.* 2. a group of persons chosen by the head of state to help run the government. *Members of the cabinet are often heads of government departments.*

cal·o·rie /kăl′ə rē/, *n.* a unit of heat used to measure the energy-producing value of food. *Exercise burns up calories.*

camp·fire /kămp′fīr′/, *n.* a fire in a camp, for keeping warm or for cooking. *It is fun to sit around a campfire at night and sing songs.*

camp·site /kămp′sīt′/, *n.* a place to camp. *We chose a beautiful campsite near a waterfall.*

can·cel /kăn′səl/, *v.* 1. to cross out; to mark with lines. *The post office cancels stamps.* 2. to stop something that was going to happen; call off. *The game was canceled due to rain.* **can·celed, can·cel·ing.**

can·di·date /kăn′dĭ dāt′/ or /-dĭt/, *n.* a person seeking an office or honor. *She is a candidate for governor.*

ca·pa·ble /kā′pə bəl/, *adj.* having the skill to; able to. *She is capable of fixing almost any machine.* **ca·pa·bly,** *adv.*

ca·pac·i·ty /kə păs′ĭ tē/, *n.* 1. the amount that can be held. *The capacity of that bottle is one quart.* 2. ability; capability. *Sarah has a capacity for solving math problems quickly.*

cap·i·tal·i·za·tion /kăp′ĭ tl ĭ zā′shən/, *n.* the process of writing or printing in capital letters. *Do you know the rules of punctuation and capitalization?*

cap·tain /kăp′tən/, *n.* a person who commands, as a ship, army, or team. *The captain is responsible for the safety of all those on board the ship.*

car·a·van /kăr′ə văn′/, *n.* a band of people, pack animals, or vehicles traveling together. *The caravan of merchants and camels stretched across the Sahara.*

car·bon /kär′bən/, *n.* a common chemical element found in all organic substances. *Diamonds are pure carbon, but carbon is also present in coal, graphite, and charcoal.*

car·bon di·ox·ide /kär′bən dī ŏk′sīd′/, *n.* a colorless, odorless gas composed of carbon and oxygen and present in the earth's atmosphere. *The carbon dioxide exhaled by animals is absorbed by green plants.*

care·ful·ly /kâr′fə lē/, *adv.* with care; cautiously or thoroughly. *Peter dusted the tiny figurines carefully.*

Car·ib·be·an /kăr′ə bē′ən/ or /kə rĭb′ē ən/, *adj.* 1. relating to the Caribbean Sea and its islands. *The Caribbean islands attract tourists from all over the world.*

car·pen·ter /kär′pən tər/, *n.* a person who can make things from wood or repair them. *We hired a carpenter to make the new cabinets.*

car·riage /kăr′ĭj/, *n.* a four-wheeled vehicle pulled by horses and used for carrying people. *Carriages were popular until the car was invented.* [Norman French *carier*, to carry.]

car·ti·lage /kär′tl ĭj/, *n.* the connective white tissue that is attached to the surfaces of bones near joints. *Cartilage helps to protect the bones from injury.*

car·ton /kär′tn/, *n.* a container made of cardboard or plastic. *Toddlers love to play games with empty egg cartons.*

cas•ta•nets /kăs′tə nĕts′/, *n. pl.* a rhythm instrument consisting of hollow shells of wood or ivory clicked together with the fingers. *Spanish flamenco dancers often perform with castanets.*

ca•su•al /kăzh′ o͞o əl/, *adj.* 1. without plan; happening by chance. *He paid a casual visit to his old friends.* 2. everyday; informal. *We wore casual clothes to the party.*

cat•a•log or **cat•a•logue** /kăt′ l ôg′ / or /-ŏg′/, *n.* a list of things arranged in alphabetical order with descriptions. *A library has a catalog of all the books in it.*

cau•tious /kô′ shəs/, *adj.* careful; keeping away from danger. [Latin *cautio*, from *cavēre*, to take care.] *The bus driver was cautious in the storm.*

ceil•ing /sē′ lĭng/, *n.* the top of a room. *In most rooms there is a light attached to the ceiling.*

cel•list /chĕl′ ĭst/, *n.* a person who plays the stringed instrument called the cello. *Cellists sit on chairs and hold their cellos between their knees.*

Cel•si•us /sĕl′ sē əs/ or /-shəs/, *adj.* relating to the Celsius temperature scale, which registers the freezing point of water at 0° and the boiling point as 100°. *Normal body temperature is about 37° Celsius.*

ă pat/ā pay/âr care/ä father/ĕ pet/
ē be/ĭ pit/ī pie/îr pier/ŏ pot/ō toe/
ô paw, for/oi noise/ou out/o͝o took/
o͞o boot/ŭ cut/ûr urge/th thin/*th* this/
hw which/zh vision/ə about, item,
pencil, gallop, circus

cen•tral /sĕn′ trəl/, *adj.* 1. in or at the middle; near the center. *The biggest stores are in the central part of the city.* 2. main; leading; chief. *What is the central idea that the author wants us to understand?*

CEO, an abbreviation for chief executive officer. *The CEO of the bank approves all loans.*

ce•ram•ics /sə răm′ ĭks/, *n. pl.* the art or technique of making objects from clay or porcelain and firing them at high temperatures. *In our class in ceramics, we made both soup mugs and figurines.*

cer•e•mo•ny /sĕr′ ə mō′ nē/, *n.* a special set of acts done in a certain way. *The wedding ceremony was held outdoors.* **cer•e•mon•ies.**

cer•tain•ly /sûr′ tn lē/, *adv.* definitely; surely. *Your grades will certainly improve if you study hard.*

change•a•ble /chān′ jə bəl/, *adj.* subject to change; variable: *changeable weather.*

chan•nel /chăn′ əl/, *n.* 1. a body of water connecting two larger bodies of water. *The English Channel lies between the Atlantic Ocean and the North Sea.* 2. any passage through which a liquid can flow. *The workers dug a channel to remove water.* 3. a frequency used for radio or TV. *We watch Channel 7 every night.*

chap•ter /chăp′ tər/, *n.* a part or main section of a book. *You will find the review questions at the end of the chapter.*

char•coal /chär′ kōl′/, *n.* a black substance made by partly burning wood in a closed container. *Many people cook outdoors in the summer using charcoal as fuel.*

check•book /chĕk′ bŏŏk′ /, *n.* a book of blank bank checks. *The monthly bank statement also tells how to balance a checkbook.*

chimes /chīms/, *n. pl.* an instrument used to make bell-like sounds. *One of the percussionists in an orchestra plays the chimes.*

chis•el /chĭz′ əl/, *n.* a tool with a strong, sharp blade. *A chisel is used for carving wood or stone.*
v. to cut or shape with a chisel. *The artist chiseled a statue out of marble.*

chord /kôrd/, *n.* three or more musical tones sounding together to produce harmony. *At our first lesson, the guitar instructor went over some basic chords.*

cir•cu•lar /sûr′ kyə lər/, *adj.* 1. round; having the shape of a circle. *A lighthouse is usually a circular building.*

cir•cum•fer•ence /sər kŭm′ fər əns/, *n.* the distance around a circle. *You can measure the circumference of a tree trunk by putting a tape measure around it.*

cir•rus /sĭr′ əs/, *n.* a high-altitude cloud consisting of narrow bands or white, fleecy patches. *Cirrus indicates fair weather, not rainfall.*

cit•i•zen•ship /sĭt′ ĭ zən shĭp′ /, *n.* the rights, duties, and privileges that come with being a citizen. *Immigrants who apply for United States citizenship promise to uphold the principles of the Constitution.*

ci•vil•ian /sĭ vĭl′ yən/, *n.* a person not serving in the military. *Most civilians do not wear uniforms.*

clas•si•fy /klăs′ ə fī′ /, *v.* to sort; arrange according to category or class. *Librarians classify fairy tales as fiction.*

cleanse /klĕnz/, *v.* to make clean; remove dirt from. *Always cleanse a cut or scrape before bandaging it.*

clear•ance /klîr′ əns/, *n.* 1. space; clearing. *There was only a foot of clearance between the branch and the roof.* 2. a sale at which items are reduced in price for quick sale. *After a clearance, a store has room to display new merchandise.*

COD, an abbreviation for cash on delivery. *Catalog orders can be sent COD.*

col•lect /kə lĕkt′ /, *v.* 1. to gather; bring or come together. *Jane collected the test papers.* 2. to gather and keep as a hobby. *Bob collects stamps.* 3. to get money that is owed. *The landlord collected the rent.*

col•lec•tive /kə lĕk′ tĭv/, *adj.* 1. of a number of persons acting as one: *the collective decision of the community.* 2. having a singular form but a plural meaning. *The word* committee *is a collective noun.*

col•umn /kŏl′ əm/, *n.* 1. a support or pillar for a building. *The ivy twined around the porch columns.* 2. a straight row that goes up and down. *Many books have two columns of print on each page.* 3. articles appearing regularly and written by one author. *Mr. Vronski writes a column for the paper.*

col•um•nist /kŏl′ əm nĭst/, *n.* a person who writes a series of articles for a newspaper or magazine. *Teresa is the advice columnist for the school newspaper.*

co•me•di•an /kə mē′dē ən/, *n.* a professional entertainer who tells jokes and does things to make people laugh. *Some comedians appear regularly on variety shows.*

com•mu•ni•ty /kə myoo′nĭ tē/, *n.* all the people who live in one area; the residents of a town. *The park is for the entire community.* **com•mu•ni•ties.** [Latin *communis,* common.]

com•pact /kəm păkt′/ or /kŏm′ păkt′/, *adj.* arranged within a small space. *Most portable appliances are compact.*
v. /kəm păkt′/, to pack together tightly. *That machine compacts garbage.*
n. /kŏm′ păkt′/, a small cosmetic case. *May I borrow the mirror in your compact?*

com•plain /kəm plān′/, *v.* 1. to find fault. *Don't complain about a problem unless you're willing to help remedy it.* 2. to report something bad. *The neighbors complained to the police about the noisy motorcycle.* **com•plains, com•plained, com•plain•ing.** [Latin *com-* (intensive) + *plangere,* to lament.]

com•plete•ly /kəm plēt′lē/, *adv.* entirely; totally. *By the end of the party, the food was completely gone.*

com•ple•tion /kəm plē′shən/, *n.* a making or being completed; finishing. *The completion of a job gives one a feeling of accomplishment.* [Latin *complet-,* perfect stem of *complēre,* to fill out, from *com-* (intensive) + *plēre,* to fill.]

com•plex•ion /kəm plĕk′ shən/, *n.* the appearance of the face with regard to color and texture. *Limiting your exposure to the sun will keep your complexion healthier.*

com•pos•er /kəm pō′zər/, *n.* a person who composes or creates music. *Leonard Bernstein, who wrote the music for* West Side Story, *earned fame as both conductor and composer.*

com•pound¹ /kŏm′ pound′/, *n.* a chemical substance formed of two or more elements. *Water is a compound of hydrogen and oxygen.*
adj. formed of two or more parts: *a compound sentence.*
v. /kəm pound′/, to add to. *The sunshine compounded our happiness.*

com•pound² /kŏm′ pound′/, *n.* a group of buildings enclosed by barriers. *The security was tight around the compound.*

com•pu•ta•tion /kŏm′ pyoo tā′shən/, *n.* the process of computing; a mathematical calculation. *The accountant used a calculator to make tax computations.*

com•pu•ter /kəm pyoo′tər/, *n.* an electronic device that stores and analyzes data or performs calculations at high speeds. *Does your school have a computer?*

con•ceit /kən sēt′/, *n.* an exaggerated opinion of one's worth; vanity. *Conceit is an unattractive quality.*

ă pat/ā pay/âr care/ä father/ĕ pet/
ē be/ĭ pit/ī pie/îr pier/ŏ pot/ō toe/
ô paw, for/oi noise/ou out/oo took/
oo boot/ŭ cut/ûr urge/th thin/*th* this/
hw which/zh vision/ə about, item,
pencil, gallop, circus

con•cern /kən **sûrn′** /, *v.* 1. to relate to; to have an effect on. *The problem of pollution concerns all of us.* 2. to make anxious; worry. *His illness concerned his parents.*

con•clude /kən **klood′** /, *v.* to end; to finish. *She concluded her speech and sat down.* **con•cludes, con•clud•ed, con•clud•ing.**

con•clu•sion /kən **kloo′** zhən/, *n.* 1. the end. *We left in a hurry at the conclusion of the dinner.* 2. an opinion arrived at by thinking carefully. *The judge's conclusion was that Mr. Benson was innocent.* [Latin *conclusio,* from *concludere,* to end, from *com-*(intensive) + *claudere,* to close.]

con•di•tion /kən **dĭsh′** ən/, *n.* 1. something that is needed before something else can be obtained. *Hard work is a condition of success.* 2. the state in which a person or thing is. *The weather conditions were good.*

con•duct[1] /**kŏn′** dŭkt′ /, *n.* behavior; way of acting. *Nancy's conduct in class was good.*

con•duct[2] /kən **dŭkt′** /, *v.* 1. to guide; to lead. *The student conducted the visitor through the new building.* 2. to carry; be a path for. *Copper conducts electricity.*

con•fide /kən **fīd′** /, *v.* to trust one's secrets to another. *Pedro confided his plan to his friend.* **con•fides, con•fid•ed, con•fid•ing.**

con•firm /kən **fûrm′** /, *v.* to make certain or sure. *The experiment confirmed her theory.*

con•fuse /kən **fyooz′** /, *v.* to mix up in the mind; throw into disorder. *The loud noises confused the wild animals.* **con•fus•es, con•fused, con•fus•ing.**

con•gru•ent /**kŏng′** groo ənt/ or /kən **groo′** -/, *adj.* having exactly the same size and shape as another figure. *Two polygons are congruent if they match exactly.*

con•nect /kə **nĕkt′** /, *v.* 1. to join; to link. *Before you turn on the water, connect the hose to the faucet.* 2. to join two ideas, events, etc., in the mind. *I connect clowns with the circus.* [Latin *com-,* together + *nectere,* to bind.]

con•ser•va•tion /kŏn′ sûr **vā′** shən/, *n.* the protection of natural resources from loss, harm, or waste. *The community's efforts toward conservation resulted in a wildlife sanctuary to protect animals.*

con•sid•er /kən **sĭd′** ər/, *v.* 1. to think carefully before doing something. *Have you considered the pros and cons?* 2. to think of someone or something as; to regard as. *I consider that a compliment.*

con•sid•er•a•tion /kən sĭd′ ə **rā′** shən/, *n.* 1. careful thinking. *They gave our plan serious consideration.* 2. regard for the feeling of others; thoughtfulness. *Selfish people have little consideration for others.*

con•sole[1] /kən **sōl′** /, *v.* to comfort in time of trouble or sorrow. *The mother tried to console the screaming toddler.*

con•sole[2] /**kŏn′** sōl′ /, *n.* a cabinet or panel that houses the controls for mechanical or electrical equipment such as a TV, stereo or computer. *Technicians operate all the theater lights from a central console.*

con•so•nant /kŏn′ sə nənt/, *n.* a speech sound made by partially or completely stopping the flow of air through the mouth, or the letter or letters that stand for such a sound. *A is a vowel, but B and C are consonants.*

con•stant /kŏn′ stənt/, *adj.* never changing or stopping; happening again and again. *The constant beat of the rain put us to sleep.*

con•stel•la•tion /kŏn′ stə lā′ shən/, *n.* a group of stars with a name. *Many constellations were named after the animals they seemed to form in the sky.*

con•tact /kŏn′ tăkt/, *n.* 1. a joining of things together; a touching. *My fingers came into contact with a cold, soft material.* 2. a connection, especially of people: *a business contact.*
v. to communicate with. *The pilot contacted the control tower for landing instructions.*

con•tent¹ /kŏn′ tĕnt/, *n.* 1. often **contents**, what is contained; what a thing holds or encloses. *The contents of the package were listed on the label.* 2. the ideas expressed; topic; substance. *The teacher liked the content of my essay but said its grammar and punctuation needed work.*

con•tent² /kən tĕnt′/, *adj.* satisfied; pleased. *We were content to win by only one point.*

con•tin•u•ous /kən tĭn′ yōō əs/, *adj.* going on without stopping; unbroken; connected. *A continuous line of people passed the window.*

con•tract /kŏn′ trăkt′/, *n.* a legal agreement. *The striking workers finally agreed on a new contract.*
v. /kŏn′ trăkt′/ or /kən trăkt′/, 1. to make a legal agreement. *We contracted to mow their lawn every two weeks.* 2. to become smaller by shrinking. *Most things expand in warm weather and contract in cold weather.*

con•trib•ute /kən trĭb′ yōōt/, *v.* to give; donate. *Each student contributed two hours of work for the bake sale.* **con•trib•utes, con•trib•ut•ed, con•trib•ut•ing.**

con•vert¹ /kən vûrt′/, *v.* to change into another form, substance, or condition. *Jim's dad converted their unfinished basement into a playroom.*

con•vert² /kŏn′ vûrt′/, *n.* a person who has accepted a new belief. *There are few converts to the new tax proposal.*

con•vict /kən vĭkt′/, *v.* to find guilty. *The defendant was convicted of a felony.*
n. /kŏn′ vĭkt′/, 1. a person found guilty of a crime. *The convict was led from the court.* 2. a person serving a prison sentence. *Some convicts work in the prison garden.*

cor•al /kôr′ əl/ or /kŏr′ -/, *n.* a hard substance formed by the skeletons of tiny sea animals. *Through the clear water, we could see fish swimming among the coral.*
adj. made of coral: *coral reefs.*

cor•rupt /kə rŭpt′/, *adj*. dishonest; influenced by bribery. *There was a citizens' campaign to remove corrupt officials from public office.*

could•'ve, could have.

cour•age /kûr′ ĭj/ or /kŭr′ -/, *n*. the quality of facing danger or a difficult task without fear. *It takes courage to admit your mistakes.* [Old French *corage*, from Latin *cor*, heart.]

cou•ra•geous /kə rā′ jəs/, *adj*. being without fear; brave; having courage. *The courageous skater attempted a triple jump.*

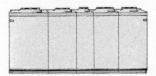

CPU, an abbreviation for central processing unit, or the part of every computer that controls the most basic operations. *The CPU is where instructions are decoded and executed.*

cra•ter /krā′ tər/, *n*. a hollow, bowl-shaped surface, such as that formed by a volcano or caused by the impact of a meteorite. *The astronauts photographed the moon's craters.*

crease /krēs/, *v*. to fold, pleat, or wrinkle. *How do you crease paper to make an airplane?* **creas•es, creased, creas•ing.** *n*. a line made by pressing, folding, or wrinkling. *Jan ironed out the creases in her skirt.*

cross-coun•try /krôs′kŭn′ trē/ or /krŏs′ /, *adj*. 1. moving across open country instead of following paths or roads: *cross-country skiing*. 2. from one side of the country to the other: *a cross-country trip*.

cru•el /krōō′ əl/, *adj*. wanting to make others suffer or cause them pain. *The cruel children threw stones at the birds.*

cruise /krōōz/, *v*. 1. to travel leisurely or aimlessly about. *The pleasure boat cruised the bay.* 2. to travel at a constant, efficient speed. *The jet cruised high above the clouds.* **cruis•es, cruised, cruis•ing.** *n*. a sea voyage taken for pleasure: *a Caribbean cruise.*

crumb /krŭm/, *n*. a small piece or fragment, especially of bread or cake. *We fed crumbs to the birds during the winter.*

cu•mu•lo•nim•bus /kyōōm′ yə lō nĭm′ bəs/, *n*. a very dense, vertically shaped cloud that may cause heavy rain or thunderstorms. *A cumulonimbus may bring hail.*

cu•mu•lus /kyōōm′ yə ləs/, *n*. a dense, white, fluffy cloud with a flat base. *A cumulus usually has a distinct shape.* **cu•mu•li.**

cup•board /kŭb′ ərd/, *n*. a cabinet with shelves, used for storing food, dishes, etc. *We keep spices in the corner cupboard.*

cur•few /kûr′ fyōō/, *n*. an order requiring persons to remain indoors during set hours, especially at night. *The soldiers had a midnight curfew.*

cu•ri•ous /kyōōr′ ē əs/, *adj*. eager to learn or find out; interested. *I was curious about how the computer program worked.*

cur•tain /kûr′ tn/, *n*. a hanging piece of cloth used to decorate a door or window or to separate the audience from the stage in a theater. *We closed the curtains to darken the room.*

cush•ion /kŏŏsh′ ən/, *n*. a soft pad or pillow. *Their poodle sleeps on a cushion in a basket.*

cus•to•di•an /kŭ stō′ dē ən/, *n*. caretaker; janitor. *The custodian of the building kept the sidewalks free of snow during the winter.*

cus•to•dy /kŭs′ tə dē/, *n.* 1. care; safekeeping; guardianship. *The judge granted the parents joint custody of the children.* 2. detention. *The police have a suspect in custody.*

cus•tom•ar•y /kŭs′ tə mĕr′ ē/, *adj.* based on custom; usual; routine. *A tuna sandwich and an apple are my customary lunch.*

cus•tom•er /kŭs′ tə mər/, *n.* any person who buys something, especially a person who buys regularly at the same place. *The store held a sale to attract new customers.*

czar /zär/, *n.* an emperor of Russia. *Czars had absolute power over their subjects.*

D d

day•dream /dā′ drēm′ /, *n.* a pleasant, dreamy thought. *She has daydreams about being a famous poet.*
v. to have pleasant, dreamy thoughts. *Try not to daydream in class.*

deal /dēl/, *v.* 1. to have to do with; to be concerned with. *The book deals with the history of America.* 2. to hand out; distribute. *Whose turn is it to deal the cards?* **deals, dealt, deal•ing.**

dealt /dĕlt/, *v.* past tense and past participle of **deal.**

ă pat/ā pay/âr care/ä father/ĕ pet/
ē be/ĭ pit/ī pie/îr pier/ŏ pot/ō toe/
ô paw, for/oi noise/ou out/ŏŏ took/
ōō boot/ŭ cut/ûr urge/th thin/*th* this/
hw which/zh vision/ə about, item,
pencil, gallop, circus

de•bate /dĭ bāt′ /, *n.* a discussion or argument on a particular subject. *We heard a debate on methods of teaching last night.*
v. to discuss or consider the pros and cons of a subject. *The students debated whether to have a dance or a field trip.*

de•bris /də brē′ / or /dā-/, *n.* remains of something broken, destroyed, or discarded. *The hurricane left much debris on the beach.*

debt /dĕt/, *n.* something owed to another person, usually money. *It is polite to repay a debt as soon as possible.*

de•bug /dē bŭg′ /, *v.* to locate and correct errors in a computer program. *If your procedure doesn't work, you'll have to debug it.* **de•bugs, de•bugged, de•bug•ging.**

dec•a•gon /dĕk′ ə gŏn′ /, *n.* a geometric figure having ten sides and ten angles. *The sides of a regular decagon are all equal.*

dec•i•bel /dĕs′ ə bəl/ or /-bĕl′ /, *n.* a unit used for measuring the relative intensity of sounds. *Ordinary conversation reaches a level of about 60 decibels.*

de•ci•sion /dĭ sĭzh′ ən/, *n.* 1. conclusion; verdict. *Has the committee reached a decision?* 2. firmness; decisiveness. *The defense lawyer was noted for her courage and decision.*

de•clar•a•tive /dĭ klâr′ ə tĭv/, *adj.* that which announces or states: *a declarative sentence.*

de•clare /dĭ klâr′ /, *v.* 1. to announce publicly and formally; to make known. *The politician declared his opposition to the new bill.* 2. to say positively and surely. *"I don't believe a word of it," she declared.* **de•clares, de•clared, de•clar•ing.**

de•fend /dǐ fĕnd´/, v. 1. to protect from harm or attack; to guard. *The soldiers continued to defend the fort.* 2. to act or speak in defense of something; to justify: *defend a decision.* 3. to represent the defendant in court. *The judge assigned a lawyer to defend him.*

de•fense /dǐ fĕns´/, n. 1. something that defends. *Warm clothing and good food are the best defense against catching colds.* 2. the defending team or side. *We all cheered as the defense came off the field.*

del•i•cate /dĕl´ ǐ kǐt/, adj. 1. light and pleasing to the senses: *a delicate perfume.* 2. carefully and expertly done; requiring careful workmanship: *delicate repairs.* 3. fragile; easily broken or hurt: *a delicate vase.*

de•light•ful /dǐ līt´ fəl/, adj. greatly pleasing; causing joy or delight. *We saw a delightful movie last night.*

del•ta /dĕl´ tə/, n. a deposit of mud and sand at the mouth of a river. *Deltas are formed when the river slows down and drops the materials that are carried by the current.*

dem•on•strate /dĕm´ ən strāt´/, v. 1. to show; make clear. *You must demonstrate a willingness to learn in school.* 2. to prove through an experiment or by using logical thinking. *The teacher demonstrated the force of gravity by dropping objects to the floor.*

de•ple•tion /dǐ plē´ shən/, n. exhaustion; a state of being used up. *Many dry areas of Africa have experienced erosion and depletion of soil.*

der•ma•tol•o•gist /dûr´ mə tŏl´ ə jist/, n. a doctor who specializes in skin care. *A dermatologist can tell you about the best skin treatments for your complexion.*

der•mis /dûr´ mĭs/, n. layer of skin beneath the surface layer. *The dermis lies beneath the epidermis.*

der•rick /dĕr´ ĭk/, n. the structure above an oil well to which drilling and pumping equipment is attached. *When the gusher was drilled, the entire derrick was hidden by a spouting stream of oil.*

des•o•late /dĕs´ ə lit/ or /dĕz´ -/, adj. 1. barren; without vegetation: *desolate terrain.* 2. uninhabited; deserted: *a desolate island.* 3. lonely; dejected. *Jessica was desolate the day after her best friend moved away.*

des•per•ate /dĕs´ pər ĭt/, adj. 1. almost despairing; frantic. *I made a desperate attempt to catch the teetering vase, but it fell before I could reach it.* 2. very bad; critical; extreme. *The driver was in a desperate situation when the brakes on the car failed.*

de•tain /dǐ tān´/, v. 1. to delay; hold back. *Their flight was detained two hours due to heavy fog.* 2. to keep in custody. *A suspect was detained for questioning.*

de•vel•op /dǐ vĕl´ əp/, v. 1. to grow; come into being. *The bud developed into a blossom.* 2. to build up; to put to use. *Reading helps to develop your mind.*

de•vel•op•ment /dǐ vĕl´ əp mənt/, n. 1. the act of developing; growth. *The children enjoyed watching the kittens' development.* 2. results; news. *What are the latest developments in the plans for a picnic?*

di•am•e•ter /dī ăm´ ĭ tər/, n. a straight line that passes through the center of a circle or other figure, dividing it into two equal parts. *The radius of a circle is half its diameter.* [Greek *dia-*, through + *metron*, measure.]

di•e•ti•tian /dĭ ĭ tĭsh′ ən/, *n.* a person who specializes in creating healthful diets. *Our school dietitian plans nutritious meals.*

dif•fer /dĭf′ ər/, *v.* 1. to be unlike. *The two nations differ in their languages and in their customs.* 2. to disagree; to have unlike ideas or opinions. *We couldn't resolve our argument, so we agreed to differ.* **dif•fers, dif•fered, dif•fer•ing.**

dif•fer•ence /dĭf′ ər əns/, *n.* 1. a way in which people or things are not alike. *There is a big difference in size between a mouse and an elephant.* 2. the amount by which one number is greater than another. *The difference between ten and twelve is two.*

dif•fer•ent /dĭf′ ər ənt/ or /dĭf′ rənt/, *adj.* 1. not alike. *Summer is different from winter.* 2. not the same; separate. *My cousin and I go to different schools.*

dif•fi•cult /dĭf′ ĭ kŭlt′/ or /-kəlt/, *adj.* 1. hard; not easy to do or understand. *Learning to play chess is difficult.* 2. hard to get along with. *He had a reputation for being difficult.*

di•ges•tive /dĭ jĕs′ tĭv/ or /dī-/, *adj.* relating to or serving the process by which food is changed so that the body can absorb it. *The digestive system turns the food that we eat into nutrients.*

ă pat/ā pay/âr care/ä father/ĕ pet/
ē be/ĭ pit/ī pie/îr pier/ŏ pot/ō toe/
ô paw, for/oi noise/ou out/o͝o took/
o͞o boot/ŭ cut/ûr urge/th thin/*th* this/
hw which/zh vision/ə about, item,
pencil, gallop, circus

di•men•sion /dĭ mĕn′ shən/ or /dī-/, *n.* a measurement of the length, width, or height of something. *The dimensions of the package are three feet in length, two feet in width, and one foot in height.* **di•men•sions.**

dip•lo•mat /dĭp′ lə măt′/, *n.* a person skilled in dealing with other persons or governments. *The diplomats tried to lessen the tension between the countries they represented.*

di•rect /dĭ rĕkt′/ or /dī-/, *v.* 1. to point out the way. *The road map directed us to the town.* 2. to be in charge of; manage. *A police officer directed traffic.* 3. to order; command. *The doctor directed Will to eat more fresh fruit.* **di•rects, di•rect•ed, di•rect•ing.**
adj. 1. straight; not roundabout: *a direct route.* 2. honest; frank: *a direct answer.* [Latin *direct-,* perfect stem of *dirigere,* to give direction to, from *dis-,* apart + *regere,* to guide.]

di•rec•tion /dĭ rĕk′ shən/ or /dī-/, *n.* 1. managing; control. *The orchestra was under the direction of a famous conductor.* 2. a point toward which one can face. *We walked in the direction of the bank.* 3. **directions,** an explanation of how to do something. *The directions were hard to follow.*

di•rect•ly /dĭ rĕkt′ lē/, *adv.* 1. in a direct line; straight. *The city is directly north of us.* 2. right away. *I'll be there directly.*

dirt•y /dûr′ tē/, *adj.* not clean; containing dirt. *Put all the dirty clothes into the washing machine.*

dis•a•gree•ment /dĭs′ ə grē′ mənt/, *n.* a dispute; difference of opinion. *We had a disagreement over whose turn it was.*

dis•count /dĭs′ kount′/, *n.* a reduction; an amount taken off a price. *Mary got a discount on the hat because it was on sale.*

dis•cuss•ion /dĭ skŭsh′ ən/, *n.* a serious or thorough conversation. *Sandy and I had a long discussion about how to clean up our neighborhood.* [Latin *discuss-*, perfect stem of *discutere,* to discuss, from *dis-*, apart + *quatere,* to shake.]

dis•guise /dĭs gīz′ /, *v.* 1. to change one's real appearance so that one will not be recognized. *In the play, the thief was disguised as a detective.* 2. to hide; mask; cover up. *He disguised his anger by smiling.* **dis•guis•es, dis•guised, dis•guis•ing.**
n. a costume used to hide one's real identity: *a clown disguise.*

disk•ette /dĭ skĕt′ /, *n.* a floppy disk on which computer data can be stored. *Dave stored his program on a diskette.*

dis•pute /dĭ spyoot′ /, *v.* to argue; debate; have a different opinion about. *Our class disputed over the best date for the picnic.* **dis•putes, dis•put•ed, dis•put•ing.**
n. argument; debate; quarrel. *Diplomats try to settle disputes between countries.*

dis•tance /dĭs′ təns/, *n.* the space between two points or places. *I live a short distance away.*

dis•tant /dĭs′ tənt/, *adj.* 1. far away or long ago. *The speaker had traveled in distant lands.* 2. not easy to talk with; keeping to oneself. *Shy persons can seem distant until you get to know them.*

dis•trict /dĭs′ trĭkt/, *n.* a part of a country, state, or county that has certain duties or functions. *We have school districts and voting districts.*

di•vis•i•bil•i•ty /dĭ vĭz′ ə bĭl′ ĭ tē/, *n.* the state of being able to divide without a remainder. *Factoring can show the divisibility of a number.*

DOB, an abbreviation for date of birth. *Write your date of birth in the space marked "DOB."*

doc•u•ment /dŏk′ yə mənt/, *n.* an official paper; any written record used as evidence for some fact. *Your birth certificate is an important document.* [Latin *documentum,* lesson, from *docēre,* to teach.]

do•nate /dō′ nāt′ /, *v.* to give or contribute to a fund or cause. *The class decided to donate the money from their bake sale to the animal shelter.* **do•nates, do•nat•ed, do•nat•ing.**

doubt•ful /dout′ fəl/, *adj.* not sure; uncertain. *I am doubtful that we can finish the game in this rain.*

down•ward /doun′ wərd/, *adv.* toward a lower place. *The car at the top of the hill rolled downward.*
adj. going toward a lower place. *This downward path leads to the house.*

drought /drout/, *n.* a period of time during which there is no rain. *The crops were ruined by a two-month drought last summer.*

du•ti•ful /doo′ tĭ fəl/ or /dyoo′ -/, *adj.* careful about performing one's duty; obedient; respectful. *Darrell is a dutiful son who always does as he is asked.*

E e

east•ward /ēst′ wərd/, *adv.* toward the east. *The river runs eastward.*
adj. in or toward the east. *The pilot set an eastward course.*

ed•i•ble /ĕd′ ə bəl/, *adj.* capable of being eaten; fit to eat. *Many wild berries are not edible.*

-eer, a suffix meaning "someone who works in or is involved with": *engineer.*

ef•fort /ĕf´ ərt/, *n.* 1. the use of one's strength or power; exertion. *Riding a bicycle uphill requires effort.* 2. an attempt; a try. *Make an effort to finish by three.* [Latin *ex-,* out + *fortis,* strong.]

e•lec•tri•cian /ĭ lĕk trĭsh´ ən/ or /ē´ lĕk-/, *n.* a person who installs and repairs electrical equipment. *The electrician rewired the old house.*

e•lec•tron /ĭ lĕk´ trŏn/, *n.* one of the tiny particles of negative matter that travel around the nucleus of an atom. *Electrons have a negative charge.*

e•mer•gen•cy /ĭ mur´ jən sē/, *n.* a serious situation that requires something to be done right away. *The police are trained to respond quickly in an emergency.* **e•mer•gen•cies.**

e•mo•tion /ĭ mō´ shən/, *n.* a strong reaction or feeling. *Anger is a common emotion.*

em•pire /ĕm´ pīr/, *n.* a number of countries having a single, powerful ruler or emperor. *Years ago, the Roman Empire included most of the world then known.*

em•ploy•ee /ĕm ploi´ ē/, *n.* a person who works for another person or for a business firm. *The bank had a picnic for all its employees.*

-ence, a suffix used to form nouns meaning: 1. act or result of acting: *dependence.* 2. state or quality: *absence.*

en•cy•clo•pe•di•a /ĕn sĭ´ klə pē´ dē ə/, *n.* a book or group of books that gives general information on many different subjects. *Topics in an encyclopedia are in alphabetical order.*

en•dan•ger /ĕn dān´ jər/, *v.* to put in danger; harm. *Pollution endangers wildlife.*

en•gi•neer /ĕn jə nîr´ /, *n.* 1. a person trained to use science and math for practical purposes such as designing and building systems or equipment. *My big sister is an electrical engineer.* 2. a person operating an engine: *a train engineer.*

en•grave /ĕn grāv´ /, *v.* to carve designs or letters into a surface. *The jeweler engraved my initials on my watch.* **en•graves, en•graved, en•grav•ing.**

en•list /ĕn lĭst´ /, *v.* 1. to join a branch of the armed forces voluntarily. *Lydia wants to enlist in the Navy when she finishes high school.* 2. to gain the support of. *The principal enlisted us all to help clean up the school yard.*

-ent, a suffix used: 1. to form adjectives meaning "causing or being": *absorbent.* 2. to form nouns meaning "one who": *president.*

en•vi•ron•ment /ĕn vī´ rən mənt/, *n.* 1. the total surroundings that allow a living organism to grow and develop. *Congress has passed bills to protect our environment from pollution.* 2. surroundings. *The library is a quiet environment for study.*

ă pat/ā pay/âr care/ä father/ĕ pet/
ē be/ĭ pit/ī pie/îr pier/ŏ pot/ō toe/
ô paw, for/oi noise/ou out/o͝o took/
o͞o boot/ŭ cut/ûr urge/th thin/*th* this/
hw which/zh vision/ə about, item, pencil, gallop, circus

en•zyme /ĕn′zīm′/, *n.* a protein substance produced by living organisms. *Enzymes help our bodies break down food.*

ep•i•der•mis /ĕp′ ĭ dûr′ mĭs/, *n.* the outer layer of the skin. *Humans as well as plants have an epidermis.*

-er, a suffix used to form nouns meaning: 1. one who: *teacher.* 2. thing that: *toaster.*

equip•ment /ĭ kwĭp′ mənt/, *n.* the things needed for a special purpose; supplies. *Paper, desks, and chairs are all office equipment.*

e•quiv•a•lent /ĭ kwĭv′ ə lənt/, *adj.* identical; equal. *Twelve inches are equivalent to one foot.*
n. something equal or identical. *The equivalent of 12 x 12 is 144.*

e•ro•sion /ĭ rō′ zhən/, *n.* the wearing or washing away of the earth's surface. *Soil conservation can help control erosion from wind or water.*

er•ror /ĕr′ ər/, *n.* a mistake. *I was happy because my spelling test had no errors.*

es•pe•cial•ly /ĭ spĕsh′ ə lē/, *adv.* mainly; in particular; unusually. *My brother likes all sports, but he especially enjoys soccer.*

es•ti•ma•tion /ĕs′ tə mā′shən/, *n.* 1. a rough calculation. *The engineer gave an estimation of the costs for the building project.* 2. judgment; opinion. *It was the engineer's estimation that the project could be finished on time.*

etch•ing /ĕch′ ing/, *n.* a design cut into a plate by the action of acid, or the print made from such a plate. *The artist printed the etching from a metal plate.*

event•ful /ĭ vĕnt′ fəl/, *adj.* filled with many events or an important happening. *Our most eventful month was May, when we moved.*

eve•ry•bod•y /ĕv′ rē bŏd′ ē/ or /-bŭd′ ē/, *pron.* all people; each person. *Everybody in our class went to see the parade.*

ex-, a prefix meaning: 1. out of; away from: *expose.* 2. former: *ex-senator.*

ex•act•ly /ĭg zăkt′ lē/, *adv.* 1. precisely; without any change. *Do exactly as the teacher says.* 2. true; quite so. *"Exactly!" exclaimed George in agreement.*

ex•am•ine /ĭg zăm′ ĭn/, *v.* to look at closely to find out the condition of; inspect. *Examine the apples before you buy them.* **ex•am•ines, ex•am•ined, ex•am•in•ing.**

ex•cel /ĭk sĕl′/, *v.* to do better than others; to perform at a high level. *Colleen excels in mathematics.* **ex•cels, ex•celled, ex•cel•ling.**

ex•cel•lence /ĕk′ sə ləns/, *n.* something in which a person surpasses others. *The school offered an award for excellence in spelling.*

ex•cel•lent /ĕk′ sə lənt/, *adj.* very good. *Their excellent singing received loud applause.*

ex•cite•ment /ĭk sīt′ mənt/, *n.* an excited condition; the state of being stirred up. *The entrance of the tigers created great excitement among the circus crowd.*

ex•clam•a•to•ry /ĭk sklăm′ ə tôr′ e/ or /-tōr′ ē/, *adj.* expressing a forceful statement or sudden cry. *An exclamatory sentence has an exclamation point at its end.*

Look at that fish!

ex•hale /ĕks hāl′/, *v.* to breathe out. *Swimmers exhale with their faces in the water.* **ex•hales, ex•haled, ex•hal•ing.**

ex•hib•it /ĭg zĭb′ĭt/, *v.* to display; to reveal publicly. *His paintings were exhibited at the art fair.* **ex•hib•its, ex•hib•it•ed, ex•hib•it•ing.** *n.* a public show or display. *Did you see the museum's new exhibit?*

ex•pe•ri•ence /ĭk spîr′ē əns/, *n.* 1. a living through an event or series of events; a doing or feeling something. *Watching the baby birds hatch was a special experience.* 2. what one learns from doing things. *I gained business experience from my paper route.*

ex•per•i•ment /ĭk spĕr′ə mənt/, *n.* a trial or test to learn, discover, or prove something. *An experiment with litmus paper will show whether a substance is an acid or a base.* *v.* to test something to learn, discover, or prove something about it. *The artist experimented with several shades of paint.* [Latin *experimentum,* from *experiri,* to try.]

ex•pert /ĕk′spûrt′/, *n.* 1. a highly skilled or knowledgeable person. *Police detectives often consult a fingerprint expert.* *adj.* having a great deal of skill or knowledge: *an expert carpenter.*

ex•po•nent /ĭk spō′nənt/ or /ĕk′ spō′nənt/, *n.* a mathematical term that shows how many times the base number is to be multiplied by itself. *In the expression y^3, the 3 is an exponent.*

ex•press /ĭk sprĕs′/, *v.* to tell; to make known. *Think for a moment before you try to express your idea.* *adj.* quick and direct: *express mail.*

ex•pres•sion /ĭk sprĕsh′ən/, *n.* 1. a particular word or phrase. *"Hit the sack" is an idiomatic expression for "go to bed."* 2. a means of expressing something; indication. *A sigh can be an expression of contentment.*

ex•tract /ĭk străkt′/, *v.* 1. to draw out or pull out by force: *extract a tooth.* 2. to obtain a substance by a chemical process: *extract aluminum from bauxite.* *n.* /ĕk′străkt′/, a concentrated substance prepared from natural food or flavoring: *vanilla extract.* 2. a passage from a literary work. *Our drama club presented extracts from Shakespeare's plays.*

F f

fa•ble /fā′bəl/, *n.* A brief tale or story, often with animal characters that speak and act like human beings, that teaches a useful lesson about human nature. *Her favorite fable was* The Tortoise and the Hare.

fab•u•lous /făb′yə ləs/, *adj.* 1. belonging to legend or myth. *Elves are fabulous creatures.* 2. amazing; wonderful. *It was a fabulous party.* [Latin *fabula,* fable.]

fac•tor /făk′tər/, *n.* 1. any of the things that cause a certain result. *Time is an important factor to consider in cooking.* 2. any of the numbers multiplied to obtain a product. *Factors of 21 are 3 and 7.* *v.* to separate into factors. *If you factor 21, you get 3 and 7.* **fac•tors, fac•tored, fac•tor•ing.**

ă pat/ā pay/âr care/ä father/ĕ pet/
ē be/ĭ pit/ī pie/îr pier/ŏ pot/ō toe/
ô paw, for/oi noise/ou out/ŏŏ took/
ōŏ boot/ŭ cut/ûr urge/th thin/*th* this/
hw which/zh vision/ə about, item,
pencil, gallop, circus

Fahr·en·heit /făr′ ən hīt′ /, *adj.* of or according to the Fahrenheit scale, where the freezing point of water is 32 degrees and the boiling point is 212 degrees: *Fahrenheit scale.*

faint /fānt/, *adj.* 1. lacking strength; weak and dizzy. *If you feel faint, sit or lie down.* 2. unclear; dim. *A faint light came from a window in the house.*
v. to lose consciousness and lie as if asleep because of illness, weakness, etc. *He fainted because he was very tired and hungry.*

fa·mine /făm′ in/, *n.* an extreme shortage of food causing widespread hunger. *The Red Cross shipped food and medicine to the areas of Africa hit by the famine.*

fan·ci·ful /făn′ si fəl/, *adj.* imaginative; unreal. *Science fiction writers create fanciful worlds.*

fash·ion /făsh′ ən/, *n.* 1. a style of dressing or behaving. *Fashions change yearly.* 2. way or manner. *She smiled in an odd fashion.*
v. to shape; to form. *Birds fashion nests of grass and twigs.*

fa·vor·a·ble /fā′ vər ə bəl/ or /fāv′ rə-/, *adj.* 1. encouraging: *a favorable answer.* 2. helpful: *favorable winds.* **fa·vor·a·bly,** *adv.*

fa·vor·ite /fā′ vər ĭt/, or /fāv′ rĭt/, *adj.* most liked; preferred. *Broccoli is my favorite vegetable.*
n. the one most liked or preferred. *Which is your favorite of the World Series teams?*

fear·less /fîr′ lĭs/, *adj.* not afraid; brave. *The fearless kitten confronted the big dog.*

fee·ble /fē′ bəl/, *adj.* without much strength; weak. *Newborn animals are often feeble.*

fer·ti·liz·er /fûr′ tl ĭ′ zər/, *n.* something added to soil to make it more productive. *Compost makes a good garden fertilizer.*

fierce /fîrs/, *adj.* 1. savage; wild. *The fierce lion growled and paced inside the cage.* 2. violent. *The fierce wind blew down trees.*

film /fĭlm/, *n.* 1. a thin, flat material coated with a chemical and used for taking photographs. *I put a new roll of film in my camera.* 2. a motion picture. *Many old films are shown.* 3. a thin coating: *a film of ice.*

fi·nal·ly /fī′ nə lē/, *adv.* at last. *I finally got the job done.*

fi·nance /fə năns′ / or /fī′ năns′ /, *n.* the management of large amounts of money. *Bankers must be skilled in finance.*

fis·cal /fĭs′ kəl/, *adj.* relating to money matters. *A government's fiscal policy determines how much money it spends.*

flex·i·ble /flĕk′ sə bəl/, *adj.* 1. capable of being bent. *The clay figures were flexible and could assume many shapes.* 2. adjustable, changeable: *a flexible schedule.*

flop·py disk /flŏp′ ē dĭsk′ /, *n.* a flexible plastic disk used to store computer data. *The information was stored on a floppy disk.*

flow·chart /flō′ chärt′ /, *n.* a diagram showing the sequence of operations. *A flow chart is helpful in writing computer programs.*

flu·id /flōō′ ĭd/, *n.* a substance such as water or air that flows easily and takes on the shape of its container. *"Drink plenty of fluids,"* the doctor advised.

flut·ist /flōō′ tĭst/, *n.* a person who plays a woodwind instrument called the flute. *The flutist and the oboist played a haunting duet.*

forc•i•ble /fôr′ sə bəl/ or /fōr′ -/, *adj.* using or applying physical force: *a forcible entry.*

fore•man /fôr′ mən/ or /fōr′ -/, *n.* a person in charge of a group of workers: *the construction foreman.*

for•get•ful /fər get′ fəl/ or /fôr′ -/, *adj.* tending to forget; unable to recall. *Because Sandra is often forgetful, she writes notes to remind herself to do things.*

for•mer /fôr′ mər/, *adj.* coming earlier in time or before in position. *The former owner of this house painted the walls blue.*
n. the first of two things talked about. *Tom was given the choice of visiting Los Angeles or New York, and he chose the former because he had never been to California.*

for•tu•nate /fôr′ chə nĭt/, *adj.* lucky. *You were fortunate to find the lost bracelet.*

frag•ment /frăg′ mənt/, *n.* 1. a piece broken off. *The vase fell to the floor in fragments.* 2. something incomplete. *An incomplete sentence is called a sentence fragment.*

freeze /frēz/, *v.* 1. to become ice; to turn to ice. *The lake froze during the night.* 2. to chill something until it becomes cold and hard as ice. *We freeze the vegetables from our garden so that they will last through the winter.* **freez•es, froze, fro•zen, freez•ing.**

fruit•less /frōōt′ lĭs/, *adj.* 1. not producing any fruit. *The fig tree was fruitless.* 2. unsuccessful; unproductive. *They conducted a fruitless search for the missing papers.*

-ful, a suffix used to form adjectives meaning "full of" or "having": *joyful.*

ful•fill /fŏŏl fĭl′ /, *v.* 1. to bring into effect; make real. *The team fulfilled their goal of a winning season.* 2. to finish; complete. *Scouts must fulfill requirements to earn badges.* [Old English *ful,* full + *fyllan,* to fill.]

fu•ri•ous /fyŏŏr′ ē əs/, *adj.* 1. very angry. *I was furious with myself for forgetting my homework.* 2. strong; violent. *The furious storm raged for hours.*

fur•nace /fûr′ nĭs/, *n.* an enclosed structure to make a fire in. *Furnaces are used to heat buildings, melt metal, and make pottery.*

G g

gal•ax•y /găl′ ək sē/, *n.* a large group of stars. *Our solar system is a part of the Milky Way galaxy.* **gal•ax•ies.**

ga•rage /gə räzh′ / or /-räj′ /, *n.* 1. a building in which cars are kept. *She backed the car out of the garage.* 2. a place where vehicles are repaired or stored. *The workers at the garage will install new brakes.* [French *garer,* to shelter, protect.]

gar•bage /gär′ bĭj/, *n.* spoiled food or waste matter that is thrown away. *We put our garbage in cans in the alley.*

ă pat/ā pay/âr care/ä father/ĕ pet/
ē be/ĭ pit/ī pie/îr pier/ŏ pot/ō toe/
ô paw, for/oi noise/ou out/ŏŏ took/
ōō boot/ŭ cut/ûr urge/th thin/*th* **th**is/
hw **wh**ich/zh vision/ə about, item,
pencil, gallop, circus

ge•og•ra•pher /jē ŏg′ rə fər/, *n.* a person who specializes in the study of geography. *The geographer studied the terrain using maps.*

ge•og•ra•phy /jē ŏg′ rə fē/, *n.* 1. the study of the earth and its features and inhabitants. *In geography we learn that trade and commerce depend upon rivers, mountains, and other natural features.* 2. the landscape of a place. *The geography of Colorado is rugged.* [Greek *geo-*, earth + *graphein*, to write.]

ge•ol•o•gist /jē ŏl′ ə jĭst/, *n.* a person who specializes in the study of geology. *The geologist explained volcanic action.*

ge•ol•o•gy /jē ŏl′ ə jē/, *n.* the scientific study of the composition and history of the earth's structure. *Scientists use geology when they try to locate water or minerals underground.*

ge•om•e•try /jē ŏm′ ĭ trē/, *n.* the mathematical study of the measurements and relationships of solid and plane figures. *In geometry we learned that a circle has 360 degrees.* [Greek *geo-*, earth + *metron*, measure.]

glaze /glāz/, *n.* a smooth, shiny coating applied to ceramics before firing. *The potter painted the bowl with a speckled blue glaze before putting it in the kiln.*

glo•ri•ous /glôr′ ē əs/ or /glōr′ -/, *adj.* 1. producing honor and glory; deserving praise. *The discovery of a way to prevent polio was a glorious triumph of medicine.* 2. beautiful; brilliant. *This is a glorious day.* [Latin *gloria*, glory.]

golf /gŏlf/ or /gôlf/, *n.* a game played with a small hard ball and a set of clubs. *The object of golf is to hit the ball into certain holes, using the fewest possible strokes.*

good•ness /gŏŏd′ nĭs/, *n.* the condition of being good. *The goodness of an apple is determined by its taste.*

gor•geous /gôr′ jəs/, *adj.* very beautiful; stunning; magnificent. *From an airplane the view of the Grand Canyon is gorgeous.* [Old French *gorrias*, elegant.]

gram•mar /grăm′ ər/, *n.* the system of rules that show how words are used in language. *A knowledge of grammar helps us to write effectively.*

graph•ic /grăf′ ĭk/, *adj.* 1. vivid; strong; clear. *Your graphic description of the painting made it easier to find in the museum.* 2. relating to art, printing, or engraving: *graphic arts.* [Greek *graphein*, to write.]

grav•i•ty /grăv′ ĭ tē/, *n.* the force that draws all objects toward the center of the earth. *A ball that is thrown into the air returns to the ground because of gravity.*

graze /grāz/, *v.* to eat grass in a field or pasture. *The cattle grazed by the river.* **graz•es, grazed, graz•ing.**

grief /grēf/, *n.* great sorrow or sadness. *Everyone felt grief when the great leader became ill.*

grown-up /grōn′ ŭp′ /, *adj.* not childish; mature; adult. *Jason felt grown-up once the training wheels were taken off his bike.*

guard•i•an /gär′ dē ən/, *n.* 1. a person or thing that takes care of or protects. *Every citizen must act as a guardian of democracy.* 2. a person appointed by a court to care for another person. *The form has a blank for the name of your parent or guardian.* [Old French *garder*, to guard.]

guide·book /gīd′ book′/, *n.* a handbook of information for tourists. *The city guidebook lists museums, restaurants, and parks.*

H h

hand·ker·chief /hăng′ kər chĭf/, *n.* a small square of cloth used for wiping the nose or worn as decoration. *Mr. Weiss wore a maroon handerkerchief that matched his tie.*

hard·ware /härd′ wâr′/, *n.* 1. articles made from metal. *Nails, bolts, and wire are hardware.* 2. machines or other physical equipment needed to perform a particular task: *computer hardware.*

her·i·tage /hĕr′ ĭ tĭj/, *n.* that which is passed down from preceding generations; tradition. *The book* Roots *deals with the heritage of black Americans.*

home·ward /hōm′ wərd/, *adv.* at or toward home. *The ship sailed homeward.*
adj. toward home: *the homeward journey.*

hon·or·ar·y /ŏn′ ə rĕr′ ē/, *adj.* given as a token of honor: *an honorary key to the city.*

hor·ri·ble /hôr′ ə bəl/ or /hŏr′ -/, *adj.* 1. causing horror; shocking; dreadful: *a horrible disease.* 2. very unpleasant: *a horrible grating noise.*

ă pat/ā pay/âr care/ä father/ĕ pet/
ē be/ĭ pit/ī pie/îr pier/ŏ pot/ō toe/
ô paw, for/oi noise/ou out/oŏ took/
oō boot/ŭ cut/ûr urge/th thin/*th* this/
hw which/zh vision/ə about, item,
pencil, gallop, circus

horse·pow·er /hôrs′ pou′ ər/, *n.* a unit of power that will raise a weight of 550 pounds one inch in one second. *An engine's strength is measured in horsepower.*

hue /hyoō/, *n.* a color or shade of a color. *The bright fabric contained some lovely red and purple hues.*

hus·band /hŭz′ bənd/, *n.* the man a woman is married to. *When they were married, her husband gave her a ring.*

hy·drau·lic /hī drô′ lĭk/, *adj.* powered by a liquid under pressure: *a hydraulic drill.*

hy·giene /hī′ jēn/, *n.* the science of keeping well; the study of rules of health. *We learn about hygiene in our health class.*

hymn /hĭm/, *n.* a song of praise. *The poet wrote a hymn in praise of nature.*

I i

-ian, a suffix used to form nouns meaning "one who": *custodian.*

-ible, a suffix used to form adjectives meaning: 1. capable of: *flexible.* 2. tending toward: *sensible.*

i·de·al /ī dē′ əl/ or /ī dēl′ /, *n.* a perfect type; an idea of something that is perfect. *Our nation was founded on the ideal that citizens can govern themselves.*
adj. perfect; exactly as one would wish. *A warm day and a clear sky are ideal conditions for a picnic.* **i·de·al·ly,** *adv.*

ig·no·rant /ĭg′ nər ənt/, *adj.* not having education or knowledge. *A person ignorant of history might think Brazilians speak Spanish.*

ig•nore /ĭg nôr′/ or /-nōr′/, v. to pay no attention to; to refuse to notice. *Anita ignored their silly remarks.* **ig•nores, ig•nored, ig•nor•ing.**

il-, a prefix meaning "not": *illicit.* **Il-** replaces **in-** before words beginning with **l.**

il•le•gal /ĭ lē′ gəl/, *adj.* not legal; against the law. *In many states, it is illegal to litter.*

il•leg•i•ble /ĭ lĕj′ ə bəl/, *adj.* not able to be read; blurred or poorly written. *The hand-writing on the old letter was nearly illegible.* **il•leg•i•bly,** adv.

il•lit•er•ate /ĭ lĭt′ ər ĭt/, *adj.* unable to read or write. *Teaching illiterate persons to read will help them vote wisely and find new jobs.*

il•log•i•cal /ĭ lŏj′ ĭ kəl/, *adj.* senseless; not according to the principles of logic. *In* Alice in Wonderland, *Alice finds herself in an illogical world.*

i•mag•i•nar•y /ĭ măj′ ə nĕr′ ē/, *adj.* not real; happening only in the mind. *Unicorns are imaginary animals.*

im•me•di•ate /ĭ mē′ dē ĭt/, *adj.* happening right away; without delay. *The immediate effect of the medicine was to stop his coughing.*

im•per•a•tive /ĭm pĕr′ ə tĭv/, *adj.* 1. expressing a command. *An imperative sentence gives an order.* 2. urgent; necessary. *It is imperative that you come at once.*

im•por•tance /ĭm pôr′ tns/, *n.* significance; value. *Never underestimate the importance of correct spelling.*

im•press /ĭm prĕs′ /, *v.* 1. to affect strongly or favorably. *Her fluent French impressed all of us.* 2. to fix firmly in the mind. *He impressed upon us the need to remain quiet.*

in-, a prefix meaning "not": *inattentive.*

in•deed /ĭn dēd′/, *adv.* in fact; really. *This meal was indeed delicious.*

in•dict /ĭn dīt′ /, *v.* to charge with a crime. *The grand jury indicted a suspect in the case.*

in•dus•tri•ous /ĭn dŭs′ trē əs/, *adj.* hard-working; diligent. *Industrious students usually enjoy school.*

in•for•ma•tion /ĭn′ fər mā′ shən/, *n.* knowledge; facts; something that is told. *They searched in the library for information about the history of Alaska.* [Latin *informare,* to inform, from *in-,* in + *forma,* form.]

in•hale /ĭn hāl′ /, *v.* to breathe in; take air into the lungs. *The doctor told me to inhale deeply.* **in•hales, in•haled, in•hal•ing.**

in•her•it /ĭn hĕr′ ĭt/, *v.* 1. to receive something from an older person. *Lisa inherited her aunt's ring.* 2. to receive from a parent as a genetic trait. *Stuart inherited his father's blue eyes.*

in•her•i•tance /ĭn hĕr′ ĭ təns/, *n.* heritage; something inherited. *Our instinct for survival is an inheritance from many previous generations.*

in•no•cence /ĭn′ ə səns/, *n.* the state of being innocent; absence of guilt or wrongdoing. *The suspect's alibi proved his innocence.*

in•no•cent /ĭn′ ə sənt/, *adj.* 1. not guilty. *She claimed she was innocent of the crime.* 2. harmless; having no bad effect: *an innocent trick.* 3. unaware of evil. *An innocent child trusts everyone.*

in•put /ĭn′ pŏot′ /, *n.* anything put into a system to produce a result, or output. *In order for the computer program to work, your input must contain all the necessary data.*

in•sert /ĭn sûrt´/, *v.* 1. to put into. *Insert the coin in the slot.* 2. to add. *Insert an example in this paragraph to strengthen it.*

in•stance /ĭn´ stəns/, *n.* an example; a case. *In most instances students adjust quickly to new schools.*

in•stant /ĭn´ stənt/, *n.* a short time; a moment. *The runner paused for an instant to catch his breath.*
adj. immediate; taking place quickly. *She demanded an instant reply.*

in•stru•ment /ĭn´ strə mənt/, *n.* 1. a tool. *A pen is a writing instrument.* 2. a device for making music. *A piano is a musical instrument.* **in•stru•ments.** [Latin *instrumentum,* tool, from *instruere,* to prepare.]

in•sult /ĭn sŭlt´/, *v.* to treat with rudeness; to hurt feelings on purpose. *It is not polite to insult someone.*
n. /ĭn´ sŭlt´/, a rude or hurtful remark or act. *I meant that as a compliment, not an insult.*

in•sur•ance /ĭn shoor´ əns/, *n.* the business of guaranteeing to cover specified losses in the future, as in case of accident, illness, theft, or death, in return for the continuing payment of regular sums of money. *Drivers in many states must maintain accident insurance.*

ă pat/ā pay/âr care/ä father/ĕ pet/
ē be/ĭ pit/ī pie/îr pier/ŏ pot/ō toe/
ô paw, for/oi noise/ou out/oŏ took/
ōō boot/ŭ cut/ûr urge/th thin/*th* this/
hw which/zh vision/ə about, item, pencil, gallop, circus

in•sure /ĭn shoor´/, *v.* to arrange for a payment of money in case of loss or illness, by paying regularly to an insurance company. *My parents insured our house against fire.* **in•sures, in•sured, in•sur•ing.**

inter-, a prefix meaning "between" or "among": *interlocking.*

in•ter•act /ĭn´ tər ăkt´/, *v.* to act on or influence each other. *After-school activities allow students to interact with each other.*

in•ter•change /ĭn´ tər chānj´/, *v.* to switch the places of. *The parts of a jigsaw puzzle cannot be interchanged.* **in•ter•chang•es, in•ter•changed, in•ter•chang•ing.**
n. /ĭn´ tər chānj´/ 1. a mutual exchange: *an interchange of ideas.* 2. an intersection: *a highway interchange.*

in•ter•est rate /ĭn´ trĭst rāt´/, *n.* the rate charged for borrowing money. *Low interest rates encourage people to borrow money.*

in•ter•face /ĭn´ tər fās´/, *v.* to join or connect at a common point or surface. *The parts of an electrical system must interface smoothly.* **in•ter•fac•es, in•ter•faced, in•ter•fac•ing.** [Latin *inter,* between + *facies,* face.]

in•ter•rog•a•tive /ĭn´ tə rŏg´ ə tĭv/, *adj.* asking a question. *An interrogative sentence ends with a question mark.*

in•ter•sect /ĭn´ tər sĕkt´/, *v.* to cross; to meet at a common point. *I'll meet you where Eighth Street intersects Main.* [Latin *inter,* between + *sect-,* perfect stem of *secare,* to cut.]

in•ter•state /ĭn´ tər stāt´/, *adj.* connecting two or more states: *an interstate highway.*

in•ter•view /ĭn′tər vyoo′/, *n.* a meeting of two people to discuss something. *The graduate had a job interview with the employer.* *v.* to meet and talk with in the hope of getting information. *The reporter interviewed the committee members.*

intra-, a prefix meaning "within": *intravenous.*

in•tra•mu•ral /ĭn′trə myoor′ əl/, *adj.* consisting of participants from the same school: *intramural sports.* [Latin *intra*, within + *murus*, wall.]

in•tra•state /ĭn′trə stāt′/, *adj.* existing within the boundaries of a state. *Intrastate telephone rates may be higher than those for out-of-state calls.*

in•tro•duce /ĭn′trə doos′/ or /-dyoos′/, *v.* 1. to present; to bring into contact with. *Mrs. Rogers, may I introduce my mother?* 2. to bring in. *New inventions introduce different ways of doing things.* **in•tro•duc•es, in•tro•duced, in•tro•duc•ing.** [Latin *introducere*, to bring in, from *intro*, within + *ducere*, to lead.]

in•tro•duc•tion /ĭn′trə dŭk′shən/, *n.* 1. being brought in or acquainted with. *Visiting the school board meeting was an introduction to politics.* 2. the first part, as of a book. *Read the chapter introduction carefully.* 3. a basic explanation: *an introduction to first aid.* [Latin *introduct-*, perfect stem of *introducere*, to bring in, introduce.]

in•trude /ĭn trood′/, *v.* to interrupt; to break in without being asked. *It's not polite to intrude on a private conversation.* **in•trudes, in•trud•ed, in•trud•ing.**

in•va•lid¹ /ĭn′və lĭd/, *n.* a sick person who needs care. *The nurse took good care of the invalid.*

in•val•id² /ĭn văl′ id/, *adj.* not valid; having no value or force. *If your pass isn't signed by the teacher or principal, it is invalid.*

in•ven•tion /ĭn vĕn′shən/, *n.* a device, method, or process that is developed or created. *The electric light and the phonograph are two inventions of Thomas A. Edison.*

in•vert /ĭn vûrt′/, *v.* to turn upside down or inside out. *If you invert a bucket of sand, the sand falls out.*

in•vest /ĭn vĕst′/, *v.* to put money into something to make a profit. *Many Americans invest in savings bonds.*

in•vis•i•ble /ĭn vĭz′ ə bəl/, *adj.* not capable of being seen. *Her hearing aid was so tiny it was almost invisible.*

in•ward /ĭn′wərd/, *adv.* toward the inside or center. *The door opened inward.* *adj.* inside a thing or person; inner: *inward doubts.*

-ion, a suffix used to form nouns meaning "the result of an action or process": *introduction.*

ir-, a prefix meaning "not": *irreversible.* **Ir-** replaces **in-** before words beginning with **r.**

IRA, an abbreviation for Individual Retirement Account. *I put the money from my summer job into an IRA.*

ir•ra•tion•al /ĭ răsh′ ə nəl/, *adj.* without reason or clear thought. *Many fears are irrational.*

ir•reg•u•lar /ĭ rĕg′ yə lər/, *adj.* not conforming to the usual rule or practice; different. *The coin was valuable because of its irregular markings.*

ir•re•sis•ti•ble /ĭr′ ĭ zĭs′ tə bəl/, *adj.* too strong to be resisted; compelling. *Although he was on a diet, his desire for the food was irresistible.*

ir•ri•gate /ĭr′ ĭ gāt′ /, *v.* to supply water to by a system of ditches or pipes. *Farmers irrigate land that does not get enough rain.* **ir•ri•gates, ir•ri•gat•ed, ir•ri•gat•ing.**

IRS, an abbreviation for Internal Revenue Service. *Most adults file income-tax reports with the IRS each year.*

isle /īl/, *n.* an island, especially a small one. *The Isle of Wight is located off the coast of England.* (Sounds like **aisle.)**

is•sue /ĭsh′ ōo/, *v.* to circulate or distribute in an official capacity; to send out. *The principal issued a memo explaining the new fire drill procedure.* **is•sues, is•sued, is•su•ing.**

i•tem /ī′ təm/, *n.* 1. a separate article. *Which item shall we buy first?* 2. a piece of news: *an item in the newspaper.*

ă pat/ā pay/âr care/ä father/ĕ pet/
ē be/ĭ pit/ī pie/îr pier/ŏ pot/ō toe/
ô paw, for/oi noise/ou out/ŏŏ took/
ōō boot/ŭ cut/ûr urge/th thin/*th* this/
hw which/zh vision/ə about, item,
pencil, gallop, circus

J j

jeal•ous /jĕl′ əs/, *adj.* feeling envy because of someone's success. *They were jealous of the star player because he played in every game.*

jew•el•ry /jōo′ əl rē/, *n.* jewels; ornaments of gold, silver, gems, etc. *The children enjoyed dressing up in their grandmother's costume jewelry.*

jour•nal /jûr′ nəl/, *n.* a personal record of activities and feelings, kept on a regular basis. *Ramon kept a journal of his summer experiences.*

jour•nal•ist /jûr′ nə lĭst/, *n.* a person whose career is in writing, editing, or publishing news stories. *My mother is a journalist who covers courthouse news for the local paper.*

K k

kiln /kĭln/ or /kĭl/, *n.* an oven used to bake or fire ceramics. *The kiln must be very hot before the pottery will harden.*

kins•man /kĭnz′ mən/, *n.* a male relative. *A kinsman is a male relative, and a kinswoman is a female relative.*

knack /năk/, *n.* a special talent for doing something. *Philip has a knack for writing short stories.*

kneel /nēl/, *v.* to rest on bent knees. *Be careful not to kneel in the dirt.* **kneels, knelt** or **kneeled, kneel•ing.**

knob /nŏb/, *n.* a rounded handle on a door, TV set, drawer, etc. *The knob on the right of the radio controls the sound.*

knowl•edge /nŏl′ ĭj/, *n.* everything that one knows or understands about something. *Her knowledge of baseball statistics is impressive.*

L l

la·bel /lā′ bəl/, *n.* a small piece of paper used for identification or instructions. *When you buy canned or packaged food, you can read the label to find out the contents.*

la·bor /lā′ bər/, *n.* physical work. *Moving these stones is hard labor.*

la·goon /lə gōōn′ /, *n.* a shallow body of water near or connected with a larger body of water. *A lagoon may be separated from the sea by sandbars.*

la·ser /lā′ zər/, *n.* an acronym for a device that strengthens light to produce a thin, powerful beam. *Lasers are used in industry, medicine, and communications.* [Light amplification by stimulated emission of radiation.]

leath·er /lĕth′ ər/, *n.* the dressed or tanned hide of an animal. *Gloves and jackets made of leather are soft, warm, and durable.*

le·gal /lē′ gəl/, *adj.* permitted by law. *A left turn at this corner is not legal.*

leg·end /lĕj′ ənd/, *n.* a popular story handed down from earlier times. *The story of King Arthur and his knights is an English legend.*

leg·i·ble /lĕj′ ə bəl/, *adj.* able to be read; clearly written. *Check to be sure that your handwriting is legible.* **leg·i·bly,** *adv.*

lei·sure /lē′ zhər/ or /lĕzh′ ər/, *adj.* free; not busy. *Our leisure time was spent reading and listening to the stereo.* [Latin *licēre,* to be permitted.]

lens /lĕnz/, *n.* a piece of clear, curved glass or plastic used to bend light rays. *Lenses are used in eyeglasses, cameras, telescopes, and microscopes.* **lens·es.**

-less, a suffix used to form adjectives meaning "without": *endless.*

li·brar·i·an /lī brâr′ ē ən/, *n.* a person who specializes in library work. *The librarian can help you find the materials you need for your report.*

li·cense /lī′ səns/, *n.* a document giving official permission; permit. *Ms. Sutherland obtained a pilot's license after she learned how to fly a plane.*

lieu·ten·ant /lōō tĕn′ ənt/, *n.* an officer usually ranking next below a captain. *A lieutenant receives orders from the captain.* [Old French *lieu,* in place of + *tenir,* to hold.]

lim·it /lĭm′ ĭt/, *n.* the greatest amount permitted. *The speed limit on this street is thirty miles an hour.*

lin·e·ar /lĭn′ ē ər/, *adj.* of or relating to a straight line. *A foot is a linear measurement.*

lin·guis·tics /lĭng gwĭs′ tĭks/, *n.* the science of language that deals with the nature and structure of speech. *Phonetics is a branch of linguistics that is especially useful in spelling.*

link·ing verb /lĭngk′ ĭng vûrb′ /, *n.* a verb, such as a form of **be,** that links the predicate of a sentence to the subject. *In the sentence "They seemed happy,"* **seemed** *is a linking verb.*

lit·er·ate /lĭt′ ər ĭt/, *adj.* able to read and write. *In school we are taught to be literate.*

liv·er /lĭv′ ər/, *n.* a large organ of the body located near the stomach that produces digestive juices. *The work of the liver includes helping to change food into fuel for the body.*

lo•cal /lō′ kəl/, *adj.* having to do with a certain place or nearby area. *Our local news program informs us about our own area.*

lo•ca•tion /lō kā′ shən/, *n.* a place; position. *This quiet field is a good location for our campsite.* [Latin *locatio*, a placing, from *locare*, to place, from *locus*, place.]

log•i•cal /lŏj′ ĭ kəl/, *adj.* using logic; sensible. *When asked to make a decision, he made the logical choice.*

lone•some /lōn′ səm/, *adj.* lonely; sad from being alone. *My little sister kept my puppy from getting lonesome while I was at school.*

loose /lōōs/, *adj.* not fastened tightly; slack. *I have a loose button on my coat.* **loos•er, loos•est, loose•ly,** *adv.*

loud•ness /loud′ nĭs/, *n.* state of being loud. *The loudness of a sound is measured in units called decibels.*

lunar /lōō′ nər/, *adj.* of or relating to the moon: *a lunar eclipse.*

-ly, a suffix used to form adverbs meaning "in a way that is" or "in the manner of": *quietly.*

M m

ma•chin•er•y /mə shē′ nə rē/, *n.* machines or machine parts. *Farm machinery has made it possible for farmers to raise larger crops.*

mag•a•zine /măg′ ə zēn′ / or /mag′ ə zēn′ /, *n.* a periodical publication containing articles, stories, poems, etc. *We receive two monthly magazines at our house.*

man•ner /măn′ ər/, *n.* way; fashion. *The students left the bus in a quiet and orderly manner.*

mar•ble /mär′ bəl/, *n.* a kind of rock or stone that can be polished to a smooth, shiny finish. *Many statues are carved from marble.*

ma•rim•ba /mə rĭm′ bə/, *n.* an instrument played by striking wooden bars arranged in a musical scale; a large xylophone. *The marimba is of African origin.*

mar•riage /măr′ ĭj/, *n.* the state of being married; life as husband and wife. *The couple celebrated fifty years of marriage.*

mass /măs/, *n.* the volume or bulk of a body or object. *The mass of an object does not change when it is broken, melted, or frozen.*

ma•te•ri•al /mə tîr′ ē əl/, *n.* the parts or substances from which a thing is made. *The material for the roof was delivered before the workers arrived.*

mead•ow /mĕd′ ō/, *n.* a field in which grass or hay grows naturally. *The cows grazed in the meadow.*

meas•ure•ment /mĕzh′ ər mənt/, *n.* 1. the act of measuring or the process of being measured. *A gallon is a unit of liquid measurement.* 2. the length, size, or amount of something. *Her waist measurement is twenty-five inches.*

mech•a•nize /mĕk′ ə nīz′ /, *v.* to equip with machinery: *mechanize a factory.*

ă pat/ā pay/âr care/ä father/ĕ pet/
ē be/ĭ pit/ī pie/îr pier/ŏ pot/ō toe/
ô paw, for/oi noise/ou out/ŏŏ took/
ōō boot/ŭ cut/ûr urge/th thin/*th* this/
hw which/zh vision/ə about, item,
pencil, gallop, circus

me•di•um /mē′ dē əm/, *adj.* having, being, or occupying a middle position; moderate. *Warm the soup over medium heat.*

mel•o•dy /měl′ ə dē/, *n.* a series of musical tones making up a tune. *He whistled the melody of a popular song.* **mel•o•dies.**

-ment, a suffix used to form nouns meaning "the result of an action or process": *advancement.*

mer•chant /mûr′ chənt/, *n.* a person who buys and sells goods. *The three fabric stores in this area are owned by the same merchant.* [Latin *mercari,* to trade.]

me•tab•o•lism /mə tăb′ə lĭz′ əm/, *n.* the physical and chemical processes that maintain life. *Doctors can check the rate of your metabolism to see how fast your body absorbs certain foods.*

me•te•or•ite /mē′ tē ə rīt′/, *n.* a piece of a meteor that does not burn up completely in the earth's atmosphere and lands on the surface of the earth. *This rock may have been part of a meteorite.*

meth•od /měth′ əd/, *n.* a system; a way of doing something. *Broiling is one method of preparing fish.*

mid-. a word element meaning "a middle part, time, or location": *midway.*

mid•sum•mer /mĭd′ sŭm′ ər/, *n.* the middle of the summer. *We had a midsummer family reunion at the beach.*

mid•way /mĭd′ wā′/, *adv.* in the middle of the way or distance; halfway. *The equator circles the earth midway between the poles.* *adj.* In the middle of a way, distance, period of time, or succession of events: *At the midway point in the baseball season.*

mile•age /mīl′ ĭj/, *n.* the number of miles covered. *What was the total mileage of the trip?*

mil•i•tar•y /mĭl′ ĭ tĕr ē/, *n.* the armed forces. *Soldiers and sailors serve in the military.* *adj.* having to do with the armed forces: *a military parade.*

min•ute¹ /mĭn′ ĭt/, *n.* 1. one of the sixty equal parts into which an hour is divided; sixty seconds. *We were given ten minutes to do each part of the test.* 2. the exact moment. *I recognized him the minute I saw him.*

min•ute² /mī nōōt′ / or /-nyōōt′ /, *adj.* tiny; very small. *Minute bits of dust floated through the ray of sunlight.*

mir•ror /mĭr′ ər/, *n.* 1. a glass or other reflective surface. *She used a mirror to see how her new hair style looked.* 2. anything that gives a true account or picture. *The book was a mirror of modern society.* *v.* to reflect. *The setting sun was mirrored on the surface of the lake.*

mis-, a prefix meaning: 1. bad; badly; wrong; wrongly: *misconduct.* 2. failure; lack: *misfire.*

mis•be•have /mĭs′ bĭ hāv′ /, *v.* to act badly or improperly. *Puppies sometimes misbehave by chewing on shoes.* **mis•be•haves, mis•be•haved, mis•be•hav•ing.**

mis•chief /mĭs′ chĭf/, *n.* 1. conduct or actions that cause or could cause harm, injury, or damage. *Mother asked me to stay out of mischief.* 2. harmless and merry teasing or pranks. *My kitten was full of mischief.* [Old French *meschief,* calamity, misfortune.]

mis•for•tune /mĭs′ fôr′ chən/, *n.* bad luck. *It was his misfortune to lose his wallet.*

mis•in•form /mĭs′ ĭn fôrm′ /, *v.* to give wrong or false information. *We were misinformed about the day of the party; it was Thursday, not Tuesday.*

mis•lead /mĭs lēd′ /, *v.* to guide in the wrong direction; confuse. *A misspelled word may mislead the reader.* **mis•leads, mis•led, mis•lead•ing.**

mis•place /mĭs plās′ /, *v.* to put in a wrong place; mislay. *Megan searched for the notebook she had misplaced.* **mis•plac•es, mis•placed, mis•plac•ing.**

mis•read /mĭs rēd′ /, *v.* to read or understand incorrectly. *Because he misread the instructions, he couldn't assemble the kite.* **mis•reads, mis•read, mis•read•ing.**

mis•trust /mĭs trŭst′ /, *n.* lack of trust. *Her mistrust showed in her frowning expression.* *v.* to view without confidence. *Don't mistrust your ability; I think you'll do a great job.*

mis•use /mĭs yōōs′ /, *n.* incorrect or improper use. *The misuse of a word can cause confusion.*
v. /mĭs yōōz′ /, to use wrongly or incorrectly. *Don't misuse the piano by banging on the keys.* **mis•us•es, mis•used, mis•us•ing.**

mod•er•ate /mŏd′ ər ĭt/, *adj.* within reasonable limits; not extreme: *a moderate price.*

mod•i•fi•er /mŏd′ ə fī′ ər/, *n.* a word, phrase, or clause that limits or qualifies the meaning of another word or group of words. *Adjectives and adverbs are modifiers.*

mod•ule /mŏj′ ōōl/, *n.* a self-contained unit of a spacecraft; a unit with a specific function. *The engineers at NASA designed a new space module.*

mo•men•tar•y /mō′ mən tĕr′ ē/, *adj.* brief; lasting a short time. *There was a momentary lull in the storm.* **mo•men•tar•ily,** *adv.*

mo•res /môr′ āz′ / or /mōr′-/, *n. pl.* the customs accepted by a particular social group. *You should respect the mores of other societies.*

mor•tar /môr′ tər/, *n.* 1. a mixture of cement or lime with sand and water. *The construction worker laid bricks with mortar.* 2. a bowl in which substances are crushed or ground. *The chef used a mortar and pestle to grind the spices.*

moun•tain•ous /moun′ tə nəs/, *adj.* having mountains; filled with or covered by mountains. *The western part of the United States contains many mountainous areas.*

mph or **m.p.h.,** an abbreviation for miles per hour. *The speed limit in our town is 30 mph.*

mul•ti•ple /mŭl′ tə pəl/, *adj.* having many parts. *His multiple interests include sports, music, and movies.*
n. a quantity into which another quantity may be divided with zero remainder. *Four is a multiple of two.* **mul•ti•ples.**

mul•ti•pli•cand /mŭl′ tə plī′ kănd′ /, *n.* a number multiplied by another. *In 2 x 7, 7 is the multiplicand.*

ă pat/ā pay/âr care/ä father/ĕ pet/
ē be/ĭ pit/ī pie/îr pier/ŏ pot/ō toe/
ô paw, for/oi noise/ou out/ŏŏ took/
ōō boot/ŭ cut/ûr urge/th thin/th this/
hw which/zh vision/ə about, item,
pencil, gallop, circus

mul•ti•pli•er /mŭl′ tə plī′ ər/, *n.* in arithmetic, a number by which another number is multiplied. *In 2 x 7, 2 is the multiplier.* **mul•ti•pli•ers.**

mu•ral /myo͝or′ əl/, *n.* a picture or design painted on a wall. *The artist designed a mural for the lobby of the auditorium.*

mus•cle /mŭs′ əl/, *n.* body tissue composed of fibers that tighten or loosen to move parts of the body. *The athlete was careful to stretch his muscles before the race.*

mu•si•cian /myo͞o zĭsh′ ən/, *n.* a person who composes or performs music. *The players in an orchestra are expert musicians.*

mut•ton /mŭt′ ən/, *n.* the meat of a full-grown sheep. *In England, roast mutton is a popular dish.*

myth /mĭth/, *n.* a story or legend that attempts to account for something in nature. *Some myths deal with the early history of a nation.*

N n

na•tion•al /năsh′ ə nəl/, *adj.* belonging to a nation. *The national flag of the United States has stars and stripes.*

nat•u•ral /năch′ ər əl/, *adj.* 1. produced by nature; not artificial. *Wood is a natural substance.* 2. having a particular character by nature. *Eileen has a natural love for art.* 3. normal; usual; to be expected. *It is natural for winters in Florida to be warm.*

neb•u•la /nĕb′ yə lə/, *n.* a cloudy mass seen among the stars at night. *On a clear night, you may see a nebula in the sky.* **neb•u•las** or **neb•u•lae.**

nec•es•sar•y /nĕs′ ĭ sĕr′ ē/, *adj.* needed; required. *A balanced diet is necessary for proper nutrition.* **nec•es•sar•i•ly,** *adv.*

neigh•bor•hood /nā′ bər ho͝od′ /, *n.* the part of a town or area where a person lives. *In a big city, some neighborhoods have apartment buildings and others have houses.*
adj. relating to the neighborhood: *a neighborhood park.*

nerv•ous /nûr′ vəs/, *adj.* 1. of the nerves. *All the nerves in the body are called the nervous system.* 2. excited; not calm. *The kitten grew nervous when everyone crowded around.*

neu•tral /no͞o′ trəl/ or /nyo͞o′ -/, *adj.* 1. not favoring either side. *During two World Wars, Switzerland remained a neutral nation.* 2. neither acidic nor alkaline: *a neutral solution.*

neu•tron /no͞o′ trŏn′ / or /nyo͞o′ -/, *n.* a part of an atomic nucleus that has no electrical charge. *Both neutrons and protons are subatomic particles.*

niece /nēs/, *n.* the daughter of one's brother or sister, or of one's spouse's brother or sister. *Your parents' nieces are your cousins.*

nim•bo•stra•tus /nĭm′ bō strā′ təs/ or /-străt′ əs/, *n.* a low, gray cloud that brings rain, snow, or sleet. *A nimbostratus sometimes indicates the arrival of snow.*

ni•tro•gen /nī′ trə jən/, *n.* a gas that forms about four-fifths of the air we breathe. *Nitrogen has no color, taste, or odor.*

nom•i•nate /nŏm′ ə **nāt**′/, *v.* to choose a candidate for an office; to name. *Mary was nominated for president of her class.* **nom•i•nates, nom•i•nat•ed, nom•i•nat•ing.**

non-, a prefix meaning "not": *nonmetal.*

non•fat /nŏn′ **făt**′/, *adj.* lacking fat solids or having the fat content removed: *nonfat milk.*

non•prof•it /nŏn **prŏf**′ĭt/, *adj.* not set up for the purpose of making a profit. *A charity is a nonprofit organization.*

non•re•new•al /nŏn′ rĭ **nōō**′ əl/ or /-nyōō′-/, *adj.* not granting an extension. *There was a nonrenewal clause in the insurance policy.*

non•re•turn•a•ble /nŏn′ rĭ **tûr**′ nə bəl/, *adj.* not able to be returned: *nonreturnable bottles.*

no•ta•ble /nō′ tə bəl/, *adj.* 1. worthy of notice; remarkable. *Writing a book is a notable accomplishment.* 2. prominent; distinguished. *He was a notable physicist.*

no•tice /nō′ tĭs/, *n.* an announcement. *The notice on the bulletin board gives the dates of the field hockey games.* *v.* to pay attention to; take notice of; see. *Joan noticed Barbara's new dress right away.* **no•tic•es, no•ticed, no•tic•ing.**

ă pat/ā **pay**/âr **care**/ä father/ĕ pet/
ē be/ĭ pit/ī **pie**/îr **pier**/ŏ pot/ō **toe**/
ô **paw, for**/oi **noise**/ou **out**/ŏŏ **took**/
ōō **boot**/ŭ cut/ûr **urge**/th **thin**/*th* **this**/
hw **which**/zh vision/ə about, item,
pencil, gallop, circus

nour•ish /nûr′ ĭsh/ or /**nŭr**′-/, *v.* to feed; to cause to grow by giving enough of the right food. *Water and sunlight nourished the flowers.* **nour•ish•es, nour•ished, nour•ish•ing.**

nov•el /nŏv′ əl/, *n.* a book-length fictional story. *Mark Twain wrote several novels.* *adj.* new or unusual: *a novel idea.*

nu•cle•us /nōō′ klē əs/ or /nyōō′/, *n.* the central, positively charged core of an atom, composed of neutrons and protons. *A nucleus contains almost all the mass of an atom.*

numb /nŭm/, *adj.* without sensation or movement. *If you don't wear warm gloves, your fingers may become numb with cold.*

nu•tri•tion /nōō **trĭsh**′ ən/ or /nyōō-/, *n.* eating; nourishment. *Proper nutrition helps to maintain good health.*

nu•tri•tious /nōō **trĭsh**′ əs/ or /nyōō-/, *adj.* providing nourishment. *Apples are a nutritious snack.* [Latin *nutrire,* to feed, nourish.]

O o

o•a•sis /ō ā′ sĭs/, *n.* a place in the desert where there is water. *Trees, shrubs, or grass might grow in an oasis.* **o•a•ses.**

ob-, a prefix meaning "toward" or "against": *object, obstacle.*

o•be•di•ence /ō bē′ dē əns/, *n.* the act of obeying rules or laws. *Crossing the street safely requires obedience to traffic laws.*

ob•ject[1] /əb **jĕkt**′/, *v.* to make objection; to protest. *They objected that the weather was too cold to play outside.*

ob•ject² /ŏb′jĭkt/, *n.* 1. a thing that can be seen or touched. *The little shop had many objects made of china.* 2. a purpose; goal: *the object of the game.*

ob•tain /əb tān′/, *v.* to get. He obtained a ticket to the play. **ob•tains, ob•tained, ob•tain•ing.**

ob•vi•ous /ŏb′vē əs/, *adj.* easy to see or figure out; clear; plain. *It is obvious that the movie is popular, since the theater is so crowded.*

oc•ca•sion /ə kā′zhən/, *n.* 1. a particular happening or event. *Holidays are special occasions.* 2. an opportunity; a good chance. *I hope you find an occasion to call us while you are traveling.*

o•cean•og•ra•pher /ō′shə nŏg′rə fər/, *n.* a scientist whose specialty is the study and exploration of the ocean. *The oceanographer told us about the Gulf Stream.* [From Greek *ōkeanos*, a great river encircling the earth ᴍ *graphein*, to write.]

of•fer /ô′fər/ or /ŏf′ ər/, *v.* 1. to say that one is willing. *We offered to help Mr. Elliott start his car.* 2. to present as a suggestion. *The President offered a plan for peace.*

of•fi•cer /ô′fĭ sər/, *n.* 1. a person in a position of authority: *a bank officer; an army officer.* 2. a policeman or policewoman. *Officer, which way is Oak Street?*

OPEC, an abbreviation for Organization of Petroleum Exporting Countries. *OPEC's decisions affect the price we pay for oil.*

op•er•a•tion /ŏp′ə rā′shən/, *n.* 1. the way in which something works. *Finally I understand the operation of an airplane.* 2. a surgical treatment. *The patient recovered quickly after the operation.* [Latin *operatio,* from *operari,* to work, from *opus,* a work.]

o•pin•ion /ə pĭn′yən/, *n.* 1. a belief or impression that cannot be proved. *Leon holds the opinion that soccer is more fun than football.* 2. a judgment or verdict. *The judge handed down an opinion in favor of the plaintiff.*

op•po•nent /ə pō′nənt/, *n.* a person or group that competes against another. *Our school's opponent for the game is Deerfield School.* [Latin *opponere,* to oppose.]

op•por•tu•ni•ty /ŏp′ər tōō′nĭ tē/ or /-tyōō′′/, *n.* a time or chance that is right for doing something. *Let's find an opportunity to talk to Amy about the picnic.* **op•por•tu•ni•ties.**

op•pose /ə pōz′/, *v.* to be against; act against. *The mayor opposed the building of a new highway.* **op•pos•es, op•posed, op•pos•ing.** [Latin *ob-,* against + *pos-,* perfect stem of *ponere,* to put, place.]

op•po•site /ŏp′ə zĭt/, *adj.* contrary; completely different; exactly reverse: *opposite opinions.*
n. the reverse of something else. *Up is the opposite of down.*
prep. across from. *The library is opposite the school.* [Latin *ob-,* against + *pos-,* perfect stem of *ponere,* to put, place.]

op•ti•mism /ŏp′tə mĭz′əm/, *n.* the belief that our world is the best of all possible worlds; a hopeful disposition. *Karen's optimism and sunny outlook on life make her fun to be around.*

or•di•nar•y /ôr′ dn ĕr′ ē/, *adj.* 1. usual; normal. *The ordinary time it takes to drive downtown is twenty minutes.* 2. not special; average: *an ordinary meal.*

-ous, a suffix used to form adjectives meaning "possessing" or "characterized by": *joyous.*

or•phan /ôr′ fən/, *n.* a child whose parents are absent or dead. Oliver Twist *is a story about an orphan.* [Greek *orphanos*, without parents.]

out•back /out′ băk′ /, *n.* a rural, undeveloped part of a country, especially Australia and New Zealand. *Great distances separate homesteads in the Australian outback.*

out•put /out′ pŏot′ /, *n.* 1. the amount of something produced or manufactured. *The supervisor praised her workers because their output had increased.* 2. the information produced from a computer. *The output was inaccurate because some of the information input was wrong.*

out•ward /out′ wərd/, *adv.* toward the outside. *Fire laws state that the doors of a public building must open outward.*
adj. of or toward the outside; exterior: *outward calm.*

o•ver•cast /ō′ vər kăst′ /, *adj.* covered with clouds or mist. *The weather report called for an overcast day with a chance of rain.*

P p

pad•dock /păd′ ək/ *n.* a fenced area used for grazing livestock. *The sheep were grazing in the paddock.*

palm¹ /päm/, *n.* the inside of a person's hand between the wrist and the fingers. *The child held her nickel tightly in her palm.*

palm² /päm/, *n.* a tree that grows in very warm places. *Coconuts grow on coconut palms.*

pam•phlet /păm′ flĭt/, *n.* a small book with a paper cover; booklet. *A pamphlet of instructions came with the camera.*

pan•cre•as /păng′ krē əs/ or /păn′-/, *n.* a long, irregularly shaped gland located behind the stomach that secretes digestive juices. *The pancreas produces enzymes.*

pan•el•ist /păn′ ə lĭst/, *n.* a member of a panel. *One panelist was an expert on foreign affairs.*

par•a•graph /păr′ ə grăf′ /, *n.* a clearly indicated part of a written work; a sentence or group of sentences that develops one main idea or topic. *The first sentence of a paragraph often is indented from the left margin.* [Greek *para*, beside + *graphein*, to write.]

par•al•lel /păr′ ə lĕl′ /, *adj.* going in the same direction but not meeting; being always the same distance apart. *Railroad tracks are parallel.*

ă pat/ā pay/âr care/ä father/ĕ pet/
ē be/ĭ pit/ī pie/îr pier/ŏ pot/ō toe/
ô paw, for/oi noise/ou out/ŏŏ took/
ōō boot/ŭ cut/ûr urge/th thin/*th* **th**is/
hw **wh**ich/zh vision/ə about, item,
pencil, gallop, circus

par•al•lel•o•gram /pär′ ə **lĕl′** ə grăm′ /, *n.* a four-sided plane figure with opposite sides parallel. *A rectangle is a parallelogram.*

par•lia•ment /pär′ lə mənt/, *n.* the legislative body of a country. *In England, the House of Commons and the House of Lords make up the British Parliament.*

par•tial /pär′ shəl/, *adj.* 1. not complete. *We saw a partial eclipse of the moon.* 2. inclined to favor one side. *An umpire should never be partial when he makes a decision.*

par•tic•i•pant /pär tĭs′ ə pənt/, *n.* a person who joins in and takes part in something. *The teachers agreed to be participants in a discussion with students.*

part•ner /pärt′ nər/, *n.* a person who shares something or joins with another. *The boys were partners on the camping trip.*

part•ner•ship /pärt′ nər shĭp′ /, *n.* a business association of two or more individuals. *Their partnership was profitable.*

pas•sage /păs′ ĭj/, *n.* 1. a way used for passing. *The passage led to the back staircase.* 2. part of a writing or speech. *The passage about whales gives much interesting information.* [Old French *passer*, to pass.]

pas•ser-by /păs′ ər bī′ /, *n.* a person who passes by. *The reporter interviewed passers-by about the upcoming election.*

pa•tience /pā′ shəns/, *n.* the calm endurance of a trying situation. *Our driver showed great patience during the traffic delay.*

pa•tri•ot /pā′ trē ət/, *n.* one who loves, supports, or defends his or her country. *George Washington was one of America's greatest patriots.*

pa•tri•ot•ism /pā′ trē ə tĭz′ əm/, *n.* love of and loyalty to one's country. *Saluting the flag is a way of expressing patriotism.*

pat•tern /păt′ ərn/, *n.* a design or figure. *The vase had a flowered pattern.*

pause /pôz/, *n.* a short stop or rest. *There was a dramatic pause in the music.*
v. to stop for a short time. *He paused to get a glass of water.* **pause•es, paused, paus•ing.**

PBS, an abbreviation for Public Broadcasting System. *We watched a science program on PBS.*

peas•ant /pĕz′ ənt/, *n.* a hired laborer who farms the land. *The peasants worked the farm for the wealthy landowner.*

per•cent or **per cent** /pər sĕnt′ /, *adv.* out of each hundred. *Ten percent means ten out of one hundred.*

per•cent•age /pər sĕn′ tĭj/, *n.* a part in its relation to the whole. *A large percentage of the people voted in the election.*

per•cus•sion /pər kŭsh′ ən/, *n.* the group of musical instruments in which sound is produced by striking. *The sections of a symphony orchestra are string, woodwind, brass, and percussion.*

221

ce /pər **fôr**′ məns/, *n*. 1. the way in
~~omeone~~ or something functions.
~~erformance on the test was very good.~~
~~e giving of a public show.~~ *On Saturday*
there is a matinee performance.

pe•ri•od•i•cal /pĭr′ ē ŏd′ ĭ kəl/, *n*. a publication
that appears at regular intervals. *Many
periodicals feature news stories.*

per•mis•sion /pər **mĭsh**′ ən/, *n*. consent,
especially formal consent. *With the permission of the principal, our class visited the
zoo.*

per•mit /pər **mĭt**′ / *v*. to let; allow; give consent
to. *Please permit me to read your magazine.*
per•mits, per•mit•ted, per•mit•ting.
n. /**pûr**′ mĭt/, a written or printed statement
that gives one permission; a license. *Most
cities require permits for parades.*

per•pen•dic•u•lar /pûr′ pən **dĭk**′ yə lər/, *adj*. at
right angles. *The walls are perpendicular to
the floor.*

per•spire /pər **spīr**′ /, *v*. to sweat. *As she
worked she began to perspire.* **per•spires,
per•spired, per•spir•ing.**

pes•si•mism /**pĕs**′ ə mĭz′ əm/, *n*. the belief that
this is the worst of all possible worlds; a
gloomy outlook. *His pessimism made
everyone unhappy.* [Latin *pessimus,* worst.]

pe•tro•le•um /pə **trō**′ lē əm/, *n*. a thick, liquid
hydrocarbon mixture found beneath the
earth's surface. *Gasoline, paraffin, and
asphalt can be produced from petroleum.*

pew•ter /**pyoo**′ tər/, *n*. an alloy of tin used for
making utensils and tableware. *The couple
received a pewter bowl as a wedding gift.*

phase /fāz/, *n*. 1. a stage in development. *The
first phase of our campaign to elect Andrew
will be distributing posters.* 2. a change in the
shape of the moon when viewed from Earth.
The moon was in its crescent phase.

phone /fōn/, *n*. a telephone. *Answer the
phone.*
v. to telephone. *Peggy's friends sometimes
phone her just to chat.* **phones, phoned,
phon•ing.**

photo /**fō**′ tō/, *n*. a photograph. *Nancy brought
in the photos of her summer vacation.*

pho•to•graph /**fō**′ tə grăf′ /, *n*. a picture taken
with a camera. *The photograph of the lake is
in color.* [Greek *photo-,* light + *graphein,* to
write.]

photography /fə **tŏg**′ rə fē/, *n*. the art or
process of taking and printing photographs.
*In our class in photography, we learned how
to develop our own film.*

ă pat/ā pay/âr care/ä father/ĕ pet/
ē be/ĭ pit/ī pie/îr pier/ŏ pot/ō toe/
ô paw, for/oi noise/ou out/o͝o took/
o͞o boot/ŭ cut/ûr urge/th thin/*th* this/
hw which/zh vision/ə about, item,
pencil, gallop, circus

phrase /frāz/, *n.* 1. a group of words that gives a single idea. *In "He swam during the summer,"* **during the summer** *is a phrase.* 2. a short expression: *a scientific phrase.*
v. to express in words. *Phrase your thoughts carefully.* **phras•es, phrased, phras•ing.**

phy•si•cian /fĭ zĭsh′ ən/, *n.* a medical doctor. *When you are ill, you should see a physician.* [Old French *fisique,* medical science, from Greek *phusis,* nature.]

pi /pī/, *n.* a Greek letter (π) used as a mathematical symbol to represent a specific number (about 3.14). *Pi is the ratio of a circle's circumference to its diameter.*

pi•an•ist /pē ăn′ ĭst/ or /pē′ ə nĭst/, *n.* one who plays the piano. *It takes years of training to become a concert pianist.*

pi•geon /pĭj′ ən/, *n.* a bird with a small head, stout body, and short legs. *Some pigeons are trained to carry messages.*

pig•ment /pĭg′ mənt/, *n.* 1. a substance used to give color to something. *There were yellow pigments in the green paint.* 2. a substance that gives color to plant or animal tissue. *Chlorophyll is the pigment that makes plants green.*

pipe•line /pīp′ līn′/, *n.* a channel or pipe used to carry water, petroleum, or natural gas. *The Alaskan pipeline supplies oil to the mainland.*

pit•i•ful /pĭt′ ĭ fəl/, *adj.* causing emotions of sorrow and compassion. *The injured dog was a pitiful sight.*

plat•form /plăt′ fôrm′/, *n.* any flat floor or surface raised above the area around it. *The train will be at the platform in five minutes.*

plumb•er /plŭm′ ər/, *n.* a person whose job is putting in and fixing sinks, pipes, and other plumbing fixtures. *We called a plumber when the basement pipes started leaking.*

plu•ral /ploor′ əl/, *n.* the form of a word meaning more than one. *The plural of* **leaf** *is* **leaves.**
adj. showing that more than one is meant. *The plural form of most words is made by adding s or es.*

P.M. or **p.m.,** an abbreviation meaning "in the afternoon or evening." *She is usually asleep by 10 p.m.* [Latin *post meridiem,* after noon.]

pol•i•cy[1] /pŏl′ ĭ sē/, *n.* a way of doing things. *The store's policy is to treat customers politely.* **pol•i•cies.**

pol•i•cy[2] /pŏl′ ĭ sē/, *n.* a contract between an insurance company and those who are insured. *The school has a fire insurance policy.* **pol•i•cies.**

pol•lu•tion /pə loo′ shən/, *n.* a harmful impurity. *Water pollution causes many fish to die.*

pop•u•la•tion /pŏp′ yə lā′ shən/, *n.* the number of people living in a country, state, town, or other area. *The town's population has greatly increased in the past five years.* [Latin *populus,* the people.]

por•tion /pôr′shən/ or /pōr′-/, *n.* a part; a share. *A portion of the school day is spent in study hall.*

pose /pōz/, *v.* 1. to hold an expression or position. *The parents posed with their children for a family portrait.* 2. to present; put forward: *pose a question.* **pos•es, posed, pos•ing.** [Latin *pausare,* to rest, influenced by *pos-,* perfect stem of *ponere,* to put, place.]

po•si•tion /pə zĭsh′ən/, *n.* 1. place; location. *The navigator marked the ship's position on a chart.* 2. a job; employment. *My brother has a new position with another company.*

pos•i•tive /pŏz′ĭ tĭv/, *adj.* 1. confident; certain; without doubt. *Gus is positive that his team will win.* 2. approving; showing agreement: *a positive answer.* 3. not negative: *a positive number.* [Latin *pos-,* perfect stem of *ponere,* to put, place.]

pos•sess /pə zĕs′/, *v.* to have; own. *Heather's family possesses a sailboat.* **pos•sess•es, pos•sessed, pos•sess•ing.**

pos•ses•sive /pə zĕs′ĭv/, *adj.* showing ownership. *A possessive pronoun indicates to whom something belongs.*
n. a word that shows possession. *Possessives such as* **teacher's** *and* **its** *are formed from nouns and pronouns.*

pos•si•bly /pŏs′ə blē/, *adv.* perhaps; maybe. *Possibly we'll finish before noon.*

post•age /pō′stĭj/, *n.* the cost of stamps needed to send a letter or package by mail. *The postage was thirty cents.* [French *poste,* mail.]

post of•fice /pōst′ ô′fĭs/ or /-ŏf′ ĭs/, *n.* 1. an office or building where people may buy stamps or mail letters or packages. *Mail these cards at the post office.* 2. the public department in charge of mail. *The post office employs thousands of workers.*

pot•ter•y /pŏt′ə rē/, *n.* pots, dishes, or ornaments made of clay that has been hardened by baking. *This shop sells beautiful pottery.*

POW or **P.O.W.,** an abbreviation for prisoner of war. *A great celebration awaited the POWs upon their return home.*

prac•ti•cal /prăk′tĭ kəl/, *adj.* 1. able to be done, used, or carried out. *Her practical solution solved the problem.* 2. dealing with facts rather than theory; concrete. *Her practical approach to children was a great help.*

pre•cious /prĕsh′əs/, *adj.* 1. having a high price; costing a great deal. *Diamonds are precious jewels.* 2. much loved; dear. *Their precious child brought happiness to the parents.* [Latin *pretium,* price.]

ă pat/ā pay/âr care/ä father/ĕ pet/
ē be/ĭ pit/ī pie/îr pier/ŏ pot/ō toe/
ô paw, for/oi noise/ou out/o͝o took/
o͞o boot/ŭ cut/ûr urge/th thin/*th* this/
hw which/zh vision/ə about, item,
pencil, gallop, circus

pre•mi•er /prē′mē ər/ or /prĕm′ē-/ or /prĭ mîr′/, *adj.* first in importance; chief. *The economy was the premier concern of the voters.*
n. /prĭ mîr′/, the chief executive of a Canadian province. *The Canadian premier plans to visit the U.S. soon.*

pre•sent¹ /prĕz′ ənt/, *adj.* 1. of the time between past and future; current: *the present moment.* 2. at hand; not absent. *All the committee members were present for the final vote.*

pre•sent² /prĭ zĕnt′/, *v.* 1. to give. *The prize was presented to the winner.* 2. to offer; to bring up for consideration. *May I present a suggestion?*
n. /prĕz′ ənt/, a gift. *The present was colorfully wrapped.*

pres•sure /prĕsh′ ər/, *n.* the act of pressing; use of force. *We applied pressure to the orange to squeeze out the juice.*

price•less /prīs′ lĭs/, *adj.* very worthy; invaluable. *The art collection was priceless.*

prim•er¹ /prĭm′ ər/, *n.* a textbook for early grades. *The children took out their reading primer and began the lesson.*

prim•er² /prī′ mər/, *n.* an undercoat of paint to prepare a surface for further painting. *The painter applied a primer coat first.*

print•er /prĭn′ tər/, *n.* the part of the computer that produces printed matter. *The printer was not working; it needed a new ribbon.*

prob•a•ble /prŏb′ ə bəl/, *adj.* likely to happen. *The dark clouds and lightning mean that rain is probable.* **prob•a•bly,** *adv.*

proc•ess /prŏs′ ĕs′/ or /prŏ′ sĕs′/, *n.* 1. a system of operations in the production of something: *the process of canning fresh fruit.* 2. a series of actions with an expected end: *the growth process.* **proc•ess•es.**

prof•it /prŏf′ ĭt/, *n.* 1. the amount of money made after all expenses have been subtracted. *The profits in some businesses are small.* 2. a benefit; an advantage. *Woo found both profit and enjoyment in his music lessons.*
v. to benefit. *I can profit from your experience.* **prof•its, prof•it•ed, prof•it•ing.**

prof•it•a•ble /prŏf′ ĭ tə bəl/, *adj.* bringing profit or benefit. *The store had a profitable year.* **prof•it•a•bly,** *adv.*

pro•gram•ming /prō′ grăm′ ĭng/ or /-grəm ing/, *n.* the designing or planning of a computer program. *Students interested in computer science should study programming.*

prog•ress /prŏg′ rĕs′/ or /prŏ′ grĕs′/, *n.* 1. a movement forward. *The train made steady progress.* 2. development; improvement: *the progress of science.*
v. /prə grĕs′/, to advance; improve. *Sarah will progress in her ability to spell.*

proj•ect /prŏj′ ĕkt′/, *n.* a plan; scheme. *The girls' next project is to build a radio.*
v. /prə jĕkt′/, 1. to throw or shoot forward. *An arrow is projected from a bow.* 2. to cause to fall on a surface. *Movies are projected on a white screen.*

proof /proof/, *n.* anything that shows that something is correct or true. *Do you have proof of your theory?*

prop•er /prŏp′ər/, *adj.* 1. correct; suitable. *A proper tool for smoothing wood is a plane.* 2. indicating a particular person, place, or thing; belonging to one or to only a few. *Proper nouns, such as* **Joan** *or* **Ohio,** *are always capitalized.*

pro•por•tion /prə pôr′ shən/ or /-pōr′-/, *n.* 1. a part. *A large proportion of the earth is water.* 2. a proper relation. *This painting is in proportion to the size of the wall it hangs on.* 3. a relation of equality between two ratios. *How do you find the missing element in a proportion?*

pro•tect /prə tĕkt′/, *v.* to guard; defend; keep from danger. *The police protect citizens from criminals.*

pro•tec•tion /prə tĕk′ shən/, *n.* watchful care; a keeping from danger. *The job of a gamekeeper is the protection of wildlife.*

pro•ton /prō′ tŏn′/, *n.* a positively charged subatomic particle. *Protons are found in the nucleus of an atom.*

prov•ince /prŏv′ ĭns/, *n.* 1. a division of a country. *Canada is divided into nine provinces.* 2. range of knowledge, activity, or authority. *The study of volcanoes falls within the province of geology.*

ă pat/ā pay/âr care/ä father/ĕ pet/ ē be/ĭ pit/ī pie/îr pier/ŏ pot/ō toe/ ô paw, for/oi noise/ou out/o͝o took/ o͞o boot/ŭ cut/ûr urge/th thin/*th* this/ hw which/zh vision/ə about, item, pencil, gallop, circus

pro•vi•sion /prə vĭzh′ ən/, *n.* a condition. *One of the provisions for ordering tickets is that you must be a student.*

pub•li•ca•tion /pŭb′ lĭ kā′ shən/, *n.* 1. the act or process of publishing printed matter. *The author was excited about the publication of her novel.* 2. a book, magazine, or newspaper. *The library has more than twenty-five thousand publications.*

punc•tu•a•tion /pŭngk′ cho͞o ā′ shən/, *n.* the use of commas, periods, and other marks to make writing clearer. *In writing, correct punctuation is as important as correct usage.*

pun•ish /pŭn′ ĭsh/, *v.* to administer a penalty for a crime or misbehavior. *I will not punish you if you tell the truth.*

pur•chase /pûr′ chĭs/, *v.* to buy. *We purchased folding chairs for the porch.* **pur•chas•es, pur•chased, pur•chas•ing.** *n.* a thing that is bought. *Mother's purchases will be delivered by the store.*

Q q

quad•ri•lat•er•al /kwŏd′ rə lăt′ ər əl/, *n.* a geometric figure with four sides and four angles. *Squares and rectangles are quadrilaterals.*

quo•ta /kwō′ tə/, *n.* 1. due share; allotment. *Not all the students used up their quota of free tickets.* 2. a maximum number. *The club has a quota of ten new members each year.*

quo•ta•tion /kwō tā′ shən/, *n.* 1. the quoting of someone else's words. *The speaker used quotations to illustrate his point.* 2. a passage repeated from a well-known literary work. *"All the world's a stage" is a quotation from a play by Shakespeare.*

R r

ra•di•us /rā′dē əs/, *n.* a straight line from the center of a circle to its edge. *The radius of a circle is half its diameter.* **ra•di•i** or **ra•di•us•es.**

rap•id /răp′ĭd/, *adj.* 1. fast; quick. *The rapid current carried the canoe down the river.*

ra•tio /rā′shō/ or /rā′shē ō′/, *n.* 1. the quotient that shows the comparison of two numbers. *The ratio of 1 to 4 is ¼.* 2. comparison in size or quantity between two things. *The recipe mixes flour and sugar in the ratio of two to one.*

ra•tion•al /răsh′ən əl/, *adj.* based on reason; logical. *After thinking it over calmly, Jeff made a rational decision to quit the team.*

re-, a prefix meaning: 1. again: *rebuild.* 2. backwards; back: *react.*

re•al es•tate /rē′əl ĭ stāt′/ or /rēl′-/, *n.* land and all buildings and properties on it. *Matt's mother sells real estate.*

re•bel /rĭ bĕl′/, *v.* 1. to resist or oppose authority. *The workers rebelled against the unfair demands of their employer.* **re•bels, re•belled, re•bel•ling.**
n. **reb•el** /rĕb′əl/, a person who reacts against authority. *Rebels challenge tradition.*

re•ceipt /rĭ sēt′/, *n.* 1. a written statement showing that money or goods have been received. *I signed the receipt when the package was delivered.* 2. the act of receiving. *On receipt of the good news, we felt happy.*

re•ceive /rĭ sēv′/, *v.* to get. *You should receive the letter in two days.* **re•ceives, re•ceived, re•ceiv•ing.**

re•ceiv•er /rĭ sē′vər/, *n.* 1. a person or thing that receives something. *The sender of a letter puts the address of the receiver on the envelope.* 2. the part in a radio, telephone, or TV that picks up the signals. *I held the receiver to my ear.*

re•cess /rē′sĕs′/, *n.* a brief rest from work. *During the morning we have a fifteen-minute recess.* **re•cess•es.**

re•cip•ro•cal /rĭ sĭp′rə kəl/, *n.* either of a pair of numbers whose product is 1. *The reciprocal of 3/4 is 4/3, since 3/4 x 4/3 = 1. adj.* mutual; felt by both sides: *reciprocal interest.*

re•flect /rĭ flĕkt′/, *v.* 1. to throw back from a surface, as light or heat. *A mirror reflects light.* 2. to give back an image of. *The trees were reflected in the clear lake.* 3. to show; make apparent. *His work reflects great effort.*

re•fract /rĭ frăkt′/, *v.* to cause the path of light to bend. *The lens of the human eye refracts light.*

re•fuse¹ /rĭ fyo͞oz′/, *n.* 1. to turn down; reject. *She refused my offer of help.* 2. to be unwilling; decline. *I refuse to let them bother me.* **re•fus•es, re•fused, re•fus•ing.**

ref•use² /rĕf′yo͞os/, *n.* useless matter; rubbish; garbage. *Please put your refuse in the wastebasket.*

re•gion•al /rē′jə nəl/, *adj.* 1. characteristic of a large geographic area. *In the sunbelt states, the growth of cities has been a regional asset.* 2. characteristic of a particular area: *a regional accent.*

reg•u•lar /rĕg′yə lər/, *adj.* 1. usual; normal; ordinary. *Our regular practice on Sunday is to have dinner in the afternoon.* 2. frequent: *regular customers.* 3. occurring at fixed intervals. *We make regular visits to the dentist.*

reign /rān/, *n.* the time during which a leader rules. *During the queen's reign, the people enjoyed many improvements.* *v.* to rule. *The king reigned for thirty years.*

re•lease /rĭ lēs′/, *v.* to let loose; to set free. *If you release the door, it will close by itself.* *n.* 1. the act of letting go or setting free. *The rangers planned the release of the bear cubs they had raised.* 2. freedom; relief. *After the test was over, I felt a sense of release.*

re•lief /rĭ lēf′/, *n.* the removal or ease of worry, pain, etc. *Imagine my relief when I remembered the right answer.*

re•main /rĭ mān′/, *v.* 1. to stay. *We remained at home because of the rain.* 2. to continue; to last without changing. *The weather remained warm until the last week of October.* 3. to be left. *All that remains of the old house is the foundation.* **re•mains, re•mained, re•main•ing.**

re•quire /rĭ kwīr′/, *v.* 1. to need. *Humans require food and water to live.* 2. to demand; to command. *Good manners require that you use a knife and a fork when you eat.* **re•quires, re•quired, re•quir•ing.**

res•i•dence /rĕz′ĭ dəns/, *n.* 1. the place where one lives; home. *His residence is on Spruce Street.* 2. the act or fact of living in a place. *His family took up residence in Spain while he was working there.*

res•i•dent /rĕz′ĭ dənt/, *n.* 1. a person who lives in a particular area. *When our family moved to California we became residents of that state.* 2. a doctor who is doing clinical training. *Ms. Wood is a third-year resident at the hospital.* [Latin *residēre*, to sit back, from *re-*, back + *sedēre*, to sit.]

res•pi•ra•to•ry /rĕs′pər ə tôr′ē/ or /-tōr′ē/, *adj.* pertaining to the process of breathing. *Smoking is hazardous to the respiratory system.*

re•spond /rĭ spŏnd′/, *v.* 1. to answer; to reply. *Susan did not respond when I asked her a question.* 2. to react. *The patient responded well to the medicine.*

re•spon•si•ble /rĭ spŏn′ sə bəl/, *adj.* 1. trustworthy; reliable. *A responsible student was chosen to collect the money for the field trip.* 2. required to answer for something. *Who is responsible for turning off the lights when we leave the room?* 3. deserving credit or blame for something. *The cold weather was responsible for the small crowd at the picnic.* **re•spon•si•bly,** *adv.*

res•tau•rant /rĕs′tər ənt/ or /-tə ränt′/, *n.* a place where meals are sold and served. *We ate dinner in a restaurant downtown.*

ă pat/ā pay/âr care/ä father/ĕ pet/
ē be/ĭ pit/ī pie/îr pier/ŏ pot/ō toe/
ô paw, for/oi noise/ou out/ŏŏ took/
ōō boot/ŭ cut/ûr urge/th thin/*th* this/
hw which/zh vision/ə about, item,
pencil, gallop, circus

re•sult /rĭ zŭlt'/, *n.* outcome; effect. *He was late to work as a result of a delay in traffic.* *v.* to happen as an effect. *The cold, damp weather resulted in icy roads.* **re•sults, re•sult•ed re•sult•ing.**

re•ver•ber•ate /rĭ vûr' bə rāt'/, *v.* to sound again; echo. *The thunder reverberated through the mountains.* **re•ver•ber•ates, re•ver•ber•at•ed, re•ver•ber•at•ing.**

re•vers•i•ble /rĭ vûr' sə bəl/, *adj.* capable of being turning backward or inside out; able to be reversed. *Jo wore her reversible coat.*

rhom•bus /rŏm' bəs/, *n.* a parallelogram with equal sides. *Every square is a rhombus.* **rhom•bus•es** *or* **rhom•bi.**

rhythm /rĭth' əm/, *n.* a regular, repeated movement in which a beat or accent rises and falls or occurs steadily. *The rhythm in music is often provided by the drums.*

ri•val /rī' vəl/, *n.* one who is trying to do better than another; one who competes. *The two friends were rivals for the same part in the school play.*
adj. competing; being rivals. *The rival stores lowered their prices to attract more customers.*

round /round/, *v.* to express to the nearest whole number or to a multiple of five or ten. *In math class we are learning to round off numbers to the nearest ten.* **rounds, round•ed, round•ing.**

rou•tine /rōō tēn'/, *n.* a standard set of activities performed regularly. *Each morning Ann went through her exercise routine.* *adj;* ordinary; not special: *a routine day.*

rpm or **r.p.m.,** an abbreviation for revolutions per minute. *A long-playing record turns at $33\frac{1}{3}$ rpm.*

ru•mor /rōō' mər/, *n.* uncertain information spread by word of mouth; hearsay. *We heard a rumor that our math quiz was canceled.*

S s

sa•li•va /sə lī' və/, *n.* the liquid that is secreted by glands in the mouth. *Saliva helps in the digestion of food.*

salm•on /săm' ən/, *n.* a large fish with silver scales and pink flesh. *Salmon swim upstream from salt water to fresh water to lay their eggs.* **salm•on** or **salm•ons.**

SALT, an abbreviation for Strategic Arms Limitations Talks. *The United States and the Soviet Union discussed the SALT treaty.*

sanc•tion /săngk' shən/, *n.* 1. approval; support; encouragement. *The governor received public sanction for his views.* 2. a course of action several nations agree to take against a nation considered to have violated international law. *Governments may impose economic sanctions on another country for violations of human rights.*

sat•is•fac•tion /săt' ĭs făk' shən/, *n.* a feeling of being satisfied or contented. *Dan gets satisfaction from doing his job well.*

sat•is•fy /săt' ĭs fī'/, *v.* 1. to please; to fill a need or desire. *You can satisfy the baby by giving her a toy.* 2. to put an end to. *Water will satisfy my thirst.* **sat•is•fies, sat•is•fied, sat•is•fy•ing**

sauce /sôs/, *n.* a liquid that is served with food. *The chicken dish had a delicious ginger sauce.*

scarce•ly /skârs′ lē/, *adv.* hardly; barely. *There are scarcely any people awake at five o'clock in the morning.*

scar•ci•ty /skâr′ sĭ tē/, *n.* a shortage in supply. *During a drought there is scarcity of water.* **scar•ci•ties.**

scheme /skēm/, *n.* 1. a plan of action; a project. *We thought of a scheme for preventing graffiti.* 2. a secret plot. *The scheme to give Mother a surprise party failed when she discovered the birthday cake.*

sci•en•tif•ic no•ta•tion /sī′ ən tĭf′ ĭk nō tā′ shən/, *n.* a method of writing numbers in terms of powers of ten. *In scientific notation the number 10,492 would be represented as 1.0492 x 10⁴.*

scis•sors /sĭz′ ərz/, *n. pl.* a cutting tool consisting of two handles and two sharp blades fastened together. *Scissors can cut through paper or fabric.*

scu•ba /skōō′ bə/ or /skyōō′ -/, *adj.* an acronym for a device with a mask, hose, and air tank used while swimming underwater. *Scuba divers often see schools of brightly colored tropical fish.* [Self-contained underwater breathing apparatus.]

sculp•tor /skŭlp′ tər/, *n.* an artist who produces figures or designs that have depth. *Sculptors may choose to work in wood, stone, clay or metal.*

sec•ond•ar•y /sĕk′ ən dĕr′ ē/, *adj.* 1. not ranking first. *Her primary concern was content, and her secondary concern was style.* 2. of or relating to the schooling one receives after elementary school: *secondary education.*

sed•i•ment /sĕd′ ə mənt/, *n.* the material that settles to the bottom of a liquid. *The river had a layer of sediment on the bottom.*

seize /sēz/, *v.* to take hold of suddenly; to grasp; to grab. *He seized her hand and shook it eagerly.* **seiz•es, seized, seiz•ing.**

self-ad•dressed /sĕlf′ ə drĕst′ /, *adj.* addressed to oneself. *If you would like a reply, please send a self-addressed envelope.*

sense•less /sĕns′ lĭs/, *adj.* without meaning; pointless: *a senseless waste of time.*

sen•si•ble /sĕn′ sə bəl/, *adj.* full of good sense; reasonable; wise. *She is too sensible to accept a ride from strangers.* **sen•si•bly,** *adv.*

se•quence /sē′ kwəns/, *n.* 1. the coming of one thing after another; succession. *Follow the sequence of steps to complete the model.* 2. order in which things follow one another. *The books are listed in alphabetical sequence.*

serf /sûrf/, *n.* in the Middle Ages, a laborer bound to a landlord. *A serf worked the lord's land and gave crops to the lord as rent.*

se•ri•al /sîr′ ē əl/, *n.* a story or show produced in installments. *Many TV dramas are serials, with a story that continues from week to week.*

ă pat/ā pay/âr care/ä father/ĕ pet/
ē be/ĭ pit/ī pie/îr pier/ŏ pot/ō toe/
ô paw, for/oi noise/ou out/ŏŏ took/
ōō boot/ŭ cut/ûr urge/th thin/*th* *th*is/
hw which/zh vision/ə about, item,
pencil, gallop, circus

ser•vant /sûr′vənt/, *n.* 1. a person whose job is to work for another person. *Cooks, maids, and butlers are servants.* 2. a person who works for a government or the public. *Firefighters are important public servants.* [Old French *servir*, to serve.]

set•tle•ment /sĕt′l mənt/, *n.* 1. a place where a number of people have gone to live; colony. *There were many English settlements in this land.* 2. a settling or being resolved. *The settlement of the dispute satisfied both countries.*

shale /shāl/, *n.* a rock composed of layers of claylike, fine-grained sediments. *Shale is found throughout the world.*

shelf /shĕlf/, *n.* a flat piece of wood, glass, or metal that is used to hold things. *The clock is on a shelf in the kitchen.* **shelves.**

shield /shēld/, *n.* 1. a piece of armor once carried on the arm by soldiers for protection in battle. *The knight's family emblem was on his shield.* 2. anything that protects. *Good nutrition is a shield against disease.* *v.* to protect; to guard. *This umbrella will shield you from the rain.*

short sto•ry, /shôrt′ stôr′ ē/ or /-stôr′ e/, *n.* a short piece of prose fiction. *Ernest Hemingway wrote some memorable short stories.*

should•'ve, should have.

shriek /shrēk/, *n.* a loud, sharp, high-pitched sound; screech. *We heard the shrieks of the gulls before we saw the ocean.* *v.* to make a loud, sharp, high-pitched sound. *The children were shrieking with laughter.*

shut•ter•bug /shŭt′ ər bŭg′/, *n.* an amateur photographer. *Most shutterbugs start out by taking pictures of family members and pets.*

siege /sēj/, *n.* the surrounding of a place for a long time in order to capture it. *The city was under siege for three weeks.*

si•lence /sī′ləns/, *n.* the absence of noise or sound; stillness. *There was silence while the principal spoke.*

sim•i•lar /sĭm′ ə lər/, *adj.* almost but not quite the same; alike but not identical. *The two girls wore similar clothes.*

sin•gu•lar /sĭng′ gyə lər/, *adj.* having to do with only one. *A singular noun names one person, place, or thing.*

sis•ter-in-law /sĭs′ tər ĭn lô′ /, *n.* the sister of one's husband or wife, or the wife of one's brother. *When my brother marries Donna, she'll be my sister-in-law.*

sky•scrap•er /skī′ skrā′ pər/, *n.* a very tall building. *The Empire State Building is one of New York's famous skyscrapers.*

sky•ward /skī′ wərd/, *adv.* in the direction of the sky. *As the plane ascended, its nose was facing skyward.*

sleet /slēt/, *n.* rain that freezes into drops of ice as it falls; a mixture of rain and snow or hail. *The sleet made the fields sparkle in the moonlight.*

sleigh /slā/, *n.* a carriage mounted on runners, used for traveling on ice or snow. *A sleigh is usually pulled by horses.*

231

smudge /smŭj/, *v.* to make dirty; smear or blotch. *Don't smudge the photographs with fingerprints!* **smudg•es, smudged, smudg•ing.**
n. a smear or blotch. *Maria got a smudge on her white shoes.*

sol•emn /sŏl′ əm/, *adj.* serious; earnest; grave: *a solemn promise.*

sol•i•tar•y /sŏl′ ĭ tĕr′ ē/, *adj.* 1. existing, living or going alone. *A solitary traveler was on the road that night.* 2. remote, secluded: *a solitary place.*

-some, a suffix used to form adjectives meaning "having the quality, condition, or action of": *bothersome, troublesome.*

so•nar /sō′ när/, *n.* an acronym for a device that uses sound waves to locate objects underwater. *Submarines use sonar to judge their distance from the ocean floor.* [**So**und **na**vigation **ra**nging.]

soph•o•more /sŏf′ ə môr′/ or /môr′/, *n.* a person in the second year of high school or college. *The sophomores took the freshmen on a tour of the high school.* [Greek *sophos,* wise + *mōros,* foolish.]

spec•trum /spĕk′ trəm/, *n.* the group of colors formed by natural light when it is broken up into its parts by being passed through a prism. *All the colors of the spectrum can be seen in a rainbow.* **spec•tra** or **spec•trums.**

speed•om•e•ter /spĭ dŏm′ ĭ tər/ or /spē-/, *n.* an instrument that indicates speed. *Every car has a speedometer.* [Speed + -meter, from Greek *metron,* measure.]

square /skwâr/, *v.* to raise a number or equation to the second power. *The number 4 squared is equal to 4 x 4 or 16.* **squares, squared, squar•ing.**

stel•lar /stĕl′ ər/, *adj.* 1. of or relating to stars. *A stellar map shows the constellations.* 2. excellent; of star quality: *a stellar cast of performers.*

steppe /stĕp/, *n.* a dry grass-covered plain found in southeastern Europe and Siberia. *Vegetation is sparse in the steppes of the Soviet Union.* **steppes.**

ster•e•o /stĕr′ ē ō/, *n.* 1. a record player giving the effect of lifelike sound by using two or more sets of equipment. *This stereo comes with two speakers.* 2. stereophonic sound: *recorded in stereo.* [From stereophonic, from Greek *stereos,* solid + *phōnē,* sound.]

stock•brok•er /stŏk′ brō′ kər/, *n.* a person who buys and sells stocks and other securities for a client. *The client trusted the stockbroker to invest his money wisely.*

stra•tus /strā′ təs/ or /străt′ əs/, *n.* a low altitude cloud in horizontal layers. *Stratus often looks like dense fog.*

strike /strīk/, *v.* 1. to hit. *A tennis player strikes the ball with a racket.* 2. to sound. *The clock strikes every hour.* 3. to stop work as a group. *The workers voted to strike for better working conditions.* **strikes, struck, strik•ing.**

ă pat/ā pay/âr care/ä father/ĕ pet/
ē be/ĭ pit/ī pie/îr pier/ŏ pot/ō toe/
ô paw, for/oi noise/ou out/o͝o took/
o͞o boot/ŭ cut/ûr urge/th thin/*th* this/
hw which/zh vision/ə about, item, pencil, gallop, circus

stub•born /stŭb′ ərn/, *adj.* not easily persuaded; having one's own definite idea. *Lee was stubborn and refused to follow my suggestions.*

stu•di•ous /stoo̅′dē əs/ or /styoo̅′-/, *adj.* devoted to study; hardworking. *The class members usually become more studious as exam time nears.*

sub -, A prefix meaning: 1. under or beneath: *submarine.* 2. a subordinate or secondary part: *subdivision.* 3. somewhat short of or less than: *subtropical.*

sub•di•vide /sŭb′dĭ vīd′/, *v.* to divide a part again into smaller parts. *The plot of land was subdivided into lots for commercial stores.* **sub•di•vides, sub•di•vid•ed, sub•di•vid•ing.**

sub•ma•rine /sŭb′ mə rēn′/ or /sŭb′ mə rēn′/, *n.* a boat that can travel underwater. *Some submarines stay underwater for many weeks. adj.* beneath the water surface; undersea. *Coral is a submarine organism.*

sub•to•tal /sŭb′ tōt′l/. *n.* a partial or incomplete total. *The clerk added the amounts to get a subtotal, then added the tax to get the total.*

sub•way /sŭb′ wā′/, *n.* an electric railway beneath the ground. *In some large cities, subways are a vital part of the transportation system.*

suc•cess /sək sĕs′/, *n.* 1. a favorable result or outcome; achievement. *Hard work often brings success.* 2. a person or thing that succeeds. *The guest speaker was a huge success.* **suc•cess•es.**

suc•cess•ful /sək sĕs′ fəl/, *adj.* having success or a favorable outcome; turning out well. *Gwen is successful as both a student and an athlete.*

suf•fer /sŭf′ ər/, *v.* 1. to feel pain or distress. *Our dog seems to suffer in the hot weather.* 2. to endure; to put up with. *The pioneers suffered many hardships.*

suf•fix /sŭf′ ĭks/, *n.* a group of letters added to the end of a word to change its meaning. *The suffix -ness changes the adjective sad to the noun sadness.* **suf•fix•es.** [Latin *suffigere,* to affix, from *sub-,* secondary + *figere,* to fix.]

suf•frage /sŭf′ rĭj′ /, *n.* the right or privilege to vote. *Women won suffrage on August 18, 1920.*

sug•ges•tion /səg jĕs′ chən/ or / sə jĕs′ /, *n.* something suggested; recommendation. *Her suggestion that we take an early plane was very sensible.* [Latin *suggest-,* perfect stem of *suggerere,* from *sub-,* up + *gerere,* to carry.]

sul•tan /sŭl′ tən/, *n.* a ruler of a Moslem country. *In ancient times, sultans had great wealth and power.*

sun•set /sŭn′ sĕt′ /, *n.* the disappearance of the sun below the horizon. *A sunset turns the sky pink and orange.*

super-, a prefix meaning: 1. above; over: *superimpose.* 2. excessive in degree: *supersaturate.*

su•per•in•tend•ent /soo̅′ pər ĭn tĕn′ dənt/, *n.* a person with the authority to supervise or direct; person in charge. *The superintendent of schools directs the activities of all the schools in a district.*

su•per•son•ic /soo̅′ pər sŏn′ ĭk/, *adj.* caused by or related to a speed greater than sound. *Some jets can fly at supersonic speeds.* [Latin *super,* over, above + *sonus,* a sound.]

su•per•star /soo̅′ pər stär′ /, *n.* a performer who has great popular appeal. *We all waited at the theater door, hoping to see the superstar.*

su•per•vise /sōō′pər vīz′/, *v.* to direct and inspect the work or performance of. *Mother supervised our cooking.* **su•per•vis•es, su•per•vised, su•per•vis•ing.** [Latin *supervis-*, perfect stem of *supervidere*, to look over, from *super-*, over + *videre*, to see.]

sure•ly /shŏŏr′lē/, *adv.* 1. undoubtedly; certainly. *Surely we will find a parking spot in this large lot!* 2. with skill; in an expert way. *Slowly but surely, Bob carved a beautiful horse from the soft wood.*

sur•vey /sər vā′/ or /sûr′vā′/, *v.* 1. to look over; to examine. *From a high tower, the ranger surveyed the forest for smoke.* 2. to measure the exact size and shape of an area of land. *A team will survey the land before the new road is built.*
n. /sûr′vā′/, 1. a study or poll: *an opinion survey.* 2. a measuring of land: *a geographical survey.*

sys•tem /sĭs′təm/, *n.* 1. a group of things or parts that work together. *The circulatory system includes the heart, the blood vessels, and the blood.* 2. an orderly way of doing things. *Use the system of keeping score that is easiest for you.* 3. an arrangement; an order: *a system of government.*

T t

ta•ble•spoon /tā′bəl spōōn′/, *n.* a large spoon used to serve food or to measure ingredients. *A tablespoon is equal to three teaspoons.*

ta•boo /tə bōō′/, *adj.* forbidden; not approved: *a taboo topic.*

tal•ent /tăl′ənt/, *n.* special ability; natural skill. *She has a great talent for writing.*

tank•er /tăng′kər/, *n.* a ship, truck, or plane that transports oil or other liquids. *The tanker in the Gulf of Mexico had an oil leak.*

tap•es•try /tăp′ĭ strē/, *n.* a heavy cloth with woven designs hung on walls for decoration. *The tapestry on the castle wall showed a hunting scene.* **tap•es•tries.**

tease /tēz/, *v.* to bother or irritate by making jokes, asking questions, poking, etc. *The sign at the zoo asked the visitors not to tease the animals.* **teas•es, teased, teas•ing.**

tea•spoon /tē′spōōn′/, *n.* the common small spoon used especially with beverages or for measuring. *In a table setting, the teaspoon goes to the right of the knife.*

te•di•ous /tē′dē əs/, *adj.* tiresome; boring. *The politician's speech became so tedious that a few listeners got up to leave.* [Latin *taedium*, tedium.]

tel•e•graph /tĕl′ə grăf /, *n.* a device for sending and receiving signals over an electrical wire. *In the code used on a telegraph, dots and dashes represent letters of the alphabet.* [Greek *tele*, at a distance + *graphein*, to write.]

tel•e•vi•sion /tĕl′ə vĭzh′ən/, *n.* a system of sending images and sound through the air by electricity or the set that receives and shows them; TV. *We watched a nature special on television.* [Greek *tele*, at a distance + Latin *vis-*, perfect stem of *videre*, to see.]

ă pat/ā pay/âr care/ä father/ĕ pet/
ē be/ĭ pit/ī pie/îr pier/ŏ pot/ō toe/
ô paw, for/oi noise/ou out/ŏŏ took/
ōō boot/ŭ cut/ûr urge/th thin/*th* this/
hw which/zh vision/ə about, item,
pencil, gallop, circus

tem•po•rar•y /tĕm′ pə rĕr′ ē /, *adj.* lasting for a brief time; not permanent. *While our teacher was ill, we had a temporary teacher.* **tem•po•rar•i•ly,** adv.

ten•ant /tĕn′ ənt/, *n.* a person who pays rent for the use of a house, apartment, or other property. *In that tall apartment building there are several hundred tenants.* [Old French *tenir,* to hold.]

tense¹ /tĕns/, *adj.* 1. tightly stretched: *a tense wire.* 2. nervous; uneasy: *a tense moment.* **tens•er, tens•est.**

tense² /tĕns/, *n.* any of the inflected forms of a verb that indicates time, continuance, or completion of an action or state: *past, present, and future tenses.*

ten•sion /tĕn′ shən/, *n.* 1. the process of stretching. *The heavy snow put tension on the electrical wires.* 2. mental strain or stress. *There was a feeling of tension in the classroom before the test.*

ter•mi•nal /tûr mə nəl/, *n.* a computer device through which data can be entered. *A computer terminal consists of a video screen and a typewriter keyboard.*

ter•rain /tə rān′ / or /tĕ-/, *n.* A tract of land, especially with respect to its physical features. *From the airplane, we could see that the terrain below us was rugged.*

ter•ri•ble /tĕr′ ə bəl/, *adj.* 1. causing terror or awe; alarming. *The monster in the movie was a terrible sight.* 2. severe; intense; extreme. *The cold at the North Pole is terrible.* **ter•ri•bly,** adv.

ter•ri•to•ry /tĕr′ ĭ tôr′ ē/ or /-tōr′ ē/, *n.* an area of land; a region. *Much of the territory in the central United States is used for farming.* **ter•ri•to•ries.**

text /tĕkst/, *n.* 1. written or printed words. *See the text under the map on page 73.* 2. the words written by an author. *The novelist revised the text of the first chapter.*

theme /thēm/, *n.* 1. subject; topic. *We selected school spirit as the theme of our discussion.* 2. a short essay. *We write one theme a week in school.*

there•fore /thâr′ fôr′ / or /-fōr′ /, *adv.* for that reason; consequently. *It turned the litmus paper blue; therefore, it must be a base.*

ther•mal /thûr′ məl/, *adj.* producing or caused by heat. *Skiers wear thermal clothing to protect themselves from the cold.* [Greek *thermē,* heat.]

ther•mom•e•ter /thər mŏm′ ĭ tər/, *n.* an instrument that measures and indicates temperatures. *The liquid in a thermometer expands and rises in the tube as the temperature rises.* [Greek *thermē,* heat + *metron,* measure.]

ther•mo•stat /thûr′ mə stăt′ /, *n.* a device that automatically controls heating or cooling equipment. *The thermostat in our house keeps the temperature at 60 degrees.* [Greek *thermē,* heat + *-statēs,* one that causes to stand.]

the•sau•rus /thĭ sôr′ əs/, *n.* a book of synonyms and antonyms. *A thesaurus is a good place to find a more exact word.*

thief /thēf/, *n.* one who steals. *Our neighbor's dog was the thief that took our newspaper from the porch.* **thieves.**

thought•less /thôt′ lĭs/, *adj.* careless; inconsiderate. *It was thoughtless of you to invite only some of your friends.*

through /thrōō/, *prep.* 1. in one side and out the opposite side. *May walked through the park to the library.* 2. from the beginning to the end: *through the night.*

through•out /thrōō out′/, *prep.* 1. during the entire time of. *Some states have warm weather throughout the year.* 2. in every part of. *We looked for you throughout the building.*

thun•der•storm /thŭn′ dər stôrm′/, *n.* a heavy rainstorm with lightning and thunder. *That tree was struck by lightning during the thunderstorm.*

tim•pa•ni /tĭm′ pə nē/, *n. pl.* a set of kettledrums. *The timpani boomed out from the back of the orchestra.*

-tion, a suffix used to form nouns meaning "an action or process": *absorption.*

tire•less /tīr′ lĭs/, *adj.* not easily tired or fatigued. *Mother was tireless with her sewing project, spending hours on it until she finished.*

tire•some /tīr′ səm/, *adj.* tedious; boring. *Filing was the most tiresome part of the library job.*

tis•sue /tĭsh′ ōō/, *n.* 1. a group of cells in a plant or animal that carry out a certain function: *skin tissue.* 2. light, soft, thin paper or cloth. *He wrapped the gift in tissue.*

tomb /tōōm/, *n.* a burial place for the dead. *Pyramids are Egyptian tombs.*

top•soil /tŏp′ soil′/, *n.* the surface layer of soil. *Flowers and shrubs grow best in rich, black topsoil.*

tour•ni•quet /tōōr′ nĭ kĭt/ or /tûr′ -/, *n.* a cloth band used to stop temporarily the flow of blood through an artery. *A tourniquet should be applied only by someone well trained in first aid.*

tra•che•a /trā′ kē ə/, *n.* the passage that leads from the back of the mouth to the lungs. *The trachea carries air to the lungs.*

traf•fic /trăf′ ĭk/, *n.* the movement of people and vehicles. *There was very little traffic on the turnpike.*

trait /trāt/, *n.* a feature or characteristic. *We all inherit physical traits from our parents.*

trans•ver•sal /trăns vûr′ səl/ or /trănz-/, *n.* a line that intersects other lines. *When a transversal crosses parallel lines it forms sets of matching angles.*

trap•e•zoid /trăp′ ĭ zoid′/, *n.* a quadrilateral having one pair of parallel sides. *A trapezoid may have no equal sides.*

trav•el•er /trăv′ əl ər/ or /trăv′ lər/, *n.* a person who travels. *Many travelers visit the United States every year.*

ă pat/ā pay/âr care/ä father/ĕ pet/
ē be/ĭ pit/ī pie/îr pier/ŏ pot/ō toe/
ô paw, for/oi noise/ou out/ŏŏ took/
ōō boot/ŭ cut/ûr urge/th thin/*th* this/
hw which/zh vision/ə about, item,
pencil, gallop, circus

tre•men•dous /trĭ mĕn′ dəs/, *adj.* 1. marvelous; wonderful. *She made a tremendous catch.* 2. terrible; dreadful. *The new dam saved the town from tremendous flood damage.* 3. extremely large; enormous. *A tremendous wave rocked the boat.*

tribe /trīb/, *n.* a group of people of the same race who are united in a community with common customs and a common leader. *The tribe moved west in their search for food.*

tril•lion /trĭl′ yən/, *n.* the number equal to one thousand billions. *The numeral for a trillion has twelve zeros.*

tril•o•gy /trĭl′ ə jē/, *n.* a group of three literary works or dramas related by theme. The Lord of the Rings *is a trilogy whose three volumes tell the legend of a ring with mystical powers.* [Greek *trilogia,* from *treis,* three + *logos,* word, speech.

tri•pod /trī′ pŏd′/, *n.* a three-legged stand for supporting a camera. *A camera tripod can be adjusted to different heights.*

tri•umph /trī′ əmf/, *n.* 1. a great victory. *Eliminating smallpox was a triumph of medicine.*
v. to win; achieve a victory; succeed. *With practice, the boy was able to triumph over his fear of swimming.*

trop•ics /trŏp′ ĭks/, *n. pl.* the region of the earth near the equator. *The weather in the tropics is usually hot and humid.*

tun•nel /tŭn′ əl/, *n.* a passage beneath the ground. *The mole dug a tunnel in the garden.*

tur•ban /tûr′ bən/, *n.* a hat made of a scarf wound around the head. *Turbans are worn in the Middle East.*

tur•bu•lent /tûr′ byə lənt/, *adj.* disturbed or violently agitated. *The ocean became turbulent as the storm approached.*

typ•i•cal /tĭp′ ĭ kəl/, *adj.* being a certain type; like others in its category. *Saturday was a typical rainy day.*

ty•rant /tī′ rənt/, *n.* a person who rules very harshly or unjustly. *The citizens of Greece rebelled against the tyrant.*

U u

ul•ti•mate /ŭl′ tə mĭt/, *adj.* 1. farthest; last; final. *Becoming a teacher is my ultimate goal.* 2. best; greatest. *Chess is the ultimate game of logic.*

un-, a prefix meaning "not" or "the opposite of": *unable; untie.*

under-, a prefix meaning "beneath" or "below in position": *underground.*

un•der•cov•er /ŭn′ dər kŭv′ ər/, *adj.* done in secret: *an undercover police investigation.*

un•der•ground /ŭn′ dər ground′/, *adv.* below the surface of the earth. *The tunnel led to an underground cavern.*

un•der•neath /ŭn′ dər nēth′/, *prep.* beneath; below; under. *Sean found the note that had been left underneath the doormat.*

un•der•pass /ŭn′ dər păs′/, *n.* a section of road that passes under another road or railroad. *The traffic noise echoed in the underpass.*

un•der•stand /ŭn′ dər stand′/, *v.* 1. to know; comprehend. *Do you understand how a vacuum cleaner works?* 2. to learn; hear. *I understand they are planning a trip.* **un•der•stands, un•der•stood, un•der•stand•ing.**

un•der•stood /ŭn′dər **stood′**/, *v*. past tense of **understand.**
adj. assumed; implied. *It is understood that all sales are final.*

un•for•tu•nate /ŭn fôr′chə nĭt/, *adj*. not fortunate; not lucky. *It is unfortunate that we missed the bus this morning.*

uni•form /yoo′nə fôrm′/, *n*. the special clothes worn by persons of a particular order or service when they are on duty. *The security guards wear uniforms so that they will be recognized.* [Latin *unus*, one + *forma*, shape.]

un•ion /yoon′yən/, *n*. 1. a joining to make a single thing. *The United States was formed by the union of the original thirteen states.* 2. a group of workers formed to protect their interests with respect to wages and working conditions. *The union of postal employees accepted the new contract.* [Latin *unus*, one.]

un•pleas•ant /ŭn plĕz′ənt/, *adj*. not pleasant; disagreeable. *That medicine had an unpleasant taste.*

un•voiced /ŭn′ voist′/, *adj*. produced without vibration of the vocal cords. *The consonant s is unvoiced, but z is voiced.*

up•ward /ŭp′wərd/, *adv*. toward a higher place, level, or position. *The balloons floated upward when they were let go.*

u•su•al /yoo′zhoo əl/, *adj*. common; ordinary. *The usual tool for driving a nail is a hammer.*

V v

va•ca•tion /vā kā′ shən/, *n*. a period of time during which one is free from work or school. *My father gets a two-week vacation every year.*

val•u•a•ble /văl′yoo ə bəl/ or /văl′ yə-/, *adj*. 1. having great value or worth; important. *He is a valuable player on the team.* 2. worth a great deal of money. *She keeps her valuable china on a high shelf.*

var•i•ous /vâr′ē əs/ or /văr′-/, *adj*. of several different kinds; different. *I found shells of various sizes and shapes on the beach.*

VCR, an abbreviation for video cassette recorder. *We rented a VCR so that we could tape the TV special.*

ve•loc•i•ty /və lŏs′ĭ tē/, *n*. the rate at which an object moves in a specific direction; speed. *The coaches measured the velocity of the pitcher's fast ball.*

ver•dict /vûr′dĭkt/, *n*. a decision reached by a jury or judge at the end of a trial. *The jury handed down a verdict of "not guilty."*

vi•brate /vī′ brāt′/, *v*. to move back and forth quickly. *The strings on a guitar vibrate when they are strummed.* **vi•brates, vi•brat•ed, vi•brat•ing.**

vic•to•ry /vĭk′tə rē/, *n*. the act of winning; defeat of the opposite side; triumph in a battle or contest. *The home team scored its first victory last night.* **vic•to•ries.**

ă pat/ā pay/âr care/ä father/ĕ pet/
ē be/ĭ pit/ī pie/îr pier/ŏ pot/ō toe/
ô paw, for/oi noise/ou out/oo took/
oo boot/ŭ cut/ûr urge/th thin/*th* this/
hw which/zh vision/ə about, item, pencil, gallop, circus

vid•e•o /vĭd′ē ō/, *adj.* of or used in the transmitting and receiving of television images. *Our local record store will soon carry a line of video equipment.*
n. a videocassette tape; a recording on videotape. *Singers often create videos of their songs.* [Latin *vidēre,* to see.]

vil•lain /vĭl′ ən/, *n.* a wicked or evil character. *When the villain appeared on stage, the audience booed.*

vi•o•lin•ist /vī ə lĭn′ ĭst/, *n.* a person who plays the violin. *Mary hopes to become a great violinist.*

vis•i•ble /vĭz′ə bəl/, *adj.* able to be seen. *Because of the fog, the lights were no longer visible.*

vi•sion /vĭzh′ ən/, *n.* 1. something that is or has been seen. *Jan was a vision of beauty in her costume.* 2. the sense of sight. *He has perfect vision in both eyes.* [Latin *vis-,* perfect stem of *vidēre,* to see.]

vis•i•tor /vĭz′ ĭ tər/, *n.* a person who visits. *The visitor brought flowers.*

visual /vĭzh′ ōō əl/, *adj.* capable of being seen; visible. *The laser light show was a visual treat for the audience.*

voiced /voist/, *adj.* sounded with the vibration of the vocal cords. *The th sound in this is a voiced consonant sound.*

vol•ume /vŏl′ yōōm/, or /-yəm/, *n.* 1. the amount of space within an enclosed area. *Can you find the volume of this cube?* 2. loudness. *Turn down the volume of the radio.* 3. one of a set of books: *a volume of the encyclopedia.*

vol•un•tar•y /vŏl′ ən tĕr′ ē/, *adj.* done by choice or on purpose. *He made a voluntary decision to stay home and study.* **vol•un•tar•i•ly,** *adv.*

vol•un•teer /vŏl′ ən tîr′/, *n.* one who offers to perform a service of his or her free will, usually without pay. *We need a volunteer to sell tickets to the school play.*

W w

-ward, a suffix used to form adverbs or adjectives meaning "in a specified direction": *downward.*

wa•ter va•por /wô′tər vā′ pər/ or /wŏt′ ər-/, *n.* water below the boiling point that is diffused as vapor in the atmosphere. *Water vapor forms in a steamy bathroom.*

wave•length /wāv′ lĕngth′ /, *n.* the distance between any point on a wave and the same point on the next wave. *Light has a shorter wavelength than sound.*

weath•er•proof /wĕth′ ər prōōf′ /, *adj.* able to be exposed to weather without damage. *Most houses are painted with weatherproof paint.*

weird /wîrd/, *adj.* strange; odd. *The group of people going to the costume party was a weird sight.*

whole•some /hōl′ səm/, *adj.* healthy. *The doctor gave us advice on the importance of exercise and wholesome meals.*

wind /wīnd/, *v.* 1. to wrap or coil around. *Wind the thread around the spool.* 2. to turn or crank. *Who will wind the clock?* **winds, wound, wind•ing.**

won·der·ful /wŭn′dər fəl/, *adj.* excellent; remarkable; marvelous. *What a wonderful sight the sunset is today!*

won·drous /wŭn′drəs/, *adj.* wonderful. *The horseback ride was a wondrous event.*

wood·cut /wŏŏd′kŭt′/, *n.* an engraved piece of wood. *The artist inked the woodcut and printed the design.*

wor·ri·some /wûr′ē səm/ or /wŭr′-/, *adj.* causing concern or worry. *His jammed locker was a worrisome problem all day.*

worth·less /wûrth′lĭs/, *adj.* without worth or value. *The photographs were worthless to everyone but the family members.*

would·'ve, would have.

wound[1] /wōōnd/, *n.* an injury to the body. *The doctor put a bandage on the wound on my arm.*

wound[2] /wound/, *v.* past tense and past participle of **wind.**

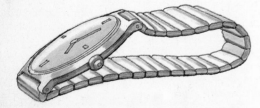

wrist watch /rĭst′wŏch′/, *n.* a watch worn on a band that fastens around the wrist. *The child was excited to get her first wrist watch.*

Y y

yield /yēld/, *v.* to surrender; give up. *A traffic sign that says "yield" warns drivers to surrender the right of way.*

ă pat/ā pay/âr care/ä father/ĕ pet/
ē be/ĭ pit/ī pie/îr pier/ŏ pot/ō toe/
ô paw, for/oi noise/ou out/ŏŏ took/
ōō boot/ŭ cut/ûr urge/th thin/*th* this/
hw which/zh vision/ə about, item,
pencil, gallop, circus

SPELLING and HANDWRITING CONNECTION

COMMON PROBLEMS CAUSED BY POOR HANDWRITING

ERROR	INCORRECT	CORRECT
1. a like u	*a soup*	*a soap*
2. e closed	*i recieve*	*e receive*
3. d like cl	*cl clog*	*d dog*
4. o like a	*a sold*	*o sold*
5. a like ce	*ce stcemp*	*a stamp*
6. n like u	*u braud*	*n brand*

CURSIVE ALPHABET

Aa Bb Cc Dd Ee Ff

Gg Hh Ii Jj Kk Ll

Mm Nn Oo Pp Qq Rr

Ss Tt Uu Vv Ww

Xx Yy Zz

This information provided for reference only.